GEORGE E

DATE DUE

NO 16 00			
DE 17 01			

DEMCO 38-296

GEORGE BERKELEY

Idealism and the man

DAVID BERMAN

CLARENDON PRESS · OXFORD

Street, Oxford ox2 6DP

York

ngkok Bombay

Calcutta Cape Town Dar es Salaam Delhi
Florence Hong Kong Istanbul Karachi
Kuala Lumpur Madras Madrid Melbourne
Mexico City Nairobi Paris Singapore
Taipei Tokyo Toronto
and associated companies in
Berlin Ibadan

Oxford is a trade mark of Oxford University Press

Published in the United States by
Oxford University Press Inc., New York

© David Berman 1994

First published in paperback 1996

British Library Cataloguing in Publication Data
Data available

Library of Congress Cataloging in Publication Data
George Berkeley : idealism and the man David Berman
Includes bibliographical references.
1. Berkeley, George, 1685–1753. I. Title.
B.1348.B463 1944   192–dc20   93–953
ISBN 0–19–826766–5

1 3 5 7 9 10 8 6 4 2

Printed in Great Britain on acid-free paper by
Biddles Ltd., Guildford and King's Lynn

Preface

This study differs from nearly all the many books which have been written on Berkeley over the past fifty years. Whereas most books dwell almost exclusively on Berkeley's philosophical writings of 1709–13, with little or no attention to either his later work or his life, this book looks at the full range of his work and links it with his life. Advancing chronologically, I have focused on Berkeley as *homo religiosus*—a focus that is by no means either forced or artificial, since it is generally agreed that religion was the main driving force in his life and thought. As my teacher, A. A. Luce, once expressed it: 'You think he is building a house, you find he has built a church'—an epigram which could well have been the motto for this book.

While aiming to present a clear picture of Berkeley's career, accessible to students and the general reader, I have also, I believe, broken new ground in a number of areas—in particular, on Berkeley's semantic revolution of 1707/8 (in Ch. 1), his philosophical strategy (in Ch. 2), his account of immortality (in Ch. 3), his Jacobitism (Ch. 4), his emotive theory of religious mysteries (Ch. 6), and the motivation of *Siris* (Ch. 7). I also pay much greater attention than usual to the Irish context of Berkeley's thought. Another distinctive feature of this study is the use made of Berkeley's symbolical frontispieces and portraits, which I try to show (in Ch. 5) illuminate his Bermuda project and his advocacy of tar-water (Ch. 7). I have also, where appropriate, introduced new Berkeley material that has come to light since Luce's *Life of Berkeley* (1949) and the Luce/Jessop edition of his *Works* (1948–57). In this respect, the present volume may claim to be the most up-to-date book on Berkeley. On the whole, my approach to his philosophical and theological work has been exegetical, although I have tried to indicate the principal objections to his theories. If I have in some instances been over-critical of his work, I have also been critical of our understanding of him. For Berkeley—the man and thinker—was deeper and more hidden, I argue, than has been generally recognized.

I have for this study drawn on work I did in the following papers or notes: 'Berkeley, Clayton and *An Essay on Spirit*', *Journal of the History of Ideas* 22 (1971); 'Berkeley's Philosophical Reception after America', *Archiv für Geschichte der Philosophie* 62 (1980); 'Bishop Berkeley and the Fountains of Living Waters', *Hermathena* 128 (1980); 'Berkeley's Prophecy', *The Scriblerian* 13 (1980); 'Cognitive Theology and Emotive Mysteries in Berkeley's *Alciphron*', *Proceedings of the Royal Irish Academy* 81 (1981); 'George Berkeley: Pictures by Goldsmith, Yeats and Luce', *Hermathena* 139 (1985); 'The Jacobitism of Berkeley's *Passive Obedience*', *Journal of the History of Ideas* 47 (1986); 'Berkeley's Semantic Revolution', *History of European Ideas* 7 (1986). I am grateful for permission (where necessary) to use some of the material from these articles.

I am also grateful to Dr Bertil Belfrage, Dr Raymond Houghton, Professor Robert McKim, and Mr Ian Tipton for commenting on an earlier version of this book.

Some of my work on this study was helped by a Royal Irish Academy/British Academy Fellowship and an award from the Trinity College Arts & ESS Benefactions Fund.

D. B.

Trinity College, Dublin
October 1992

Contents

List of Figures

Berkeley's Works

My quotations from Berkeley's writings are, with two exceptions, taken from *The Works of George Berkeley* (Edinburgh, 1948–57), 9 vols., edited by A. A. Luce and T. E. Jessop.

The two exceptions are: (1) Berkeley's manuscript notebooks, the *Philosophical Commentaries* (Ohio, 1976), edited by George Thomas, with notes by A. A. Luce; reprinted in Garland, vol. 8; and (2) *George Berkeley's Manuscript Introduction* [to the *Principles*] (Oxford, 1987), edited by Bertil Belfrage. Although these texts are printed by Luce and Jessop in the *Works* (vols. i and ii), the more recent editions are more accurate and complete.

Since most of Berkeley's writings are composed of numbered sections, my references are usually to these sections, or, as in the case of the *Philosophical Commentaries*, to entry numbers.

There are a number of accessible paperback editions of Berkeley's important writings; probably the most useful is the Everyman *Berkeley: Philosophical Works* (London, repr. 1989) edited by M. R. Ayers. Three other recent editions are those edited by Kenneth Winkler (Indianapolis, 1982), Roger Woolhouse (London, 1988), and G. J. Warnock (Glasgow, repr. 1989). There is, unfortunately, no recent edition of Berkeley's principal theological work, *Alciphron*, apart from that in volume iii of the *Works*. However, an abridged edition, *Berkeley's Alciphron in Focus* (London, 1993), with critical essays, edited by the present writer, is now available.

Abbreviations and Short Titles

Alc.	*Alciphron, or the Minute Philosopher* (1732)
DHP	*Three Dialogues between Hylas and Philonous* (1713)
NTV	*An Essay toward a New Theory of Vision* (1709)
PC	*Philosophical Commentaries* (written *c*.1707–8)
PHK	*A Treatise concerning the Principles of Human Knowledge* (1710)
TVV	*Theory of Vision Vindicated and Explained* (1733)
Works	*The Works of George Berkeley*, ed. A. A. Luce and T. E. Jessop (9 vols.; Edinburgh, 1948–57)

Armstrong	D. M. Armstrong and C. B. Martin (eds.), *Locke and Berkeley* (New York, 1968), Garland, xiv
Clark	S. R. L. Clark (ed.), *Money, Obedience and Affection*, Garland, ii
Creery	W. E. Creery (ed.), *George Berkeley: Critical Assessments* (3 vols.; London, 1991)
Engle	G. W. Engle and G. Taylor (eds.), *Berkeley's Principles of Human Knowledge: Critical Studies* (Belmont, Calif., 1968)
Essay	Locke, *An Essay concerning Human Understanding* (1690), ed. P. Nidditch (Oxford, 1975)
Fraser	A. C. Fraser, *Life and Letters of Berkeley* (Oxford, 1871), in Garland, x
Garland	G. Pitcher (gen. ed.), *The Philosophy of George Berkeley*, a 15-vol. series issued by Garland Publishing (New York, 1988–9)

Images   R. Houghton, D. Berman, and M. Lapan, *Images of Berkeley* (Dublin, 1986)

Life   A. A. Luce, *The Life of George Berkeley* (1949; repr. with a new introduction by D. Berman, London, 1992)

Mill   'Berkeley's Life and Writings' (1871 review-article of Fraser), in Mill's *Collected Works*, vii, ed. J. M. Robson (Toronto, 1978), 451–71

Stock   [J. Stock], *An Account of the Life of George Berkeley* (1776); repr. in Berman, *George Berkeley: Eighteenth-Century Responses*, Garland, i. 1

Turbayne   C. M. Turbayne (ed.), *Berkeley: Principles, Text and Critical Essays* (Indianapolis, 1970)

1

Early Life and Intellectual Background
(1685–1713)

I

George Berkeley, Ireland's most famous philosopher, was born in (or near) the town of Kilkenny on 12 March 1685. His early years were spent at Dysart Castle, overlooking the river Nore, two miles from Thomastown in Co. Kilkenny. Little is known of his early life or his parents. His father came from Staffordshire in England, but Berkeley considered himself Irish, or what we would now call Anglo-Irish.[1] As a young man, he refers in his notebooks to 'We Irish men'.[2] He also noted 'Mem: that I was [sceptical *crossed out*] distrustful at 8 years old and consequently by nature disposed for these new Doctrines' (*PC*, no. 266). In 1696 he entered Kilkenny College, formerly the school of Jonathan Swift (1667–1745) and William Congreve (1670–1729), where he remained for four years. Here, too, we have little information, although we may assume that he showed early signs of ability, since he was placed, unusually, in the second highest class.

His youthful promise is also evident in the one recorded incident from this period. In July 1699 he and some school friends explored the nearby cave of Dunmore, about which 'rarity' he wrote a lively and detailed account. Composed from memory nearly seven years later, his essay was delivered to a student society at Trinity College, Dublin. Apart from describing the 'dark and dismal place', he refers to crystallization and petrifaction, and to

---

[1] *Life*, pp. vi, 20–6; on Berkeley's father, see my 'Mrs Berkeley's Annotation in her Interleaved Copy of *An Account of the Life of George Berkeley* (1776)', *Hermathena* 122 (1977), 18.

[2] See *PC*, nos. 392–4, 398.

the theories of René Descartes (1591–1650) and John Woodward (1645–1728). The essay also contains Berkeley's one reference to his father (*Works*, iv. 261), who seems to have been a gentleman farmer and subsequently a commissioned military officer. The essay, his first extant, was sent for publication to the *Philosophical Transactions* in London; but since it was not printed there, we may assume that it was turned down.[3] Nor was this to be Berkeley's only literary disappointment.

From Kilkenny Berkeley came to Dublin where he matriculated at Trinity College on 21 March 1700. His official association with the College was to last until 1724, when he was appointed Dean of Londonderry. But it was between the years 1707 and 1713 that his connection with Trinity was closest and most fruitful. (The title-pages of his three most influential books— printed in 1709, 1710, 1713—describe him as 'George Berkeley, M.A. Fellow of Trinity-College, Dublin'.) He was elected a Scholar in 1702 and took his B.A. degree in 1704. He then remained in the College, doing what would now be called post-graduate research. He seems to have been a member of at least two College societies, one of which was formed 'to discourse on some part of the new Philosophy'.[4] His essay on Dunmore cave is from this period. So too are the minor mathematical works, *Arithmetica* and *Miscellanea Mathematica*; the latter, published in Latin in 1707, includes his 'De Ludo Algebraico', which sets out his idea for an algebraic board game. These were his first publications and are interesting for the glimpses they give of his reading and his college associates.

In issuing these mathematical publications Berkeley probably hoped to strengthen his chances of obtaining a College Fellow-ship. There were a limited number of Fellows, and he had to wait until late 1706 for a vacancy. He then 'sustained with

[3] T. K. Hoppen, *The Common Scientist ... a Study of the Dublin Philosophical Society 1683–1708* (London, 1970), 196.

[4] The rules of this society, dated 7 Dec. 1706, are printed by Luce in Berkeley's *Philosophical Commentaries ... An Editio Diplomatica* (London, 1944), p. 3. The more elaborate statutes of the other society, dated 10 Jan. 1705, are on pp. 470–2; one statute reads: 'That no member reveal the secrets of the assembly'.

honour the very trying examination, which the candidates for that preferment are by the statutes required to undergo', and was admitted to Fellowship on 9 June 1707 (Stock, 2).

At about this time we begin to have a clearer picture not only of his career, but especially of his intellectual development. For from about 1706 to 1709 Berkeley was working out his immaterialist philosophy, for which he is best known, and we can see him doing this in two private notebooks, which fortunately have been preserved, and are now in the British Library, London. First published in 1871 by A. C. Fraser—who called them Berkeley's *Commonplace Book of Occasional Metaphysical Thoughts*—they have since been significantly re-edited at least four times, an indication both of their importance and of their problematic character. Now generally called the *Philosophical Commentaries*, the two notebooks are composed of some nine hundred entries or notes, many in the form of questions or pithy sentences, sometimes of an enigmatic nature. Nearly all the entries have marginal signs, most of which are elucidated at the beginning of the second notebook (fo. 3), where Berkeley has the following key:

I — Introduction
M — Matter
P — Primary & Secondary Qualities
E — Existence
T — Time

S — Soul — Spirit
G — God
Mo — Moral Philosophy
N — Natural Philosophy

The marginal signs give some idea of the main subjects and scope of the *Philosophical Commentaries*. However, in order to appreciate the work's excitement and disorder one needs to look at the entries themselves. Here, as a sample, are nos. 7, 17, 423, and 625:

+   Why time in pain, longer than time in pleasure?

M   ffall of Adam, rise of Idolatry, rise of Epicurism & Hobbism, dispute about divisibility of matter &c expounded by material substances.

S   If uneasiness be necessary to set the will at work. Qu: How
      shall we will in Heaven.

M.+ Matter once allow'd. I defy any man to prove that God is not
      matter.

The *Commentaries* range over nearly every topic of the three philosophical classics which Berkeley published between 1709 and
1713, although there is much in the *Commentaries* which Berkeley
never published. They give us a unique, inside view of a great
philosophy in the making, and of the man behind the philosophy.
But it is at this point, when Berkeley appears more clearly, that
he has also becomes the subject of scholarly controversy. One small
but consequential question concerns the meaning of the marginal
plus sign (+) present above in entries 7 and 625. According to
most commentators, Berkeley used it to stand for: discard or, at
least, discount. As A. A. Luce, the most distinguished editor of
the *Commentaries*, once noted: 'In effect the sign was an obelus, and
it is of great importance in our study of development and revision;
for it calls attention to Berkeley's discarded views.'[5] However, this
interpretation has come under strong attack, which caused even
Luce to modify somewhat his earlier, clear-cut view.[6]

There have also been wider, biographical disputes. Thus for
some writers—again notably A. A. Luce—the *Philosophical
Commentaries* show Berkeley to be a shrewd, commonsense man
with a solid, commonsense philosophy; whereas for others they
reveal a radical and subversive thinker, a visionary who—as
W. B. Yeats expressed it—proved

---

[5] Luce, *Dialectic of Immaterialism* (London, 1963), 56.
[6] See Luce, 'Another Look at Berkeley's Notebooks', *Hermathena* 110 (1970),
8–14. The strongest criticism of Luce's interpretation is Bertil Belfrage, 'A New
Approach to Berkeley's Philosophical Notebooks', in E. Sosa (ed.), *Essays on the
Philosophy of George Berkeley* (Dordrecht, 1987), 217–30. For a more conciliatory
discussion, see E. J. Furlong, 'Some Puzzles in Berkeley's Writings', *Hermathena* 120
(1976), 68–71 and M. R. Ayers, who is probably expressing the consensus amongst
scholars when he states: 'The meaning of the symbol '+' is controversial, but it is
difficult to believe that it does not in general indicate entries for which Berkeley at some
time felt that he would have (or had had) no further use, whether because they
expressed falsehood . . . or because they adopted the wrong tone . . . or for some other
reason.' (*Berkeley: Philosophical Works* (1989), p. xxiv).

> All things a dream,
> That this pragmatical preposterous pig of a world . . .
> Must vanish in an instant, if the mind but change its theme.[7]

More will be said about this debate in Chapter 8, but here I want to complete my sketch of the uncontroversial outline of Berkeley's early life, work, and influences. Our next view of him, after his election to the coveted Fellowship, is through a short paper, 'Of Infinites', which he read to the Dublin Philosophical Society on 19 November 1707. Some three months later, on 11 January 1708, he delivered a sermon (his first extant) in the College Chapel on the afterlife. In February 1709 he was made a deacon. In the following year he was ordained, although, as we shall shortly see, in somewhat peculiar circumstances.

He was now launched on his college career, as lecturer in Greek, Hebrew and Divinity, and as Librarian and Junior Dean. More importantly, he was preparing for publication his first two major books, *An Essay Towards a New Theory of Vision* (Dublin, 1709) and *A Treatise concerning the Principles of Human Knowledge* (Dublin, 1710). The genesis of both books can be observed in the *Commentaries*; that of the latter work can also be traced in two other manuscripts: early versions of the Introduction and of sections 85 to 145. Neither book, and particularly not the *Principles*, was well received. Thus Berkeley's friend, Sir John Percival (1683–1748), reported to him from London in August 1710:

. . . I did but name the subject matter of your book [the *Principles*] to some ingenious friends of mine and they immediately treated it with ridicule, at the same time refusing to read it . . . A physician of my acquaintance undertook to describe your person, and argued you must needs be mad, and that you ought to take remedies. A Bishop pitied you.[8]

On the whole, Berkeley's early work was ridiculed unread; as a poet later put it, he was vanquished 'by a grin'.[9] Yet even a serious

---

[7] 'Blood and the Moon', *The Variorum Edition of the Poems* (London, 1957), 481. Yeats's picture is opposed by Luce, especially in the preface to *Berkeley's Immaterialism* (1945, reissued New York, 1968).

[8] Benjamin Rand, *Berkeley and Percival* (Cambridge, 1914), 80.

[9] John Brown in 1745; see below Ch. 5 § V for this quotation and more on the reception of Berkeley's philosophy.

philosopher such as Samuel Clarke (1675–1729), to whom he had sent the *Principles*, rejected Berkeley's philosophy, but refused to explain his objections to the book.

Berkeley's next work, *Passive Obedience* (Dublin, 1712), which contains his principal views on moral and political philosophy, provoked a more ominous response. He had delivered three dis-courses in the Trinity College Chapel in which he argued that active rebellion against any ruling government is always wrong, indeed sinful. This engendered suspicions that he was a Jacobite, that he supported the exiled Stuarts. Partly for this reason, he published the discourses, combining them into one work. Although *Passive Obedience* seems to have been more popular than his earlier books—since it went into three editions in two years—it did little, as we shall see in Chapter 4, to dispel the Jacobite rumours.

Berkeley's next project was a popular rewriting of his imma-terialist position. Believing that his *Principles* had been rejected partly because of style and presentation, he recast the work in the *Three Dialogues between Hylas and Philonous* (London, 1713). While the *Three Dialogues* are more elegant and accessible, and can almost be read as pure literature, they must give way to the *Principles* as the authoritative statement of his philosophy. Hence my exposition of his philosophy in Chapters 2 and 3 is based primarily on the *Principles*. It should also be borne in mind that the *Principles*, as we have it, is only the first part of a work which was to include at least one and (at one time) two other parts.[10] Even in the second (1734) edition of the *Principles*, the last authorized by Berkeley, 'Part I' is still displayed in the text. Concerning Part II, Berkeley told a correspondent in 1729 that he had 'made considerable pro-gress in it; but the manuscript was lost about fourteen years ago, during my travels in Italy, and I never had leisure since to do so disagreeable a thing as writing twice on the same subject' (*Works*, ii. 282).

---

[10] In entry 508 of the *Commentaries*, Berkeley notes, 'the Being of a God & the Freedom of Man: these to be handled in the beginning of the Second Book.' On the third part, which was to deal with natural philosophy, see nos. 583 and 853.

II

Berkeley left Ireland for London in early 1713, to improve his health, to meet 'men of merit', and to publish his *Three Dialogues*. He may also have thought that he could improve the reception of his *Three Dialogues* by having them published in London rather than Dublin. Berkeley's departure from Ireland ends what can be considered the first, and, from the point of posterity, most important phase of his career. Had Berkeley published nothing else after his *Three Dialogues,* his claim to philosophical fame would nonetheless have been assured. Let us then look at the intellectual background and influences from which his three philosophical classics emerged.

It would be most useful to know what philosophical teaching Berkeley received as an undergraduate at Trinity College. Unfortunately, we have little information, although we do have a letter from one of his College contemporaries, named John Shadwell, describing the course of philosophy in 1703 as a farrago of conflicting hypotheses drawn from Aristotle, Descartes, Colbert, Epicurus, Pierre Gassendi, Malebranche (1638–1715), and Locke (1632–1704). Among the writers and subjects neglected, Shadwell mentions Plato, Francis Bacon (1591–1626), Robert Boyle (1627–92), and the Humanities; but he notes that there were persons in the College illustrious in every point of learning such as the Provost and Professor of Theology, Peter Browne (1666–1735).[11]

It is generally agreed that John Locke and the Cartesians, particularly Father Nicolas Malebranche, were the most important influences on Berkeley. Locke's influence has never been in question, and especially not since the publication of Berkeley's *Philosophical Commentaries*, where Locke is the most cited philosopher. In his published writings, too, Berkeley refers to Locke, sometimes in highly laudatory terms. We know that Locke's *Essay concerning Human Understanding* (London, 1690) was studied very early at Trinity College, largely through the good offices of William Molyneux (1656–98), who, in a letter to Locke of 1692, points out that he had recommended the *Essay* to St George

---

[11] See *Analecta Hibernica* (Dublin, 1931), ii. 74.

Ashe (1658?–1718), the Provost of Trinity College; and Ashe 'was so wonderfully pleased and satisfied, that he ordered it to be read by the bachelors in the college, and strictly examines them in their progress therein'.[12] But Berkeley's attitude to Locke was mixed. He admired Locke's candour and concern for clarity; he adopted much of Locke's terminology (for example, that of primary and secondary qualities); he adapted important Lockean doctrines, such as the Lockean theories of meaning, substance, and time. But he also strongly attacked Locke, particularly on abstract general ideas.

The influence of Malebranche is harder to pin down, since Berkeley's references to him are fewer and invariably hostile, even dismissive. But in his pioneer work, *Berkeley and Malebranche* (Oxford, 1934; new edn., 1967), A. A. Luce has established the crucial influence of Malebranche's *Treatise Concerning the Search After Truth* (English trans. London, 1694), especially on Berkeley's rejection of matter and understanding of ideas. 'Ideas' are central for Berkeley, as they are for Malebranche and Locke. Berkeley's conception of idea is indebted to both men, Luce argued, but particularly to Malebranche. In the *Essay*'s 'Epistle to the Reader', Locke characterizes an idea as 'some immediate Object of the Mind, which it perceives or has before it'. Malebranche agrees, but goes further; for him ideas also have a certain substantiality and independent reality, lacking in Lockean ideas but present (as we shall see) in Berkeleian ideas. In short, as Luce nicely put it, 'Locke taught him, but Malebranche inspired him'; to which Luce later added 'Bayle alarmed and alerted him' (1967 edn., p. viii). The addition was occasioned partly by the research of Richard Popkin, which suggested that Berkeley's early, Malebranchian development of immaterialism was modified by reading the great sceptic, Pierre Bayle (1674–1706), who alerted Berkeley to the sceptical dangers inherent in Cartesianism and especially in Malebranche's version.[13] There is no doubt that Berkeley was

[12] *The Correspondence of John Locke*, ed. E. S. De Beer (Oxford, 1976–89), iv. 602.
[13] Popkin, 'Berkeley and Pyrrhonism', in Turbayne, 100–27. For a useful recent account of the Continental influence on Berkeley, see G. Vesey, *Berkeley* (Open University text; Milton Keynes, 1982).

sensitive to the dangers of scepticism; this is clear even from the subtitle of his *Three Dialogues* which states his 'opposition to Sceptics and Atheists'. But since Berkeley refers to Bayle only twice, it is hard to delineate precisely his influence.

While Locke, Malebranche, and Bayle should be seen as the chief influences on Berkeley's thought, it is also important to see his work in both a wider and narrower context. The wider context would include the work of Plato (whom Berkeley is supposed to have called his favourite author), Aristotle, Scholastic philosophers, G. W. Leibniz (1646–1716), and Isaac Newton (1642–1727). There are also the classic enemies of Christian philosophers; thus in entry 824 of the *Commentaries* Berkeley writes:

M. My Doctrines rightly understood all that Philosophy of Epicurus, Hobbs [1588–1679], Spinoza [1632–77] &c wch has been a Declared Enemy of Religion Comes to ye Ground.

There has been a regrettable tendency amongst recent commen⁄tators to identify Locke, rather than the traditional materialists, as the main or even exclusive target of Berkeley's immaterialism.[14]

Commentators have also tended to ignore the local, Irish influences on Berkeley's thought. This, too, I shall be showing, is a mistake; for Berkeley's philosophy emerged in the one great age of Irish philosophy. It was born in the 1690s with William Molyneux, Robert Molesworth (1656–1725) and John Toland (1670–1722); grew into adulthood in the early eighteenth century with Berkeley, William King (1650–1729), Peter Browne, Francis Hutcheson (1694–1746); and died in the late 1750s with Robert Clayton (1695–1758) and Edmund Burke (1729–97). Irish philos⁄ophy engaged a host of lesser⁄known figures, too, such as Edward Synge (1659–1741), Philip Skelton (1707–87) and John Ellis (1690–1764). It also found lasting popular expression in the satirical writings of Jonathan Swift—for example, his 1708 'Argument [against] abolishing Christianity'. Neither before this

---

[14] See my 'On Missing the Wrong Target', *Hermathena* 113 (1972), 54–67; repr. in Creery, vol. iii.

sixty-year period, nor after, has Ireland produced such continuous creative philosophy, or a philosopher of Berkeley's stature.[15]

There are two main tendencies in Irish philosophy: one liberal, the other traditional, both of which drew heavily on Locke. The liberals, such as Molesworth and Toland, represent the Enlightenment, especially in their sympathy for toleration and rationalism, and their hostility to the priestly and dogmatic aspects of religion. The traditionalists, such as King and Browne, are more inclined to fideism, empiricism, and intolerance. In Berkeley we can see the creative mingling of both tendencies. I shall be exploring the Irish impact—particularly of Toland, King, and Browne—on Berkeley in this chapter as well as in Chapters 4 and 6.

I have already mentioned William Molyneux's indirect influence, in having Locke's *Essay* studied at Trinity College. But Molyneux had a much more direct influence on Berkeley, particularly on his first major book, the *New Theory of Vision*. Berkeley's indebtedness to the *Dioptrica Nova* (London, 1692) of the 'ingenious Mr Molyneux' (*NTV*, sect. 4) can be seen throughout the *Theory of Vision*, starting with the key section 2, which is taken nearly verbatim from Molyneux's *Dioptrica* (p. 113). Molyneux's article on the moon illusion, published in the *Philosophical Transactions* in 1687, also influenced (albeit deleteriously) Berkeley's own explanation in sections 70 and 77.[16] A more profound influence was Molyneux's famous problem: whether a blind man made to see would be able to identify by sight alone objects which he formerly knew only by touch. Berkeley comments on this problem in fifteen entries of his notebooks, and uses it crucially in the *Theory of Vision*. The Molyneux problem was very much an Irish problem. One of the earliest published answers to it was in a 1695 letter by Edward Synge (later Archbishop of Tuam), who then used a variant of the problem in a 1698 work

[15] See my 'Enlightenment and Counter-Enlightenment in Irish Philosophy' and 'The Culmination and Causation of Irish Philosophy', in *Archiv für Geschichte der Philosophie* 64 (1982), 149–65 and 257–79.

[16] See my 'Berkeley and the Moon Illusions', *Revue Internationale de Philosophie* 154 (1985), 219–21; repr. in Creery, vol. i.

against Toland to justify belief in religious mystery, a justification which Berkeley was to employ (as we shall see in Chapter 6) in his *Theory of Vision*, section 148, and in *Alciphron* (1732), iv. 15.[17]

III

The importance of the Irish background can also be seen in two early episodes that enable us to gain a sharper picture of Berkeley the man, his thought, and the connection between them. The first of these also shows the influence of Locke; the second concerns Berkeley's irregular ordination. Let us begin, then, with what appears to be Berkeley's philosophical debut: the little paper, 'Of Infinites', which he read to the Dublin Philosophical Society on 19 November 1707. Although 'Of Infinites' was slight—scarcely four pages (in *Works*, iv, 235–8)—the meeting was probably of considerable significance for Berkeley. For one thing, this was no mere student club, but rather a Society composed of the leaders of church, state and thought in Ireland. The Society had been established in 1683, largely by William Molyneux, as a counter- part to the Royal Society in England. Among the Society's officers when Berkeley read his paper was the Earl of Pembroke, then Lord Lieutenant of Ireland, to whom Locke had dedicated his *Essay* seventeen years earlier and to whom Berkeley, too, was to dedicate his main philosophical work, the *Principles*. Two other officers, perhaps even more consequential, were Peter Browne, then Provost of Trinity College, and William King, Archbishop of Dublin, both philosophers of standing in and outside Ireland. King's reputation was based on his *De Origine Mali* (Dublin, 1702), a work discussed on the Continent by Leibniz and Bayle (and by Berkeley in his *Commentaries*). Browne's fame rested on his *Letter in Answer to* [John Toland's] *Christianity not Mysterious* (Dublin, 1697). Berkeley would later, in 1732 and 1733, cross

---

[17] Molyneux's problem was first printed in Locke's *Essay*, II. ix. 8 (2nd edn., 1694); on the Irish reaction, including extracts from Synge's letter and his response to Toland, see D. Berman and A. Carpenter, 'Eighteenth-Century Irish Philosophy', in S. Deane (gen. ed.), *The Field Day Anthology of Irish Writing* (Derry, 1991), i. 768–72, 777–9, 786–8.

swords (in print) with Browne, and it is likely that he did so with Browne and King at this meeting.

When Berkeley read 'Of Infinites' on 19 November 1707 he was very much a follower of Locke on the question of linguistic meaning, a crucial issue for philosophers and theologians at the time. Locke held an extreme cognitivist view on meaning, according to which a word can have meaning only if it stands for, or communicates, an idea. Thus in *Essay*, III. x. 26, Locke writes: 'He that hath Words of any language, without distinct Ideas in his Mind, to which he applies them in Discourse, only makes a Noise without any Sense or Signification . . .'. Similarly, Berkeley says in 'Of Infinites': "Tis plain to me we ought to use no sign without an idea answering it' (*Works*, iv. 235–6). But when Berkeley delivered his first (extant) sermon in the Trinity College Chapel on 11 January 1708 he had changed his mind. For here he happily uses certain words which he knows do not stand for ideas. Thus he asserts that 'we have no determin'd idea of the pleasures of Heaven'; and yet he speaks of them again and again (see *Works*, vii. 11–13). He also endorses St Paul's 'empty tho' emphatical description' of Heaven, namely, 'tis wt eye hath not seen nor ear heard neither hath it enter'd into the heart of man to conceive.' (ibid. 12). Clearly, Berkeley has here abandoned the Lockean, cognitivist, position, the position he had held so confidently only seven weeks earlier. How did this volteface occur? What, to be more exact, happened between 19 November 1707 and 11 January 1708 to bring about Berkeley's semantic revolution?

The issue is important to us, because by means of his new nonLockean, noncognitive semantics Berkeley was halfway to one of his major contributions to theology: the emotive theory of religious utterances. Very briefly, according to this theory, religious words such as 'grace' can be significant even if they do not inform or stand for ideas, provided they evoke appropriate emotions, attitudes, or actions.[18] Berkeley seems to have reached this theory by stages over a period of months. We find this emotive theory first fully expressed in the *Manuscript Introduction* to the *Principles*, written

[18]   For a more complete account, see below Ch. 6 §§ III–V.

near the middle or end of 1708, some six or ten months after the first sermon. But how did Berkeley come to the first stage in his theory, the abandonment of the cognitive theory that all significant words stand for ideas?

Now one obvious place to look for evidence of some change in Berkeley's thinking is in his *Commentaries*, the two notebooks he kept during this period. In the earlier notebook, the Lockean theory of meaning was very important to him. Thus towards the end of this notebook (entry 378) he sets out a fifteen-step demon-stration, which begins: 'All significant words stand for Ideas'. By entry 696 he was still a Lockean cognitivist; for there he warns his future reader not to 'regard my Words any otherwise than as occasions of bringing into his mind determin'd [ideas *crossed out*] significations so far as they fail of this they are Gibberish'. But by entry 720 this austere cognitivism has been repudiated. For in this important entry Berkeley writes:

I When I say I will reject all Propositions wherein I know not . . . fully & adequately & clearly . . . This is not to be extended to pro-positions in the Scripture. I speak of Matters of Reason & Philosophy not Revelation, In this I think an Humble Implicit faith becomes us just (where we cannot [fully *crossed out*] comprehend & Under-stand the proposition) such as a popish peasant gives to propositions he hears at Mass in Latin. This proud men may call blind, popish, implicit, irrational. for my part I think it more irrational to pretend to dispute at cavil & ridicule . . . holy mysteries i.e. propositions about things out of our reach that are altogether above our knowledge . . .

Here, I take it, Berkeley has reached, or nearly reached, the non-cognitive position of the first sermon, where he appears to be following the advice contained in entry 720.

Are there, then, any clues as to the nature of Berkeley's semantic revolution in the entries between 696 and 720? Entry 715 seems to be the most promising. It reads: 'N.B. To use utmost Caution not to give the least Handle of offence to the Church or Church-men.' The Church would have been the Anglican Church, and the two most influential Church-men in Berkeley's vicinity, as I have suggested, were King and Browne, both of whom were elected officers of the Society at the previous meeting on 12 November 1707.[19] To see why Berkeley's 'Of Infinites' might well have given 'Handle' to these two churchmen one must appreciate one of its main theses, a thesis taken, as Berkeley puts it, from 'the incomparable Mr. Locke's treatise of Humane Understanding, b. 2, ch. 17. sec. 7' (*Works*, iv. 235). Briefly, Locke had distinguished between two conceptions of infinity: (1) that of an 'endless growing idea', a never ending progression, for example, 1, 2, 3 . . .; and (2) that of a positive, completed totality, such as an infinite number. For Locke and the cognitivist Berkeley, only the first conception was legitimate, since, as Berkeley says, 'we have an idea of the former, but none at all of the later' (ibid.). Following Locke, Berkeley distinguishes between the two by calling the first (legitimate) conception 'infinity' and the second (illegitimate) conception 'infinite'. He then concludes his paper with the advice: 'Now I am of opinion that all disputes about infinites would cease . . . would [mathematicians] . . . condescend to learn from Mr. Locke what distinction there is betwixt infinity and infinite'(p. 238).

Now, unlike the young cognitivist Berkeley and his esteemed mentor, Mr. Locke, William King held that the word 'infinite' can be legitimately used. 'Who doth not know what I mean', writes King in a manuscript sent to Locke himself in 1692 by Molyneux,

when I ask if the world be infinite? The design of Ideas is to distinguish as a mark one thing from another. If I have knowledge of but a mole on a man's face by which I may know him from all others I have idea enough of him.[20]

King then acutely observes that Locke himself had contended in *Essay*, II. xiii. 23, that he had an

idea of [empty] Space [i.e., a vacuum] because we reasoned and argued about it. But here tho we reason and argue about infinite . . . yet he will not allow us to have an idea of it.

[19] Hoppen, 192–3.
[20] Locke, *Correspondence*, iv. 539.

King was not the only Irish philosopher to have previously quarrelled with the Lockean thesis of Berkeley's 'Of Infinites'. Browne, too, criticized Locke's notion of infinity in his 1697 *Letter in Answer to* [Toland's] *Christianity not Mysterious*, a work which established Browne's reputation and reached a third edition in 1703. Infinity, considered as an attribute of God, cannot he adequately understood as 'continu'd accumulation,' Browne argues, 'therefore it were more conducive to true knowledge, to own our ignorance and say it [infinity] is a Perfection which we know nothing of; but we form a gross, scanty notion of it, by perpetual addition', a notion which is 'answerable' as a representation of God's unknown infinity.[21] Although Browne and King are not making the same point, they both seem to agree (against Locke) that a word may be used meaningfully even though it does not stand for an idea which resembles the thing signified.

Here we can begin to see the crucial theological issue, a crux which had been brought to the fore by John Toland, the Irish freethinker from Co. Donegal, who, in *Christianity not Mysterious* (1696) had used Locke's cognitive theory of meaning to undermine belief in Christian mysteries. In short, since mysteries, such as the Holy Trinity, do not stand for distinct ideas, Toland argued that Christianity either employs meaningless doctrines or it is not mysterious. This line of argument is fairly apparent even from the full title of his book: *Christianity not Mysterious: or, a Treatise showing That there is nothing in the Gospel Contrary to Reason, nor above it: And that no Christian Doctrine can be properly called A Mystery.* Thus the Christian mysteries were for Toland meaningless 'Blictri' words—or 'Gibberish', to use Berkeley's expression— because like Blictri they do not stand for any distinct idea.[22] Shortly after issuing his notorious challenge in 1696, Toland returned to his native country, where he made himself so unpopular that an

---

[21] Browne, *A Letter in Answer to ... Christianity not Mysterious* (3rd edn., 1703), 35–6.

[22] In *Christianity not Mysterious* (London, 1696) Toland writes: 'if we have no Idea's of a thing, it is ... lost Labour for us to trouble our selves about it: For what I don't conceive, can no more give me right Notions of God, or influence my Actions, than a Prayer deliver'd in an unknown Tongue can excite my Devotion' (p. 28).

order was issued for his apprehension. His book was burned by the public hangman. It was even suggested that Toland himself should be burned. Certainly Browne called for his legal prosecution in his bellicose *Letter* of 1697. Toland prudently took the hint. He fled to England, never to return to Ireland. But he was not forgotten: in 1708 Swift called him the 'great Oracle of the antiChristians'.[23]

In 'Of Infinites', the young Junior Fellow, George Berkeley, seemed to be playing into the hands of the heretic Toland. If the word 'infinite' is meaningless, and if there is no legitimate notion of a positive infinity, then how can we say that God is infinite or that the mysterious joys of Heaven are infinite? My suggestion is that until 19 November 1707 Berkeley had not considered this; but that he very much did so when Browne and King taxed him with these destructive Tolandian consequences at that November meeting. They made Berkeley see what his (future) friend, Alexander Pope (1688–1744), was later to express in the couplet:

> What partly pleases totally will shock
> I question much if Toland would be Locke.[24]

We can witness Berkeley questioning much, I think, in entry 720 of the *Commentaries* and in his first sermon; for in the sermon he goes out of his way to apply the term 'infinite'—which he had earlier regarded as illegitimate—to the mystery of Heaven, confidently speaking of 'things of infinite weight' and of 'infinite eternal bliss'. He also comes as close as he ever did to the negative theology of King and Browne, which, as we shall see in Chapter 6, he later forcefully attacked in *Alciphron*, dialogue 4. Thus he says in the 1708 sermon that we have no determined idea of the pleasures of heaven 'because of their surpassing, transcendent nature which is not suited to our present weak & narrow faculties'

---

[23] Swift, 'An Argument [against] Abolishing Christianity', *The Works of Jonathan Swift*, ed. W. Scott (London, 1883), viii. 75.

[24] *The Works of Alexander Pope*, ed. W. Warburton (London, 1757), iii. 32; Pope intended (but decided against) using the couplet in his *Essay on Man* (1732–4), a poem on which Berkeley is said to have given him advice; see Joseph Warton, *An Essay on . . . Pope* (London, 1782), ii. 295.

(*Works*, vii. 13). This would certainly have appealed to those churchmen, the Provost (Browne) and the Archbishop and Visitor of Trinity College (King), both of whom could well have been listening attentively in the College Chapel on 11 January 1708.

Like Browne, Berkeley seems to allow in the 1708 sermon that things 'beyond this World' are 'a dark and empty Void to us', as Browne expressed it in his *Letter* against Toland (p. 46). And yet we must, of course, believe (what Berkeley calls) that 'empty tho emphatical description' of Heaven offered by St Paul, a description which Browne approvingly quotes in his *Letter* (p. 96). Berkeley also seems to be moving in the sermon to a more pragmatic, Kingean approach to theological language. The word 'infinite' and St Paul's description do have a use, even if they cannot 'so forcibly engage us' as cognitive terms (*Works*, vii. 13). Yet while Berkeley here held a non-cognitive view of statements about religious mystery, he does not seem to have formulated the specific emotive component which we find in the *Manuscript Introduction*, although the pragmatic approach (perhaps suggested by King) was pointing him in that direction.[25]

IV

In reconstructing Berkeley's semantic revolution, I have supposed a confrontation between Berkeley and his clerical superiors, King and Browne, at the 19 November 1707 meeting of the Dublin Philosophical Society. Part of my reason for supposing this is that we have direct evidence of later confrontations. Probably the most acrimonious of these occurred as a result of Berkeley's ordination by St George Ashe, Bishop of Clogher and Vice-Chancellor of Trinity College, in early 1710. Because this was done within King's jurisdiction (in Trinity College) but without his permission, King ordered Berkeley to be prosecuted in his court. To avoid this, Berkeley wrote a letter of apology, dated 18 April 1710, to the Archbishop. In his *Life of Berkeley*, A. A. Luce tends to play down this affair:

[25] See below, Ch. 6; on King's pragmatism, see my introduction to King's *Sermon on Predestination* (Dublin, 1976), 15–20.

The incident did not reflect in any way on Berkeley, who was the victim of a trial of strength between the university and the Archbishop. King was not an enemy of the college or of Berkeley. (pp. 43–4)

However, evidence has subsequently come to light which shows that King's attitude to Berkeley was decidedly unfriendly, at least in March 1710. The evidence is contained in a letter to Bishop Ashe, sent from Bath on 27 March 1710, in which King angrily writes:

... your Ldp alledges that Mr Berkly [*sic*] was in a great haste [to be ordained.] I believe he was as soon as my back was turned, but tho it be three years as you intimate since he was fellow, yet he never aplyed to me nor I suppose wou'd if I had bin in Dublin, and yet phaps it had not bin the worse for him, if I had discoursed him as I do others before Ordination but its plain to avoid that, he desired to be ordained by another, a reason that I think your Ldp shou'd consider well before you approve it.[26]

Clearly, King saw the episode at least partly in personal terms, as a trial of strength between himself and the young Junior Fellow. But why would King believe that Berkeley resisted being 'discoursed' by him and waited three years until his 'back was turned'? In his *Commentaries*, Berkeley himself notes that

+ I am young, I am an upstart, I am a pretender, I am vain, very well. I shall Endeavour patiently to bear up under the most lessening, vilifying appellations the pride & rage of man can devise.   (no. 465)

I do not know whether Berkeley had the Archbishop in mind in the latter part of this note; but it does seem reasonable to suppose that King had experienced something of Berkeley's 'vain', rebellious side before the ordination incident, and the 19 November 1707 meeting of the Dublin Philosophical Society may well have been the occasion.

According to Berkeley's daughter-in-law, Eliza, King was Berkeley's enemy, but Berkeley 'refused to make the least answer to the scurrilous things written against him by that worse than

---

[26] The letter is in the Library of Trinity College, Dublin, MS 750/11; for further details on it and the episode, see my 'Berkeley and King', *Notes and Queries* NS 29 (1982), 528–30.

savage monster Archbishop King of Dublin . . . saying, "The noticing them would be like preserving a *dirty* fly in AMBER"'.[27] It is hard to know how much confidence to place in this late (1797) statement from someone who had not met either Berkeley or King. However, King's comments (quoted above) support it. We also know that there was another uneasy encounter between the two men in 1710, arising from Berkeley's *New Theory of Vision* (1709). This comes out in Berkeley's important letter to Sir John Percival, of 1 March 1710, from which we learn that the Appendix Berkeley added to the second edition of the *New Theory of Vision* was 'to answer the objections of the Archbishop of Dublin' (*Works*, viii. 31).

Prima facie, Berkeley seems to be accommodating in the Appendix; thus he writes:

to prevent being misunderstood for the future, I was willing to make any necessary alterations or additions in what I had written. But that was impracticable, the present edition having been almost finished before I received this information. Wherefore I think it proper to consider in this place the principal objections that are come to my notice. (*Works*, i. 237)

But what Berkeley goes on to say could hardly have satisfied King. In two out of three cases his answer to King is little more than extensive quotations from well-known philosophers, Descartes and Gassendi. A man of King's position and reputation would hardly have been pleased with this lesson, or with Berkeley's final message: 'if they who are pleased to criticize on my essay would but read the whole over with some attention, they might be better able to comprehend my meaning . . .' (ibid. 239).

That Berkeley himself was not happy with the Appendix is shown by his omitting it from subsequent (1732) editions of the *New Theory of Vision*, and without incorporating its points in the body of the work. By then, however, Archbishop King had been dead for three years, although he was far from forgotten by Berkeley, since in that 1732 publication Berkeley forcefully attacks King's

---

[27] *Poems by the Late George-Monck Berkeley*, ed. Eliza Berkeley (London, 1797), p. ccxxvii.

(and Browne's) theological position. In Chapter 6 I shall be examining this sequel to their debate. I must first consider Berkeley's chief claim to fame, his immaterialist philosophy—which showed him to be, according to J. S. Mill (1806–73), 'the one of greatest philosophic genius' (Mill, 451). This is the subject of the next chapter.

2

Philosophy in the Heroic Period (1709–1713)

Berkeley's philosophical system, like his philosophical prose, is disarmingly and deceptively simple. For him, there are only two sorts of things in the world: ideas and spirits. The elements of his system are set out in the first two sections of the *Principles of Human Knowledge*. Ideas are dealt with in section 1, spirits in section 2.

Berkeley's use of the word 'idea' will probably strike a modern reader as unusually wide. For first and foremost amongst ideas, according to him, are ideas of sense, or sensible experiences, about which he writes:

By sight I have the ideas of light and colours with their several degrees and variations. By touch I perceive, for example, hard and soft, heat and cold, motion and resistance . . . Smelling furnishes me with odours; the palate with tastes, and hearing conveys sounds to the mind.

Then there are 'ideas formed by help of memory and imagination, either compounding, dividing, or barely representing those orig⁄inally perceived [by sense] in the aforesaid ways'. These ideas, of memory and imagination, are distinguished from sensible ideas in being derived from sensible ideas and in being less vivid and orderly than them.

In section 2 Berkeley turns to the other ontological category: spirit or mind. Whereas 'ideas or objects of knowledge' are passive and are perceived, minds are active and perceive. There are two sorts of minds: finite and infinite. Human beings, or finite minds, are able to produce only derivative and faint ideas, of memory and imagination. God creates ideas of sense, which constitute the physical world, in human minds. Whereas our feeble ideas are 'unsteady', the ideas God produces are 'more affecting, orderly and distinct'; they are impressed upon our minds according to the laws of nature.

Minds are 'entirely distinct' from the ideas which they perceive, create, or act 'about'. In this sense, Berkeley is in the dualistic tradition of Descartes. Indeed, there is little in sections 1 and 2 which would have greatly surprised a contemporary reader of the *Principles*. The surprising inference comes in section 3 and is summed up in Berkeley's famous formula '*esse* is *percipi*', the being of the physical world consists in being perceived. Hence a table is simply a collection of sensible ideas; it exists only in being perceived by a mind: 'That neither our thoughts,' writes Berkeley,

nor passions, nor ideas formed by the imagination, exist without the mind, is what every body will allow. And it seems no less evident that the various sensations or ideas imprinted on the sense, however blended or combined together (that is, whatever objects they compose) cannot exist otherwise than in a mind perceiving them.   (sect. 3)

Yet even this might not have seemed that shocking to a contemporary reader accustomed to distinguishing between the material things which exist in the external world, independent of any perceivers, and our ideas or experiences of them. Nor does Berkeley deny the existence of matter, by name, until section 9 of the *Principles*, although the denial is implicit in section 3. This was no accident. Berkeley was a deep and subtle strategist. In this case we know something of his specific strategy from an important private letter to his friend, Percival, of 6 September 1710:

whatever doctrine contradicts vulgar and settled opinion had need been introduced with great caution into the world. For this reason ... I omitted all mention of the non-existence of matter in the title-page [of the *Principles*] dedication, preface and introduction, that so the notion might steal unawares on the reader.[1]

---

[1] *Works*, viii. 36. Compare *PC* 163, where Berkeley observes how one must do more than merely demonstrate a proposition's truth in metaphysics as distinct from mathematics, where 'men have no prejudices, no anticipated opinions ...'; in metaphysics one has to deal with 'scruples and establish'd opinions wch contradict' the truth.

Some commentators, notably A. A. Luce and M. R. Ayers, have argued that Berkeley's diplomatic strategy is also present in a more positive way in his 'survey of the objects of human knowledge' in section 1. This raises a complication which I have so far intentionally glossed over, namely, that in section 1 Berkeley seems to allow a third type of ideas: 'such as are perceived by attending to the passions and operations of the mind'. Yet, as Ayers points out, 'The rejection of [these] "ideas of reflection" is essential to Berkeley's published philosophy'. Thus, later in the *Principles*, sect. 27, Berkeley clearly states that the mind's acts are not, as ideas are, perceived. Hence, it would seem that mental operations and emotions should be classed with perceivers and active beings, rather than with ideas. Now Luce and Ayers argue—convincingly, I think—that this ambiguity and apparent conflict was deliberate. Berkeley's phrase 'such as are perceived by attending to the passions and operations of the mind' was, Luce states, 'diplomatic'; for Berkeley 'understood the art of "humouring" his readers'. And we know from the *Commentaries*, no. 571, that Berkeley 'had considered with care how he would "begin the 1st Book"'. In short, Luce says, he wished 'to appear at the outset to accept Locke's ideas of reflection; but he does not accept them'.[2] Similarly, Ayers holds that the 'ambiguity accords with Berkeley's evident intention that this [opening] paragraph should read like a statement of Lockean principles'.[3]

Berkeley's strategic humouring of his readers occurs even more strikingly in his *New Theory of Vision*. I shall say more about his views on vision in Chapter 6 § 1, when I describe the important theological use to which he put them; but the main point I want to make here concerns strategy. Thus when Berkeley published the *New Theory of Vision* in 1709 he already held, as is clear from the *Commentaries*, that the entire physical world was minddependent. Yet while he did not believe that tangible objects exist outside

[2] 'Is there a Berkeleian Philosophy?', *Hermathena* 25 (1936), 200–1.
[3] *Berkeley: Philosophical Works* (London, 1989), 77 n. For alternative accounts of the ambiguity, see *Works*, ii, 41 n. and E. J. Furlong, 'An Ambiguity in Berkeley's *Principles*', *Philosophical Quarterly* 14 (1964), 334–44.

the mind, he none the less states this as his view in the *New Theory of Vision*. In the following year (1710), Berkeley himself commented on this curious inconsistency in the *Principles*, section 44:

> That the proper objects of sight neither exist without the mind, nor are the images of external things, was shown even in that treatise [of vision]. Though throughout the same, the contrary be supposed true of tangible objects: not that to suppose that vulgar error, was necessary for estab⁄lishing the notion therein laid down; but because it was beside my purpose to examine and refute it in a discourse concerning *vision*.

It seems generally agreed that Berkeley also hoped that by presenting his daring doctrine in stages or by degrees he would be more likely to have it accepted (see *Works*, i. 149–50, 248).

There is also strategic intent, I believe, in section 2 of the *Theory of Vision*, which bears comparing with that in section 1 of the *Principles*. Section 2 reads:

> It is, I think, agreed by all that distance, of itself and immediately, can⁄not be seen. For distance being a line directed end⁄wise to the eye, it projects only one point in the fund [the retina] of the eye, which point remains invariably the same, whether the distance be longer or shorter.

Now Berkeley does hold that distance cannot immediately be seen; indeed, he makes explicit use of this premise in section 11 (and in section 18) for his argument against the accepted account of how we judge distance. According to this account, accepted by Descartes in *Optics* (1637), most of our judgements of distance are accomplished by an innate geometry: in short, rays coming from objects project on to the eyes angles by means of which the mind is said to judge objects to be near or far away. Berkeley's main argument in the *Theory of Vision* against the innate⁄geometry theory is:

1. We do not immediately see objects at a distance (sect. 2).
2. What we judge distance by must itself be perceived (sects. 10–12).
3. But we do not perceive projected lines or angles.
4. Therefore, we do not judge distance by an innate geometry.

Now what needs to be pointed out is that Berkeley is not entitled to use the justification 'agreed by all' for his major premise, i.e. (1). For, to begin with, by the 'fund', or retina, Berkeley's con- temporary readers must have understood a part of the human body existing outside the mind. The question then is: what are the projected lines, points, and retina? Are they visual or tangible? Now they cannot be visual for Berkeley, since that goes against his central thesis in the *Theory of Vision*. For how can there be a visual line projected from the outward object to a perceived visual point on the visual retina if, as Berkeley holds, all visual data are mind-dependent? A visual line and point on the retina would be outside, independent of the mind. Yet neither can Berkeley legitimately hold that the points are tangible; for then he would have to say that we immediately see tangible points on the retina, which he regards as absurd (see NTV, sect. 49).

So here again he was introducing his doctrine in a cautious, tactical, accommodating way. He is, I think, alluding to this initial accommodation of the *New Theory of Vision* in his later *Theory of Vision Vindicated and Explained* (London, 1733): 'It seemed proper [he writes in section 35], if not unavoidable, *to begin* in the accustomed style of optic writers, admitting divers things as true, which in a rigorous sense are not such, but only received by the vulgar and admitted for such ... [achieving] philosophical exactness [he adds] is ... done by degrees' (my emphasis). So as Berkeley proceeds in the *New Theory of Vision* he quietly offers his own justifications (e.g., in sects 41–3 and 79– 82) for the claim in section 2. In short, Berkeley exploits at least two 'vulgar' errors in the *New Theory of Vision*.

Berkeley outlines his general strategic approach most openly in two early manuscript notes, the first of which is extremely revealing also as autobiography:

He that would win another over to his opinion must seem to har- monize with him at first and humour him in his own way of talking. From my childhood I had an unaccountable turn of thought that way. (*Works*, ix. 153)

The second private note is from the *Commentaries*, no. 185:

M. P. Mem: to allow existence to colours in the dark, persons not thinking &c but not an absolute actual existence. 'Tis prudent to correct mens mistakes without altering their language. This makes truth glide into their souls insensibly.

This note is summed up, to some extent, in Berkeley's recommendation in *Principles*, sect. 51, that we should *'think with the learned, and speak with the vulgar'*. If we put this maxim together with the notes, published glosses, and 1710 observation to Percival (all quoted above) we can identify three main components in Berkeley's persuasive strategy. It involves (1) appearing at first to agree with the beliefs with which one disagrees, (2) by using the erroneous language of that belief; but then (3) correcting the false belief by degrees so that the correct belief can 'steal unaware on the reader', gliding 'insensibly' into his mind. In this way Berkeley hoped to persuade and, perhaps we should add, teach his readers. His timespan for accommodation and correction is not always the same. While false beliefs are usually corrected in the same work, this is not the case, for instance, with the principal 'vulgar error' in the *Theory of Vision*, which was corrected in the *Principles*.

I have said a good deal about Berkeley's strategy for a number of reasons: (1) I do not think that Berkeley scholars have recognized either its extent or seriousness; (2) it has important theological implications which I shall be discussing in the next chapter; (3) it has a bearing on Berkeley's controversial interpretation of the freethinkers in *Alciphron* (1732), a question I shall be taking up in Chapter 6; (4) it also has a bearing on the Yeats/Luce debate on Berkeley the man, which I shall be considering in Chapter 8; finally (5) it may throw light on some disputed issues in Berkeley's philosophy, for example, on his concept or concepts of mind and his use of arguments from relativity in the *Principles* and *Three Dialogues*.[4]

What I mean in (1) by the 'seriousness' of the strategy can be brought out straightaway by looking at the Introduction to the

---

[4] See e.g. C. M. Turbayne's 'Berkeley's Two Concepts of Mind', in Turbayne, 155; for a criticism of Turbayne's view, see G. Pitcher, *Berkeley* (London, 1977), 224–7.

Principles, where, in the last section, Berkeley warns his reader about the 'embarras and delusion of words', and entreats him 'to attain the same train of thoughts in reading, that I had in writing them', so that he will be 'out of danger of being deceived by my words'. But in the very next sentence, as we have seen above, Berkeley deceives his reader with the misleading (Lockean) suggestion that there are ideas 'perceived by attending to the passions and operations of the mind'. Berkeley is like the Schoolman, mentioned in section 20 of the Introduction, who uses certain words not to communicate but 'to dispose me to embrace his opinion'. Yet in Berkeley's case, the reader is not aware from the operative words which belief Berkeley wishes him to embrace. Indeed, in order for Berkeley's strategy to succeed, his reader must *not* have the same thoughts in reading Berkeley's words that Berkeley had in writing them.

If I am correct, then, Berkeley was engaged in important strategic deception. But this raises a number of serious problems of both a moral and biographical nature. Thus it may well be wondered how Berkeley's apparent willingness to engage in such deception coheres with his stern moral views in *Passive Obedience*, where (as we shall see in Chapter 4) he argues against making any exceptions to negative moral principles such as 'Thou shalt not commit adultery' or 'Thou shalt not resist the supreme power' (sect. 3). But does Berkeley regard lying as subject to the same prohibition as adultery or rebellion? According to Joseph Kupfer, he does: 'Like Kant, Berkeley concludes, for example, that "we ought not lie" is a [universal] moral rule.'[5] Yet it is by no means clear that this is Berkeley's view. He does not mention lying in *Passive Obedience*, with adultery or rebellion, as something that should never be done. The closest that he comes is 'Thou shalt not forswear thyself' (in sect. 3); but falsely swearing is not the same as deception or even lying. And, in any case, Berkeley is quite clear in *Alciphron* (1732) that in certain instances deception or dissembling is acceptable. For

---

[5] 'Universalization in Berkeley's Rule Utilitarianism', *Revue Internationale de Philosophie* 28 (1974), 511 and 530; in Clark, 93 and 112.

Would you undeceive a child that was taking physic? Would you officiously set an enemy right that was making a wrong attack? Would you help an enraged man to his sword? (*Alc.* iii. 16)

In the matter of deception, therefore, Berkeley was following Plato, rather than anticipating Kant.[6] Indeed, it is notable that in *Alciphron* iii. 16 Berkeley seems to have a therapeutic notion of philosophy itself. As 'bodily distempers are cured by physic', he says, so 'those of the mind are cured by philosophy'. In short, 'philosophy is a medicine for the soul of man'. But like all medicines it needs to be given at the right time and in the correct dosage. And it may be necessary, at times, not to undeceive the patient 'that was taking physic'.

II

By section 9 of the *Principles*, however, Berkeley has set aside strategy and let the cat plainly out of the bag. 'Matter' is now mentioned for the first time: 'the very notion of what is called matter', he states, 'involves a contradiction in it.' In the next 22 sections he then pursues his quarry, pausing in section 36 to present an abstract of his positive position. The diagram in Figure 1 may be useful in showing his overall positive and negative position.

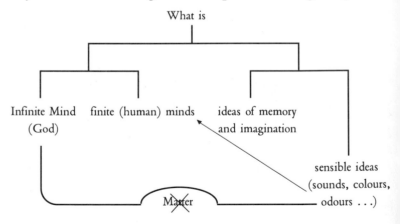

Fig. 1. Berkeley's immaterialist position

6 See Plato, *The Republic*, Book I (331 C); and Kupfer, pp. 93–4.

It is important to keep in mind Berkeley's strong assertion in section 9, because it is sometimes wrongly thought, particularly by casual readers of Berkeley's books, that he has a softer attitude towards matter: that he only doubts its existence. But this is not so, even though in some sections of the *Principles* (e.g. 18 and 20), and in the first of the *Three Dialogues*, he is making limited sceptical points. But Berkeley is not merely sceptical about matter: he clearly denies its existence and regards himself as diametrically opposed to the sceptic. This central, anti-sceptic theme is dramatized in the *Three Dialogues*, where the opponent of Berkeley, Hylas (or the materialist), at first regards Philonous (the lover of mind and defender of Berkeley's immaterialism) as a sceptic. But Hylas is forced as the dialogue proceeds to concede that he (the defender of matter) is closer to scepticism than Philonous.

Berkeley also believes that his immaterialism is not only further from scepticism but—perhaps even more surprisingly—closer to common sense than is materialism. For if, as Berkeley says, one were to ask an ordinary person, the so-called 'man in the street', what he thinks are the real physical things, he would reply that they are those things he immediately perceives (*Works*, ii, 262), rather than (as most philosophers would say) objects represented by our immediate experience. Berkeley agrees with this common-sense response, but he thinks that it needs to be united with a crucial truth agreed on by 'the philosophers', namely, that the things *immediately perceived, are ideas which exist only in the mind*'. These 'two notions put together [Berkeley says] do in effect constitute the substance of what I advance'. (ibid.)

This anti-scepticism and pro-commonsense theme is taken up in the concluding passage of the *Three Dialogues* (a passage which may also allude to Berkeley's strategy of apparent accommodation), where Philonous says, 'the same principles which at first view lead to *scepticism*, pursued to a certain point, bring men back to common sense' (*Works,* ii. 263).

Of course, to say that Berkeley opposed scepticism in the interest of common sense is not to say that he was successful, or that his philosophy does not logically involve or lead to scepticism. The charge of scepticism was persistently levelled against him. Thus David Hume, the leading philosopher writing after Berkeley—and himself a sceptic—held that most of Berkeley's books 'form the best lessons of skepticism, which are to be found either among the ancient or modern philosophers, BAYLE not excepted'. However, Hume recognized that this was by no means Berkeley's intention; for, as he goes on to say, Berkeley 'professes . . . in his title-page

to have composed his book against the skeptics as well as against the atheists and freethinkers. But that all his arguments, though otherwise intended, are in reality merely skeptical appears from this, *that they admit of no answer and produce no conviction.* Their only effect is to cause that momentary amazement and irresolution and confusion which is the result of skepticism.[7]

Whether Hume is correct, we can see only after we have examined some of Berkeley's powerful arguments.

Now one main argument for immaterialism can be formulated as follows:

1. Everything which we perceive or know of the physical world is got through our senses.
2. Our senses present us with ideas of sense; that is, the only immediate objects of our senses are sensible ideas.
3. These mind-dependent sensible ideas are all that minds can know of the physical world.
4. Therefore we can know nothing of matter or of an unthinking being which exists outside or independently of mind.
5. Therefore matter is inconceivable or unintelligible.

Is this a convincing argument? Possibly so, but a reader may well feel suspicious of step (2); for surely, it might be objected, we see and touch objects, tables and trees, which are outside our minds. Sometimes Berkeley takes this objection to be evidently wrong, for the simple reason that what we immediately perceive can only, he thinks, be a perception, or sensible idea, and hence mind-dependent. He also (as we have seen above) takes (2) to be a crucial truth agreed on by 'the philosophers'. In the first of the

[7] *An Inquiry concerning Human Understanding* (1777; Indianapolis, 1955), 163.

Three Dialogues, however, Berkeley does give us something more like an argument for (2), which runs as follows:

1. Pain, everyone agrees, is subjective or mind-dependent.
2. When, therefore, we put our hands close to a fire and feel the pain, we do not say the pain is in the fire: rather, we say that the pain is in us, in our minds.
3. But when we feel the pain we also feel extreme heat, which we cannot separate from the pain.
4. But if the two cannot be separated, then both must exist in the same place, that is, in the mind. (See *Works*, ii, 175–6.)

So heat and other qualities, such as odours, tastes, sounds, which seem inextricably connected with pain or pleasure, must be mind-dependent, sensible ideas. (For example, an extremely loud sound is painful, so is a very sour taste.) Berkeley's main argument, however, is a good deal more complicated, even when supple-mented by the above. For one thing, he was aiming to show not merely that we cannot know anything of matter, but that any distinct conception of matter involves a contradiction. He was, in short, aiming to explode every apparently plausible conception of matter. It is not always appreciated that Berkeley had in view not just one target, but different materialistic targets and sometimes a shifting target. Accordingly, the same argument may not be applicable against every targeted conception of matter. But, in general, Berkeley has two criticisms: that every conception of matter is either meaningless or contradictory. As he emphatically puts it in section 24: 'It is on this therefore that I insist, to wit, that the absolute existence of unthinking things are words with-out a meaning, or which include a contradiction.'

Now to say that something is meaningless, unintelligible, or empty (Berkeley seems to use these expressions interchangeably) is not the worst thing one can say about an alleged thing. For one might still hold that it (whatever 'it' is) none the less exists, even though you or I cannot understand 'it'. After all, our human minds are finite; hence we are unlikely to understand everything that exists. As Berkeley himself says in the *Three Dialogues*, 'Many things, for ought I know, may exist, whereof neither I nor any other man hath or can have any idea or notion whatsoever' (*Works*, ii. 232). But this is not to say that the charge of meaninglessness is not serious. It is, because if X is cognitively meaningless, then in affirming X I seem to be saying nothing. I might as well say that 'Gloop' or 'Blictri' (a classic nonsense word) exists. Hence, if the asserter of X wants to be taken seriously, he must have some distinct sense or use for X. But when matter is given a distinct sense—and it will need to be, if it is to be taken seriously—then, Berkeley holds, it can be shown to be contradictory. And if X is contradictory, then it cannot exist. (To say that something is contradictory is, for nearly all philosophers, the worst thing one can say about it.) So Berkeley goes through various conceptions of matter, showing them to be either meaningless or contradictory. He sometimes, as we will see, uses this technique as a gladiator might use two weapons: one to draw his opponent out (the charge of meaninglessness), the other to dispatch him (the charge of contradiction).

The process begins in *Principles*, sect. 3, where Berkeley considers the first putative concept of matter (although he does not call it such.) This is 'the absolute existence of unthinking things without any relation to their being perceived'. But what could such a thing be? It cannot be an idea, for an idea is perceived; nor can it be a mind, since a mind is a thinking thing. Hence the expression seems to refer to nothing; it is, he says, 'unintelligible'. However in section 4 we have quite a different conception of material things, since here we have 'houses, mountains, rivers, and in a word all sensible objects [which] have an existence, natural or real, distinct from being perceived ...'. This conception, he urges, involves a 'manifest contradiction', since it is saying that houses are and are not perceived. Similarly in section 7 Berkeley attacks a conception of matter according to which sensible qualities are said to exist in an unthinking substance. But this again is a 'manifest contradiction', since it implies that a non-percipient being, which cannot sense, is having sensations.

If we look at the key sections 3 to 24 in this way, we find Berkeley arguing that a certain conception of matter is either:

(sect. 3) unintelligible; (4) contradictory; (6) unintelligible; (7) contradictory; (8) inconceivable or contradictory; (9) contradictory; (10) inconceivable; (11) inconceivable; (16) unintelligible; (17) unintelligible or contradictory; (22) contradictory; (23) contradic⁄ tory; (24) contradictory or meaningless.

Seeing the multiplicity of Berkeley's materialistic targets should also help us to appreciate that he is not simply attacking one philosopher—who, according to most textbooks, was Locke. Berkeley never, in fact, identifies his materialistic opponents by name in these sections. They are simply described as 'philoso⁄ phers', 'materialists', 'some there are', or 'modern philosophers'. The only writer specifically adverted to in the entire body of the *Principles* (i.e., excluding the Introduction) is the author of the 'celebrated' *Principia* (1687), Isaac Newton, whose views on motion and space are respectfully but firmly criticized in sections 110–16. In section 93, Berkeley comes close to naming his opponents when he speaks of 'your Epicureans, Hobbists, and the like . . .'. In the *Three Dialogues* he is more specific, mentioning 'Vanini, Hobbes and Spinoza' (*Works*, ii. 213). In neither work, however, is Locke mentioned as a target of immaterialism.[8]

Locke is indeed singled out for criticism in the Introduction to the *Principles*, sects. 11–13, on the subject of abstraction. Here Berkeley quotes from Locke's *Essay*—the only work, apart from Scripture, which he does quote in the *Principles*—and then goes on to attack that 'late deservedly esteemed philosopher'. For Locke, general words such as 'motion' and 'triangle' stand for abstract general ideas. Locke's position can be situated between Platonism, which holds that there are general ideas or forms actually existing in the world, and nominalism, according to which only particular things exist. Locke's compromise, sometimes called conceptualism, is that while only particular things really exist 'out there', we are able to form abstract general ideas from them, and it is these

---

[8] This has not prevented able philosophers, like George Pitcher, from making assertions such as 'Berkeley bluntly contends, against Locke, that our own ideas of sense cannot possibly resemble Lockean material objects . . .'; see his *Berkeley*, 115, and my review in the *Journal of the History of Philosophy* 18 (1980), 352–3.

psychological constructions to which general words refer. Berkeley opposed this view on both introspective and logical grounds. He also regarded it as one of the major causes of confusion and error in philosophy and the sciences.

Yet while Berkeley is a nominalist, he is not opposed to all sorts of abstraction: Legitimate abstraction occurs when something can indeed be imagined in abstraction—for example, we can imagine the head of a camel without its body, or the smell of a rose without the (visual or tangible) rose. But this is not the case with motion. One cannot imagine mere motion, or motion as such. One needs to imagine something in motion. And it must be one kind of motion: either falling, jumping, rolling, flying, or so on. Similarly, one cannot have an abstract general idea of a triangle; it needs to be a particular kind of triangle. Locke played into Berkeley's hands in *Essay*, IV. vii. 9, when he wrote that it required 'some pains and skill to form the *general Idea* of a Triangle (which is yet none of the most abstract, comprehensive, and difficult), for it must be neither Oblique nor Rectangle, neither Equilateral ... nor Scalene: but all and none of these at once'. By simply quoting the last part of this statement (in *Principles*, Introduction, sect. 13) Berkeley felt he was able to strike the ' killing blow' to the theory; for Locke seems to have described an idea which is contradictory and therefore impossible.

Commentators have differed in assessing Berkeley's critique of abstraction as well as its role in his immaterialism. For Hume, it was 'one of the greatest and most valuable discoveries that has been made of late years in the republic of letters'.[9] For A. A. Luce, Berkeley's distinguished follower, it is important but 'not all-important ... The refutation of matter does not rest on the refutation of abstract ideas; but the one refutation greatly helps our appreciation ... of the other.'[10] In *Principles*, sects. 5 and 6, Berkeley emphasizes the pernicious role of abstraction in fostering the belief in physical objects existing outside the mind. 'For can

---

[9]   *Treatise of Human Nature* (1739; Oxford, 1967), 17.

[10]   *Berkeley's Immaterialism*, 36; for a more positive view, see G. Pappas, 'Abstract Ideas and the *Esse* is *Percipi* Thesis', *Hermathena* 139 (1985), 47–62; also in Creery vol. 2.

there be a nicer strain of abstraction than to distinguish the existence of sensible things from their being perceived, so as to conceive them existing unperceived? . . . For my part I might as easily divide a thing from it self' (sect. 5).

In section 8 Berkeley introduces a new conception of matter which appears to evade the objections he brought against those in sections 3, 4, and 7. This fourth conception posits specific material things, and so cannot be charged with unintelligibility (as that in section 3). Nor can it be charged with contradiction (as that in section 4), because it does not assert that ideas exist unperceived. Nor does it suppose (as the conception in section 7 does) that an unthinking thing has, or perceives, ideas. All this theory asserts is that there are things existing outside the mind, of which our sensible ideas are 'copies or resemblances'. Here we have one of the most influential materialist theories, often called the representationalist theory of perception.

Representationalism posits three terms: (1) the mind, (2) its sensory experiences, and (3) the external, material object. Thus:

(1) mind ◄— (2) sensory experience ◄— (3) material object

Here (2) is said to represent and be the means whereby (1) knows (3). This theory of perception departs from direct realism, which has two terms: a (i) mind which directly knows (ii) external objects, somewhat in the way a searchlight (the mind) illuminates objects in the dark. Representationalism was widely held in the seventeenth and eighteenth centuries. Berkeley, however, regarded it as not only flawed theoretically, but also dangerous on account of its sceptical implications; for since we do not directly perceive (3) we must always be doubtful about the extent to which (2) represents or resembles (3).

Berkeley's principal attack on the representationalist theory is based on his so-called 'likeness principle': 'an idea can be like nothing but an idea' (sect. 8). How can a sound or an odour be like something which one cannot hear or smell? But if the external objects, (3), are like the representing ideas or experiences, (2), then they are ideas, and hence mind-dependent. If, on the contrary, these alleged objects are not like our ideas, then we seem (once again) to be saying that a sound is like something that cannot be heard, or that an external object is like nothing we can experience or know. In the first case, we seem to be uttering a contradiction, in the second case, nonsense.

In section 9, Berkeley introduces another theory of matter, this time in the context of the socalled primary/secondary quality distinction, a central distinction in the new science and philosophy. Briefly and simply, there were, according to Descartes, Malebranche, Boyle and Locke, some qualities which were essential and intrinsic to bodies, for example, extension, solidity, number. These Locke called 'primary qualities', which he distinguished from 'secondary qualities', the powers in bodies which produce colours, odours, sounds, and sensations of hot or cold. So colours, odours, and so on are not essential or really in bodies; they are ideas in our minds, ideas of the secondary qualities. Hence in a world without perceivers there would be bodies, according to Malebranche and Locke, but they would contain only such qualities as extension and solidity, rather than colours, tastes, sounds, and smells. This, then, gives rise to a new conception of matter, namely, 'an inert, senseless substance, in which extension, figure, and motion, do actually subsist'. Against this theory Berkeley argues that we cannot separate or abstract the supposed primary from the ideas of secondary qualities.[11] And since it is allowed that the latter exist in the mind, then so must the former. For it is not in our 'power to frame an idea of a body extended and moved, but [we] must withal give it some colour or other sensible quality which is acknowledged to exist only in the mind' (sect. 10). We cannot think of a visual object that has no colour; nor can we consider a tangible object without some degree of warmth or coldness, roughness or smoothness.

In sections 14 and 15 Berkeley deploys another *ad hominem* argument against matter based on the primary/secondary quality distinction. In the same way that 'modern philosophers' prove

---

[11] As with matter, Berkeley's attack on the primary/secondary quality distinction is not directed against one philosopher. Thus, while he uses (or misuses) Locke's terms for the distinction, his characterization of it is, in some respects, closer to Malebranche's; see my 'On Missing the Wrong Target', 62–5.

that colours, tastes, hot and cold are mind-dependent, 'the same thing can be proved' of primary qualities, such as extension and shape. If I have eaten something sweet, I will then find a grapefruit very sour. Similarly, if my hand has been near a coal fire, and I place it in lukewarm water, I will find the water cool. If heat and cold, sweetness and sourness, are not really in bodies because they are altered by the state of the mind perceiving them; then 'why may we not as well argue [Berkeley says] that figure and extension are not patterns . . . in matter, because to the same eye at different stations . . . they appear various?'.

It is likely that Berkeley took this relativistic line of argument from Pierre Bayle's famous *Dictionnaire Historique et Critique* (1697); for in his article on Zeno the Eleatic Bayle observes that because 'the same bodies appear sweet to one man, bitter to another', the Cartesians have inferred that bodies are 'neither sweet nor bitter in their own nature', and that this can also be said of 'sounds, odours, heat, cold, hardness and softness . . . savours and colours, etc.'. But 'why [asks Bayle] should we not say the same of extension?'—the main primary quality of the Cartesians. For 'a body which seems to us very little, appears very great to a fly.'[12]

In fact, Berkeley is not very happy with this Baylean relativity argument; and not only because it depends on the (*ad hominem*) concession from his opponents that sounds, odours, and so on are mind-dependent. It is the argument's sceptical or inconclusive nature that worries Berkeley. For 'it must be confessed', he says, that 'this method of arguing doth not so much prove that there is no extension or colour in an outward object, as that we do not know by sense which is the true extension or colour of the object' (*PHK*, sect. 15). This confession shows that Berkeley's concern is not merely to cast sceptical doubt on the existence of matter, but to deny it. Yet there is a problem, since in the *Three Dialogues* (and in *PHK*, sects. 11 and 12) Berkeley uses relativity arguments without any apparent qualms about their sceptical or inconclusive nature. One plausible way of resolving this problem is to suppose that he was using them strategically.

---

[12] *The Dictionary, Historical and Critical* (London, 1738), v. 612.

Let us consider one final conception of matter, examined in section 16, according to which 'extension is a mode or accident of matter, and ... matter is the *substratum* that supports it'. It is easy to confuse this conception with the materialistic theory we previously considered from section 9; but the two, as we can see, are significantly different:

matter-A = substance + primary qualities (sect. 9);
matter-B = substance, which happens to support the quality (or accident) extension (sect. 16).

As the two conceptions are different, so Berkeley attacks them differently. Matter-A is contradictory, he holds, because it implies that a senseless substance necessarily has sensible qualities like extension. Matter-B, which Berkeley calls the 'received opinion', merely identifies matter with substance; hence it cannot be charged with contradiction. But matter-B has protected itself, so to speak, at the cost of losing meaningfulness; for what meaning can be given to mere substance, mere something, or to its supporting qualities? 'It is evident [writes Berkeley] support cannot here be taken in its usual or literal sense, as when we say that pillars support a building: in what sense therefore must it be taken?' How can substance literally support a quality if the supporter or support is not itself extended? But matter-B cannot be extended, since it is by definition different from, indeed it is the alleged support of, extension itself. Matter-A evades this difficulty, since it combines substance and extension; but then we have another conception, liable, once again, to the charge of contradiction.

A great deal more might be said about Berkeley's critique of matter. Indeed, most of the recent books on Berkeley deal very largely with it.[13] I hope I have said enough to show some of the argumentative force of this critique. More will also be said in the next chapter, where I shall be developing its theological impli- cations. First, something needs to be said about its weaknesses.

It is to Berkeley's credit that he himself stated, and tried to answer, most of the formidable objections to his philosophy.

[13] For a closely argued examination of this subject, see K. P. Winkler, *Berkeley: An Interpretation* (Oxford, 1989), ch. 6.

This he aims to do in sections 34–85 of the *Principles*, where he considers sixteen difficulties, and also in the *Three Dialogues*, particularly the third dialogue. These passages corroborate his auto-biographical statement that he had a 'turn' for harmonizing or getting into the mind of his opponent. In some cases, Berkeley seeks to obviate misunderstanding by explicating his own position. Thus in section 49 he poses this, fifth, objection: 'if extension and figure exist only in the mind, it follows that the mind is extended and figured.' To this he replies that for him ideas exist in the mind not 'by way of mode or attribute, but only by way of idea'. The phrase 'in the mind' should not be taken in the literal sense—as, for instance, 'the apples are in the basket'; it should be taken more in the sense of 'I shall keep you in mind'. The relationship between mind and its ideas is, for Berkeley, a perceptual one.

Perhaps the most persistent and damaging objection to imma-terialism is that it amounts to subjective idealism, in short, that it reduces the real physical world into a dreamy imaginary world; or, more soberly put, that it offers no tenable way of distinguishing between the objective world and the subjective, between reality and appearance. In one form or another, this criticism (discussed in sections 34–41) has been levelled against Berkeley from Andrew Baxter and Kant, in the eighteenth century, to Lenin and Geoffrey Warnock, in our own century.

It is a complicated issue, and one that I cannot adequately go into here. That it has some justification cannot, I think, be denied. Thus when Berkeley is trying to show that the physical world is mind-dependent he is happy to accept its apparent sub-jectivity. This is particularly clear in the *Three Dialogues* where, as we have seen above, he argues for the mind-dependence of heat and cold by showing their necessary connection with pain, which is plainly subjective. When, on the other hand, Berkeley is anxious to show that his philosophy is in line with common sense, then he stresses that sensible objects are entirely distinct from the mind. Yet there does seem to be a tension between these two aims, a tension that is explored in careful detail in Ian Tipton's *Berkeley: The Philosophy of Immaterialism* (London, 1974) and George Pitcher's *Berkeley* (London, 1977).

The tension comes out in a number of ways. For example, can you and I see the same (numerical) object, for example, this paper? Given a strict interpretation of *esse* is *percipi*, it would seem that we cannot, since you perceive one sensible idea (or collection of sensible ideas) and I perceive another. How could we both see the same mind-dependent idea? (One might as well claim that we could literally feel the same pain.) Nor will it necessarily or obviously help matters if we bring in God's idea of the paper, since, as Denis Grey has nicely put, 'God's point of view . . . carries no peculiar logical privileges; it is simply one among others'.[14] Now Berkeley is reluctant to accept this uncommonsensical position, because it deprives his philosophy of public objects. (It would also undermine his use of the so-called continuity argument for God's existence, which I shall be examining in Chapter 3 § I.) Yet it is by no means clear how successful he is in resisting the position. And it is interesting that in his 1713 *Clavis Universalis*, Berkeley's fellow immaterialist, Arthur Collier (1680–1732), accepted it: 'the sound which one [person at a concert] hears, is not the very same with the sound which another hears'.[15]

Another major objection often levelled against Berkeley is that the same arguments that he uses against matter could, with minor tailoring, be used against his notion of God or spirit. Very briefly, if matter is to be dismissed as meaningless because we have no idea of it, then should we not also dismiss spirit, since, as Berkeley states in *Principles*, sect. 2, we can have no idea of it? Now Berkeley replies to this objection at length in the *Three Dialogues* (*Works*, ii. 321–4), where, among other things, he notes that he rejects matter not *only* because he has no idea of it, but also because it involves a contradiction. Hence there is no clear-cut parity of reasoning, he claims, between spirit and matter.

I shall be saying something more about this complex topic in the next chapter; but here I should like to point to a more straightforward instance of inconsistency, that is, in Berkeley's use of Occam's razor, the argument from economy. He uses it in

[14] 'Berkeley on Other Selves: A Study in Fugue', *Philosophical Quarterly* 4 (1954), 30.
[15] See *Clavis Universalis*, ed. Ethel Bowman (Chicago, 1909), 11.

Principles, sect. 53, when attacking a materialist theory held by some 'Schoolmen' and 'others among the modern philosophers'— by which he probably means Malebranche. Briefly, according to this theory, God immediately causes all things, but he none the less created innumerable material beings, which, writes Berkeley, are 'made to no manner of purpose, since God might have done everything as well without them'. So even if it is possible that such useless material things exist, it is still, concludes Berkeley, 'a very unaccountable and extravagant supposition'. Occam's razor dictates that the useless things should be excised. Yet in sections 151 and 152 Berkeley takes quite a different view when, shifting from offence to defence, he tries to explain why God has created innumerable things which seem to have no purpose, such as seeds and embryos that never come to maturity and 'rains falling in desert places'. He writes:

we must not imagine, that the inexplicably fine machine of an animal or vegetable, costs the great Creator any more pains or trouble in its pro-duction than a pebble doth: nothing being more evident, than that an omnipotent spirit can indifferently produce every thing by a mere *fiat* or act of his will. Hence it is plain, that the splendid profusion of natural things should not be interpreted, weakness or prodigality in the agent who produces them, but rather be looked on as an argument of the riches of his power.   (sect. 152)

But then the materialist might ask, by parity of reasoning, why it is not 'an argument of the riches of his power' that God creates useless material beings? Indeed, why not (*apropos* representation-alism) suppose:

mind ◄— ideas ◄— material object ◄— material object-X

as this four-term theory would provide an even more 'splendid profusion of natural things'?

Berkeley's account of causality may also be criticized. At the least, it is embarrassingly uncommonsensical, since according to him there is no agency in physical objects; thus fire does not burn paper. Since the fire is a passive idea or collection of ideas, it cannot do or bring about anything. Ideas have no efficacy, only spirits have. There is, in fact, only a train of passive ideas, each idea disconnected from that preceding and succeeding it. The burning-paper idea simply follows the fire idea. That paper has always burned when in contact with fire should not make us think that there is any intrinsic causal connection between the two phenomena. Instead, according to Berkeley, we should regard it as a sign of God's goodness in imprinting sensible ideas in such an orderly fashion, according to the laws of nature—which he determines and decides to abide by. (Of course, God could, according to Berkeley, change his mind in very exceptional cases, thereby producing a miracle; see *Principles*, sect. 63.)

Even more embarrassing for Berkeley (the defender of common sense) is the question: do we move our own limbs? He wishes to return an affirmative answer, since a negative one seems so uncommonsensical. Thus in *Commentaries*, no. 548 he states: 'S We move our Legs ourselves. 'tis we that will their movement. Herein I differ from Malbranch.' But how can I move my legs if they are merely collections of ideas, i.e., how can one move an inert idea (or ideas) of sense? If I do not really move my pen, why should I think I move my fingers or legs? Since pens and fingers are both collections of sensible ideas, should not Berkeley say that they are both caused or created by God?

Now in his more theological mood, which we see at the end of the *Principles*, Berkeley happily embraces this position, since, as he says, it makes us realize our 'absolute and entire dependence' on God, '*in whom we live, and move, and have our being*' (sect. 149). But it would also mean, strangely, that the only real sort of causation in the world is creation: either the creation of sensible ideas by God, or the creation of imaginative and remembered ideas by human minds. Yet even this had theological advantages for Berkeley. It helped him to answer one of the great objections to theism, 'That impious maxim [as Hume put it] of ancient philosophy, *Ex nihilo, nihil fit*, by which the creation of matter was excluded ...'.[16] In short, how can one conceive God's creation of matter out of nothing? Yet if one cannot conceive it, as many

---

[16]   Hume, *Inquiry*, 172 n.

theists conceded, then is it not meaningless to assert it? Or, to put this in a more positive way: is it not then more reasonable to believe instead in the eternity of matter?

Locke had grappled with this problem towards the end of *Essay*, IV. x, where he admits that he has not provided an altogether satisfactory answer. The problem had been raised again more recently and insidiously by Anthony Collins (1676–1729), Locke's friend and Berkeley's future *bête noire*, in his 1708 *Answer to Samuel Clarke*. Here Collins suggests that if we do not 'have an Idea of the *Creation of matter ex nihilo*, we must inevitably conclude Matter a Self-existent Being', and that we have no good grounds for believing in God.[17] Now, at one level, Berkeley has an amazingly simple solution to this ancient and modern problem. If there is no matter, then surely the problem of conceiving its creation *ex nihilo* dissolves. This is Berkeley's message in section 92 of the *Principles*, where he speaks of the 'doctrine of matter' as the main 'foundation' upon which have

... been raised all the impious schemes of *atheism* and irreligion. Nay so great a difficulty hath it been thought, to conceive matter produced out of nothing, that the most celebrated among the ancient philosophers, even of these who maintained the being of a God, have thought matter to be uncreated and coeternal with him. How great a friend material substance hath been to *atheists* in all ages, were needless to relate. All their monstrous systems have so visible and necessary a dependence on it, that when this corner-stone is once removed, the whole fabric cannot choose but fall to the ground ...[18]

In fact, it is not quite as simple as that. For even if matter does not exist, Berkeley still has the problem of conceiving how God created *ex nihilo* the world of sensible ideas: 'all the choir of heaven and furniture of earth, in a word all those bodies which compose the mighty frame of the world', as he eloquently expresses

---

[17] See Collins's *Answer* (2nd edn. 1709), 78–9, and my *History of Atheism in Britain* (London, 1990), 79–81.

[18] In the *Three Dialogues* Berkeley describes the problem of how a spirit can produce 'corporeal substance ... out of nothing' as the atheist's 'most plausible argument against creation' (*Works*, ii. 256).

it in *Principles*, sect. 6. It is here that Berkeley's seemingly strange view of causality pays rich dividends. As he says in entry 830 of his *Commentaries*:

G. Why may we not conceive it possible for God to create things out of Nothing. Certainly we ourselves create in some wise whenever we imagine.

Our imaginative creation provides us with a glimpse or paradigm of creation *ex nihilo*, which, by analogy, we can extend to God. By eliminating efficient causality as a source of agency, Berkeley forces us, in effect, to appreciate that our only real or direct grip on agency or causal efficacy is in mental agency, in our imaginative creation.

On the debit side, Berkeley seems obliged to admit that for him there is no real pulling or pushing or cutting of things; instead there is only a train of inert ideas in our minds, created either by God (if sensible ideas) or by us (if imaginative). Clearly, this is very far from common sense; hence on this issue Berkeley can hardly say, as he does in *Commentaries*, no. 405, 'I side in all things with the Mob'. Yet the theological rewards in not siding, but only speaking with the mob, were great. And they were recognized very early on. For in a letter of 11 September 1710 John Chamberlayne wrote to Percival: 'I believe Mr Berkeley's doctrine of ideas does, besides other absurdities, solve that unphilosophical notion of the creation of matter from nothing.'[19] And yet there is still the question whether Berkeley is entitled to receive this reward. That is, can he really reject all causal efficacy in the physical world but allow it in our creation of imaginative ideas? Do we really 'create in some wise whenever we imagine'? This is a question that I shall consider in the next chapter, which is on Berkeley's immaterialist theology.

[19] Rand, *Berkeley and Percival*, 11 n.

3

Theology in the Heroic Period
(1709–1713)

In Chapter 2 we were largely concerned with Berkeley's attack on matter and with his alternative account of the physical world as collections of sensible ideas. This forms the basis of his philosophy. For positivists or phenomenalists, such as J. S. Mill and the late A. J. Ayer, this also constitutes Berkeley's most valuable contri' bution. Indeed, phenomenalism has been defined as Berkeley's philosophy without God.[1] But Mill and Ayer recognized that Berkeley himself would never have accepted positivism or phe' nomenalism *per se*. For Berkeley also believed in minds or spirits which cannot be known or experienced by sense. There are, then, two components in Berkeley's immaterialism. The first might be called 'positivistic immaterialism', the second 'spiritualistic immaterialism', the main part of which concerns the infinite spirit, God.

Berkeley was a strong believer in natural or rational theology. He held that the existence of God and the immortality of the soul could be demonstrated, and that he had done so in the *Principles* 'in a way not hitherto made use of' (*Works*, viii. 36). He has at least one and possibly two proofs for the existence of God based on the positivistic side of his immaterialism. The first, sometimes called the passivity argument, is set out in *Principles*, sects. 145–7. It can be succinctly outlined as follows:

1. The physical world is simply collections of sensible ideas.
2. Sensible ideas are inert.

[1]   G. Warnock, *Berkeley* (London, 1969), 225.

3. Hence a sensible idea cannot cause itself or another sensible idea.
4. But there must be some cause of the physical world.
5. The cause cannot be matter, since that does not, and cannot, exist.
6. Therefore it could only be mind.
7. But finite, human minds are able to produce only faint ideas, of memory and imagination.
8. Hence the vast world of sensible ideas, which appears so orderly, must be created by an infinite, intelligent mind—God.
9. Therefore God exists.

Although this argument has distinctively Berkeleian premises, it also shares something (notably premise 4) with the traditional cosmological and teleological arguments of Aquinas and Locke, among others. By comparison, the second argument is even more Berkeleian. It is partially enshrined in the pair of engaging limericks[2] by Monsignor Ronald Knox:

> There was a young man who said, 'God
> Must think it exceedingly odd
> If he finds that this tree
> Continues to be
> When there's no one about in the Quad.'

> *Reply*

> Dear Sir:
> Your astonishment's odd:
> *I* am always about in the Quad.
> And that's why the tree
> Will continue to be,
> Since observed by

> *Yours faithfully,*

> GOD

---

[2] Quoted in Bertrand Russell's *History of Western Philosophy* (New York, 1964), 648.

This argument can be more formally stated in these steps:

1. The physical world is simply collections of sensible ideas.
2. Sensible ideas cannot exist in themselves.
3. They must exist in, or be perceived by, some mind or minds.
4. But a vast number of physical objects, or collections of sensible ideas, exist when not perceived by any human mind.
5. They cannot exist in, or be perceived by, material bodies, since material bodies do not exist.
6. Therefore these objects, or collections of sensible ideas, must be perceived by some infinite mind—God.
7. Therefore God exists.

In short, God seems to be the only way of accounting for the existence, and continued existence, of objects not perceived by human minds. Without an infinite God, how could one explain, as Knox expresses it, 'why the tree will continue to be'? For many people Berkeley is distinctively the philosopher of Knox's limerick and this proof—sometimes called the continuity argument—for God's existence. This view of Berkeley goes back at least to Mill's 1871 review-article, in which he outlines the continuity argument and calls it Berkeley's 'favourite argument for Theism', for which, 'above all, he prized his immaterial theory' (Mill, 465).

However, some recent scholars have disputed whether Berkeley really thought he had such an argument. For as Jonathan Bennett has persuasively argued, the key passages in which the argument is supposed to occur—notably in the *Three Dialogues (Works*, ii. 173–7)—are by no mean decisive. Bennett and other commentators have all questioned whether Berkeley was even particularly concerned to assert the existence, or continued existence, of objects not perceived by any human mind.[3] Of course, if Berkeley was indifferent to the continuity of objects, then he could hardly have regarded the continuity argument as his 'favourite argument'. Without continuous objects the continuity argument would make no sense, whereas a denial of continuity would not jeopardize the passivity argument.

[3] See Bennett, ' Berkeley and God', in Armstrong and Engle; Bennett is supported by J. O. Urmson, *Berkeley* (Oxford, 1982), 20.

Does Berkeley, then, believe in continuity: that the tree in the Quad continues to be when unperceived by us, because it is perceived by God? Certainly, it sounds very odd to say that the tree ceases to exist when no human mind is perceiving it. Hence one would expect Berkeley, the self-proclaimed champion of common sense, to reject such a doctrine. On the other hand, there is much that Berkeley says that goes against continuity. Now one brief way of suggesting why God cannot, for Berkeley, continuously perceive objects might use the argument from the *Three Dialogues*, as out-lined in the previous chapter, which infers from the essentially painful nature of intense heat that it is mind-dependent. For if intense heat is painful, then it seems to follow that if God expe-riences such an idea, then he must also be experiencing pain. But this is something which Berkeley (like most theists) cannot accept, since it would call into question God's perfection. As he says in the *Three Dialogues*: 'that God . . . can suffer pain, I positively deny.' (*Works*, ii. 240). Yet if Berkeley's God cannot perceive the intense heat of the sun, say, then he can hardly be continuously perceiving the sun (as we understand it) when no human being is perceiving it.

Berkeley scholars are very much divided on whether Berkeley did or did not subscribe to continuity and to the continuity argument. J. D. Mabbott, however, seems to offer an interpretative *via media*. He holds that while Berkeley does assert continuity and the con-tinuity argument, he did this to humour his readers 'in their own way of talking'; really, Berkeley believed that God is only the cause of sensible ideas, not their perceiver. For if God perceived ideas, then he must be passive—which Mabbott takes to be unacceptable to Berkeley. Nor, according to Mabbott, does Berkeley need to say that God perceives ideas. For Berkeley can still speak, in one sense, of the tree in the Quad that no finite mind is perceiving, but then he must mean that the tree exists not as a collection of ideas but as powers in God. 'So the trees in the park are [Mabbott suggests] permanently represented only by a "resolve" of the will of God.'[4]

[4] Mabbott, 'The Place of God in Berkeley's Philosophy', in Armstrong, 368, and Turbayne, 206.

Berkeley discusses this powers theory in his *Commentaries*, and it is possible that it might have found a place in Part II of the *Principles*—just as the mind-independence of tangible objects was strategically accepted in the *New Theory of Vision*, although later consistently denied in the *Principles*. Yet to speak of the (continuous) tree in the Quad as (permanent) powers is hardly in accord with common sense, or step (4) in the continuity argument.

The traditional interpretation has, however, received some support from the recent discovery by Dr Bertil Belfrage of a hitherto unknown Berkeleian manuscript. The manuscript (probably dating from the 1720s) is in the Columbia University Library, among the books and papers of Samuel Johnson, Berkeley's friend and disciple, who became first President of King's College, now Columbia.[5] It is, almost certainly, a copy by Johnson taken from an original by Berkeley. Since the manuscript (as we have it) is short and summarizes much of Berkeley's spiritualistic immaterialism, I shall quote the whole of it:

It is my Opinion, 1. That There is an Infinite Omnipotent, Incorporal Being, which comprehends & contains all things: He is present everywhere; not that He is coextended with the Universe, but after the manner of a Spirit, by Thought & Power, perceiving all things & actuating all things: He comprehends every Created Being in the Immensity of His Intellect, & the Influence of His Power reacheth to all real [or natural] Effects; Insomuch that there is no Created Thing or Part of the Sensible World whatsoever which existeth out of the Divine Mind.

2. That the Things perceived by Sense are the true & real Things; That these Things do really exist out of our Minds, but then it must be in the Mind of God,—which, as hath been said includeth all Things.

3. That it is repugnant to the very Nature of Sensible things that they should exist independently of, or without a Mind; that therefore, from the very being of Sensible or Corporeal Things, it must necessarily be inferred, That there is a mind wherein they exist.

[5] Belfrage, 'A Summary of Berkeley's Metaphysics in a Hitherto Unpublished Berkeleian Manuscript', *Berkeley Newsletter* 3 (1979), 1–4.

Berkeley's words from opinion 2 (that the 'Things perceived by Sense . . . do really exist out of our Minds . . . in the Mind of God') suggest that he did believe in continuity; and opinion 3 suggests that he thought he had an argument for God's existence based on it. Although this new evidence is by no means conclusive, it does seem to bear against Mabbott's view, particularly if—as seems likely—Berkeley wrote it relatively late and without the aim of publishing it.

The traditional interpretation has also received support from E.J. Furlong, among others, who ably defends it against Bennett's objections. Furlong also questions whether Berkeley thought he had two separate arguments for the existence of God. According to Furlong, Berkeley saw passivity and continuity as two aspects of one argument, the first emphasizing God's will, the second his intellect.[6]

What most commentators seem to agree on is the implausibility of continuity within Berkeley's system. As Mill noted in his 1871 essay: 'The part of Berkeley's theory on which he grounded what he deemed the most cogent argument for a Deity, is obviously the weak and illogical part of it' (pp. 463–4). It is illogical, according to Mill, because the continuity argument requires a permanent, numerically identical tree; but Berkeley cannot consistently allow such a thing. Since for him a tree is a collection of sensible ideas, there is no sense in saying that 'it' is perceived by God when not perceived by any human mind. Berkeley equivocated, Mill maintains, in his use of the crucial word 'idea':

By means of this word he gives a kind of double existence to the objects of sense: they are, according to him, sensations, and contingencies, or possibilities, of sensation, and yet they are also something else; they . . . are laid up in the Divine Mind as a kind of repository, from which it almost seems that God must be supposed to detach them when it is his will to impress them on us . . . (Mill, pp. 464–5)

This latter line of argument comes out most clearly in a portion of the *Three Dialogues (Works*, ii. 252–4) where Berkeley tries to

---

[6] Furlong, 'Berkeley and the Tree in the Quad', *Philosophy* 41 (1969), 169–73; also in Armstrong and Engle.

answer a difficulty for his immaterialist philosophy raised by Lady Percival in 1710, concerning the Mosaic account of the creation. How, she asked, could physical objects have existed in the six days which preceded God's creation of human beings? Part of Berkeley's answer is 'to acknowledge a two-fold state of things, the one ectypal or natural, the other archetypal and eternal . . . The former was created in time; the latter existed from everlasting in the mind of God.' To this he adds that the things created in the first six days might have begun 'to exist in the mind of other created intelligences, beside men'—by which he seems to mean angels of different orders (*Works*, viii. 38).

Yet can God's eternal, archetypal tree be numerically the same as the ectypal one I now see? Berkeley needs to give a positive answer, if he is to assert coherently the continuous existence of the tree, but, according to most commentators, he is unable to do so. For how can I perceive God's idea (tree) without becoming part of God's mind? And even if God could, to use Mill's term, 'detach' his idea (tree) from himself when he creates it in me, then that idea would then be mine and not numerically the same as his. Hence it seems meaningless to talk of God's constantly perceiving the same tree which minds A and B perceive only intermittently.

And yet perhaps Berkeley's position is not as weak as Mill suggests. For consider the question which Berkeley asks in *Commentaries*, entry 645: 'Qu: whether there can be Volition without perception'; to which he answers some thirty entries later: 'Distinct from or without perception there is no Volition' (no. 674). I take this to mean that a mind cannot will, cause, or create an idea without perceiving the idea it creates. How could one create an imaginative idea of a red dot, for example, without perceiving it? And if we can judge God' s mental activity by analogy with our own—which we are entitled to do, according to Berkeley (*Works*, ii. 231)—then we may assume that God, too, must perceive the ideas he creates in finite minds. As Berkeley states in the *Three Dialogues*: 'whatever ideas we perceive from without are in the mind that affects us' (*Works*, ii. 240). Yet if God is aware of the idea he creates in my mind, then he and I are aware of the numerically same idea. To assert the contrary seems to imply that God creates an idea of which he is not aware, that he is an absolute creator but, at best, only a relative perceiver. Such a view seems mistaken, if only because it limits God's omniscience. Yet if God and I can perceive the same idea, then there seems no insuperable reason why God cannot create and perceive the same idea in other finite minds. Thus the way seems open for the continuity of the idea (tree).

However, to say that God can produce or preserve continuity is not to imply that he does, or must do so. And even if my defence of Berkeley is plausible—and the issue is far more com-plex than I have suggested—it would not be enough for the continuity argument, since there is still no good reason to accept step (4). For how, given the truth of '*esse* is *percipi*', can Berkeley legitimately say that certain objects exist unperceived by any human mind? While it may be uncommonsensical to think that objects go out of existence when unperceived by finite minds, this is scarcely a justification Berkeley can use; rather it could be used by his opponents as a *reductio ad absurdum* against his immaterialism. In short, while Berkeley may be able to justify his belief in con-tinuity by recourse to God, he cannot reasonably base his belief in God, it would seem, on his belief in continuity.

II

In any case, it is clear that God replaces matter in Berkeley's phi-losophy. God fills the vacuum left by the elimination of matter. Once we realize that matter cannot and does not separate us from God, we should become clearly aware of these 'great truths', as Berkeley calls them: that God 'is present and conscious to our innermost thoughts; and that we have a most absolute and imme-diate dependence on him' (*PHK*, sect. 155). Probably no major philosopher of the past three hundred years has assigned such a central and operative role to God in his system. The description, 'God-intoxicated man', which was applied to Spinoza, could with equal or more justice be applied to Berkeley. His conviction of the existence and presence of God seems to have been unusually powerful, so powerful that he questions whether some or most putative theists really believe in God. He suggests that many people have 'through a supine and dreadful negligence sunk into a sort of demy-atheism':

For what else can it be but some lurking infidelity, some secret misgivings of mind, with regard to the existence and attributes of God, which permits sinners to grow and harden in impiety? Since it is downright impossible, that a soul pierced and enlightened with a thorough sense of the omnipotence, holiness and justice of that *Almighty Spirit*, should persist in a remorseless violation of his laws. (*PHK*, 1st edn., sect. 155)

Berkeley, we may presume, having no misgivings himself, was 'pierced' with a 'thorough sense' of God. The language here and elsewhere (e.g. *Works*, vii. 10–11) is verging on the mystical. It is as though (to use one of his favourite analogies) Berkeley felt himself to be a sighted man in a land of blind or seriously myopic people. These people claim to be able to see; but since they often stumble and bump into objects, their avowals cannot be taken seriously. Similarly, Berkeley cannot take seriously the avowals of most theists, given their (godless) behaviour. His resounding, almost mystical, belief in God is given clearest expression in *Principles*, sect. 149:

It is therefore plain, that nothing can be more evident to any one that is capable of the least reflexion, than the existence of God, or a spirit who is intimately present to our minds, producing in them all that variety of ideas or sensations, which continually affect us, on whom we have an absolute and entire dependence, in short, *in whom we live, and move, and have our being*. That the discovery of this great truth which lies so near and obvious to the mind, should be attained to by the reason of so very few, is a sad instance of the stupidity and inattention of men, who, though they are surrounded with such clear manifestations of the Deity, are yet so little affected by them, that they seem as it were blinded with excess of light.

But if Berkeley had an almost mystical awareness of God—and it could be that his language is more conventionally rhetorical than personally expressive—it is a mysticism grounded on reason. Thus the exuberance of section 149 is based on Berkeley's argument in section 148 that we have more reason to believe in God than the existence of other (human) minds. And just as the sighted man in the land of blind people can persuade the inhabitants that he does see objects, so Berkeley uses reason to persuade putative theists, or 'demy-atheists', of the actual presence of God.[7] This is his primary aim. Thus, in the final section of the *Principles*, speaking of the 'main drift and design' of his labours, he says that he will esteem them 'altogether useless and ineffectual, if by what I have said I cannot inspire my readers with a pious sense of the presence of God . . .'.

As matter lost its hold, so, Berkeley hoped, God would establish his. Here, too, we can observe a certain strategic intent. Berkeley wished to inspire his readers with the 'presence of God', but he recognized that it had to be done gradually. By not mentioning his bold denial of matter by name in the early parts of the *Principles*, he hoped his positivistic immaterialism would glide into his readers' minds. Similarly, Berkeley does not mention God by name, as the substitute for matter, until section 62, although—as with matter in section 3—God is clearly implied in various circumlocutions in earlier sections. Thus he seems to have hoped that the spiritual-istic immaterialism would also gently glide into his readers' minds.

In section 6 Berkeley does state that if sensible objects 'do not exist in my mind or that of any other created spirit, they must either have no existence at all, or else subsist in the mind of some eternal spirit . . .'. His next relevant reference to God, in section 26, is even more understated. Here God is described as a 'cause of these [sensible] ideas whereon they depend' and 'an incorporeal active substance or spirit'. In sections 29 and 30 he is described, respectively, as a 'will or spirit that produces' ideas, and as 'the mind we depend on [that] excites in us the ideas of sense . . .'. In sections 32 and 33 Berkeley's language becomes more theological, when he speaks of 'the goodness and wisdom of that governing spirit . . .' and 'the Author of Nature'. Yet it is perhaps only in section 149, which I quoted above, that the theocentric force of Berkeley's immaterialism becomes fully apparent.

---

[7]   Compare *NTV*, sect. 148 and *Alc.* iv. 15; see also below Ch. 6.

A similar theological strategy is to be found, more simply and clearly, in Berkeley's *New Theory of Vision*, where he tries to show that vision—the visual data of sense—constitutes a language which tells us about tangible things. This eventually issued in what Berkeley calls 'a new and unanswerable proof of the existence and immediate operation of God' (*TVV*, sect. 1). But this proof only becomes evident in the third edition of the *Theory of Vision* and in *Alciphron* iv, published together in 1732. In the first two (1709) editions of the *Theory of Vision* Berkeley draws no explicit theological conclusion. Where he refers to vision as a language in sections in 147 and 152, he speaks of 'the universal language of nature' and 'the voice of nature'. In the third edition, however, these become 'the universal language of the Author of nature' and 'the voice of the Author of nature'. Here we have an excellent example of Berkeley's seeming 'to harmonize with [his reader] at first and humour him in his own way of talking'. By speaking of the language of nature he was using the old metaphor. But if vision is really, literally, a language, as Berkeley holds in *Alciphron*, iv. 12, then there must be a language-speaker. The logic is theological, therefore, although it is expressed initially in more naturalistic prose. (As Luce put it: 'You think Berkeley is building a house; you find he has built a church.'[8])

So both here and in the *Principles*, I believe, Berkeley hoped his strategy of verbal accommodation and gradual revelation would win over the 'demy-atheists', those who 'can't say there is not a God, but neither are they convinced that there is' (*PHK*, 1st edn., sect. 155). But there were dangers in strategically understating— even if only at the outset—the theistic component of immateri-alism; for some early readers, as Harry Bracken has shown, failed to see the central role (or any significant role) of God in Berkeley's philosophy.[9]

---

[8] *Berkeley's Immaterialism*, 69.
[9] Bracken, *The Early Reception of Berkeley's Immaterialism* (The Hague, rev. edn., 1965), 23 and 57.

III

But for present-day readers there is no such difficulty. The difficulty is in justifying this central role of God. Berkeley's concept of God has been criticized on various grounds, but I should like to consider briefly one main line of argument, which I alluded to at the end of the previous chapter. Is Berkeley entitled to speak of active spirit, given his rigorous view of causality (or the absence of it) in the physical world? If Berkeley is sure that fire does not really burn, how can he be so confident that God really causes, or creates, sensible ideas? Is Berkeley, in short, entitled to premises (4) and (6) in the passivity argument, as outlined above? Why must there be a cause or causes of the physical world? Berkeley would probably answer that everything must have a cause. But that is a principle which, since Hume, is no longer self-evident. It is also not entirely evident why, even if matter does not exist, the cause could only be mind (or one Mind).

However, the crucial issue is whether Berkeley has some satisfactory reason for holding that spirit can cause. Why not accept Hume's more economic (agnostic) position, according to which the world (as far as we can tell) is composed neither of matter nor active minds but only of collections—to use Berkeley's expression (*Works*, ii. 233)—of 'floating ideas, without any substance to support them'? I think Berkeley's most persuasive response to the Humean position is that we do have some grip on spiritual agency, because we know that we finite spirits can cause or create (weak) imaginative ideas. Then by magnifying our weak spiritual agency we can form by analogy some notion of divine agency. But the question is: how do we know that we really create imaginative ideas such as pink dragons? Here, again, Hume would say that the imaginative idea may be granted, but why suppose that we have created it?[10] If we are wrong, as Berkeley holds, to believe that fire causes paper to burn—which seems so patently evident to most people—then how can we be so confident that we really produce ideas of imagination?

---

[10] See Hume, *Inquiry*, sect. vii, 79–80.

Berkeley's reply is that we know this because we experience in ourselves such imaginative creation. Thus in the *Three Dialogues* he states that 'it is very conceivable' that ideas should 'be produced by a Spirit; since this is no more than I daily experience in myself, inasmuch as . . . by an act of my will [I] can form a great variety of them, and raise them up in my imagination . . .' (*Works*, ii. 215). Yet the expression 'experience in myself' is ambiguous. It could mean that I have direct introspective experience of myself actually creating imaginative ideas, or that I have indirect experience of it. Now it is hard to see how Berkeley could legitimately claim the former, given his insistence in the *Principles* that spirit and ideas are 'entirely distinct' (sect. 2), and that what we perceive is inert, rather than active. For 'Such is the nature of *spirit* or that which acts, that it cannot be of itself perceived, but only by the effects which it produceth' (sect. 27). Yet if this is so, then by 'experience in myself' Berkeley cannot mean that he has direct introspective experience of active imaginative creation. He is only entitled to say that he experiences first something like a wish to produce an imaginative idea and then the idea arising in his imagination; from which he infers that he is the cause of the imaginative idea. However, if this is what Berkeley means, then he has lost his grip on spiritual agency. He has no more access to spiritual agency than the materialist has to physical agency. In both cases it is a leap in the dark, an inference to something they know not what.[11]

There is another way of illustrating Berkeley's fundamental dilemma. Suppose he insists that he has a direct (non-ideational) experience of himself as spirit. Will this not offer an obvious opening to the materialist, who could then claim that he, too, has a direct (non-ideational) experience of matter?

---

[11] Berkeley's account of spirit, as something which 'cannot be of itself perceived', raises theological problems: e.g. can God perceive human spirits and their acts? If he cannot, then will this not limit God's omniscience, as well as going against the usual notion that he can 'see into our hearts'? Yet if he can, then this would seem to call into question Berkeley's dictum (in sect. 27) that a spirit cannot be directly perceived.

IV

In the Preface to the *Principles* Berkeley states that his work should be particularly useful 'to those who are tainted with scepticism, or want a demonstration of the existence and immateriality of God, or the natural immortality of the soul'. In the *Three Dialogues* (*Works*, ii. 257) he also stresses the importance of 'a plain demon-stration of the immediate Providence of an all-seeing God, and the natural immortality of the soul', 'those great articles of religion'. A great deal has been written on the first 'great' article, on Berkeley's proofs for the existence of God, but relatively little on immortality—possibly because Berkeley himself says relatively little about it, despite the importance he assigns to it.[12] If it were not for this belief in immortality, he writes in *Guardian*, no. 89, 'I had rather be an oyster than a man, the most stupid and senseless of animals . . .'.[13] This *Guardian* essay and his sermon on eternal life cast interesting light on the subject, but they are more literary and edifying than philosophical. The 'comfortable truth' of immortality is attested, he says in the *Guardian* essay, in three ways: by 'instinct, reason and faith' (*Works*, vii. 222). By 'instinct' he seems to mean that there is an innate desire for immortality in human beings, although he recognizes that some (perverse) people 'prefer the thought of annihilation' (ibid. 223).

Berkeley tells us more in the sermon, where, by supplying a theological premise, he converts the first attestation into a probable argument for immortality. The premise is that God would not have given us an 'appetite without a possibility of satisfying it'; from which it follows that since he has 'implanted in us a strong desire for immortality we have grounds to think there is a probability of having this . . . contented' (*Works*, vii. 109). In the sermon Berkeley also elucidates somewhat the third attestation, faith, although he is here mainly concerned to show that the resurrection of the body is a doctrine less strange and improbable than it may appear 'at first sight' (*Works*, vii. 107–8).

---

[12] For a notable exception, see Harry Bracken, 'Berkeley on the Immortality of the Soul', *The Modern Schoolman* 37 (1960), 77–94 and 197–212.

[13] *Works*, vii. 222; on Berkeley's *Guardian* (1713) essays, see below Ch. 4 § II.

Berkeley's most significant discussion of faith in a future life is in his first extant sermon, his *Manuscript Introduction*, and especially *Alciphron* vii. He general thesis is that it is meaningful and desir-able to believe in an afterlife (even though we have little or no cognitive grasp of it), since the doctrine can produce the right sort of emotions, habits, and actions. In his first sermon Berkeley tries to justify belief in an afterlife in a way reminiscent of Pascal's famous wager argument. Though the pleasures of Heaven promised in the Gospels are such as 'eye has not seen . . . [the] prize is good enough to warrant the laying out all our care . . . on the least hazard of obtaining it . . . tho' 'twere an hundred to one but we are cheated in the end' (*Works*, vii. 12–13). In the *Manuscript Introduction* and *Alciphron* vii the doctrine of the afterlife is explained emotively (as we shall see in Chapter 6) as well as being justi-fied pragmatically; and its utility is seen in terms of this-worldly advantages, rather than those likely to accrue in the next world. It is also important to note that for Berkeley the afterlife is a matter of faith or mystery, not rational theology. He clearly distinguished these areas (at least in his published works) when discussing the two great articles of religion: God and immortality. Thus God's grace and three-in-one nature are matters of faith or mystery; where-as his wisdom and goodness can be proved by reason. Similarly, we can know by reason that we are immortal, according to Berkeley, but what our otherworldly existence will be like is a matter of faith and mystery.

Berkeley's reasoned proof that the soul is immortal is clearly set out in *Principles*, sect. 141, although, as with his account of God, he has been gradually moving towards it in earlier sections. His discussion may be seen as one of the last statements in an extensive and often acrimonious debate on the soul, a debate started by Locke's suggestion in *Essay*, IV. iii. 6, that matter suitably dis-posed might be made to think if God superadded a faculty of thinking to it. Although Berkeley does not directly address Locke's suggestion, he is alluding to it in *Principles*, sect. 85, and also, possibly, in 141 where he states: 'It must not be supposed, that they who assert the natural immortality of the soul are of opinion, that it is absolutely incapable of annihilation, even by the infinite power of the Creator . . .'.

Berkeley's thesis is that the soul is not absolutely immortal but only 'not liable to be broken, or dissolv'd , by the ordinary Laws of Nature or motion'. His justification is similar to the well‑established Platonic‑Cartesian line of argument, although Berkeley gives the dualistic argument a mildly immaterialist slant: 'it hath been made evident, that bodies of what frame or texture soever, are barely passive ideas in the mind, which is more distant and heterogeneous from them, than light is from darkness.' Berkeley then claims to have 'shewn that the soul is indivisible, incorporeal, unextended'—although exactly where, or how, he does not tell us—from which it follows that the soul is 'incorruptible'. A helpful gloss on this statement is available, however, in the *Three Dialogues*: 'I say [the soul is] *indivisible*, because unextended; and *unextended*, because extended, figured, movable things are ideas; and that which perceives ideas . . . is plainly itself no idea' (*Works*, ii. 231). In short, since the inactive natural world 'cannot possibly affect an active, simple, uncompounded substance', the soul must be 'indissoluble by the force of nature' (sect. 141).

Here, as in the opening of the *Principles*, we can see Berkeley's allegiance to dualism, which was then accepted by nearly all philosophers and theologians in their account of immortality.[14] In recent years, this dualistic or Cartesian theory of mind has come under considerable pressure from philosophers such as Gilbert Ryle, who in his *Concept of Mind* (1949; London, 1966) ridiculed it as 'the dogma of the Ghost in the Machine' (p. 17). If minds are disembodied, purely mental beings, then how can they be identified, re‑identified, and distinguished one from another? Is it not the case that our criteria for such identification are based on observing bodily people? And could a bodiless person even know that a particular thought was its own? Yet unlike many contem‑porary philosophers, notably Antony Flew,[15] Berkeley saw no

[14] See my 'Die Debatte über die Seele', in J. P. Schobinger (ed.), *Grundriss der Geschichte der Philosophie, Die Philosophie des 17. Jahrhunderts* (Basle, 1988), iii. *England*, 760–81.

[15] See A. Flew, *The Logic of Mortality* (Oxford, 1987), ch. 7.

difficulty in conceiving the soul's disembodied existence following what 'is vulgarly called Death'.

This striking phrase is from Berkeley's 1729 letter to Johnson, in which he writes: 'Now, it seems very easy to conceive the soul to exist in a separate state (i.e., divested from those limits and laws of motion and perception with which she is embarrassed here), and to exercise herself on new ideas, without the intervention of these tangible things we call bodies' (*Works*, ii. 282). What Berkeley has in mind is vividly described in his *Guardian* essay (no. 27), where he tries to give his reader some 'faint and glimmering idea' of the soul's emerging into Heaven and experiencing what—in the words of his favourite Scriptural quotation—'eye hath not seen, nor ear heard . . .'. He asks us first to suppose '. . . a person blind and deaf from his birth', who, when adult, is deprived of his feeling, tasting, and smelling, and at the same time gains his sight and hearing, and then to suppose the same person's eyes, at their first opening, 'to be struck with a great variety of . . . pleasing objects, and his ears with melodious . . . music. Behold him amazed, ravished . . .'. We may then have 'some distant representation' of the Heavenly state (*Works*, vii. 183–4).

V

In this section I shall argue that Berkeley had a more distinctive proof for immortality than we find in *Principles*, sect. 141. The proof, drawn less from Plato or Descartes than from Locke, is based on Berkeley's radical theory of time, concisely outlined in *Principles*, sects. 97–8. I shall also try to show that the radical theory and equally radical theological application make sense when seen as a reply to William Coward's heterodox views on immortality, published between 1702 and 1706. Neither of these points has been appreciated by scholars.

For Berkeley, time is constituted by the succession of ideas in a mind. Hence time is subjective. Your time is different from mine. There is, in short, no external, absolute, public time. Berkeley rejected both absolute time and absolute space. He thought they were false abstractions, like the absurd abstract general idea of a triangle. Psychological time exists; it is experienced. Absolute, public time abstracts from all experiences; hence it makes no sense. On Berkeley's theory, I do not move through the great containers of space and time. Rather, time is in me: it is simply the succession of my ideas. A number of striking consequences follow from this. Since ideas can succeed each other more or less swiftly, time can also vary (see *PC*, nos. 7 and 16). Hence, if my ideas are brisker and faster moving than yours, then I have (or live) more time than you. It also follows that, contrary to Locke's claim in *Essay*, II. i, each of us always thinks (sect. 141). Why? Because, once again, time is in us. It only makes sense to say that I am not thinking between time-3 and time-4, if time is out there, independent of me. But, for Berkeley, there is no such independent absolute time.

A good deal might be said about this extraordinary theory, both about its weaknesses and its possible anticipation of twentieth-century theories in physics.[16] My aim, however, is to consider its implications for immortality. Yet it must be stated that Berkeley himself does not explicitly or precisely draw out such theological implications. That he did have further novel things to say on time, and that they were at least partly theological, is clear from his 1730 letter to Johnson, in which he writes: 'One of my earliest inquiries was about Time, which led me into several Paradoxes that I did not think fit or necessary to publish; particularly the notion that the Resurrection follows the next moment to death' (*Works*, ii. 293). Exactly what Berkeley has in mind here is not clear; nor is it likely to become so if we do not bear in mind that the word 'paradox' does not have the same meaning for us as it had in the eighteenth century. Now it means something which seems to be absurd or self-contradictory, although it might possibly be true; whereas, according to N. Bailey's *Universal English Dictionary* (10th edn., London, 1742), it is 'a strange Sentiment,

---

[16] See Tipton, *Berkeley*, in Garland, vol. 15, 272–89; Popper, 'A Note on Berkeley as Precursor of Mach and Einstein', in Armstrong, Engle, and Turbayne; and Jessop, 'Berkeley and Contemporary Physics', *Revue Internationale de Philosophie* 7(1953), 95–6.

contrary to common Opinion, but yet true'—a usage which Berkeley must be following in *Alciphron*, iv. 15 n. (see also *Works*, viii. 36).

Hence it is worth trying to understand Berkeley's 'several Paradoxes'. Connecting his 'notion' about the Resurrection with his theory of time takes us some of the way. If time is subjective, then there would seem to be no time after what is 'vulgarly called Death' and before the Resurrection, if no ideas intervene. Hence an allegedly dead person has not really stopped existing *qua* mind. This would happen only if there were public or absolute time in which the stopping could take place. This, I take it, is what Berkeley is saying in entry 590 of the *Commentaries*:

T No broken Intervals of Death or Annihilation. Those Intervals are nothing. Each Person's time being measured to him by his own Ideas.

So it seems that once a mind is created it need not and perhaps cannot cease existing. I might say that my deceased father has not existed, or has had no thoughts, for the past seventeen years, but that is to judge him falsely either by my time or by putative public time. I might as well say about someone who is deeply asleep, that he is, *qua* mind or self, dead. Berkeley himself argues roughly in this way in the *Principles*, sect. 98, when commenting on the accepted theory that time is 'infinitely divisible'. For that doctrine, he says, 'lays one under an absolute necessity of thinking, either that he passes away innumerable ages without a thought, or else that he is annihilated every moment of his life'. Berkeley scholars have not, I think, explicated this dilemma or two-part *reductio ad absurdum*.

Part of the explanation, I take it, is to be found in the Lockean–Newtonian theory of absolute time or, as Locke and Newton also call it, duration. That Newton and Locke are his targets in this area is clear (in Newton's case) from *Principles*, sect. 111, and (in Locke's case) from Berkeley's 1730 letter, quoted above, where he says: 'A succession of ideas I take to constitute Time, and not to be only the sensible measure thereof, as Mr Locke & others think' (*Works*, ii. 293). Now, both Locke and

Newton held that duration or absolute time was infinitely divisible. Duration, Locke states in *Essay*, II. xv. 9, is 'capable of addition or division *in infinitum*'. So on this theory my ideas or thoughts exist in the absolute container time of which any portion or 'length' to use Locke' s term in *Essay*, II. xiv. 21) is infinitely divisible.

However, this cannot be said of *my* ideas, or psychological time, as Locke himself realized. Ideas are not infinitely divisible. At some point in the division, the idea will (as psychologists now say) go below the level of threshold; it will cease to be perceived, and hence it will simply cease to be. For Locke, ideas are grosser than the temporal container in which they exist or flow. The train of my ideas, like those of other minds, is embedded in the common absolute time or duration. Since my ideas succeed each other and are distinguishable, there must be some (microscopic) bit of duration which separates them. But this does not mean that I am aware of that which separates two successive ideas. For me, the two ideas appear to be contiguous; although, according to Locke, this is not so. For, to adapt his thought experiment in *Essay*, II. iv. 10, suppose that two thin walls are constructed within a few feet of each other. Imagine, too, that you are at some distance from them when they are penetrated by a stone. You will hear only one bang; but there must have been two. There is some time between the two bangs, but you compressed it into one moment. Similarly, between any two ideas, or psychological moments, there must be some time, just as for Locke and Newton there must be some space between any two bodies, even though they sometimes appear to be contiguous or touching. Berkeley is certainly aware of the latter, parallel case; for in entry 632 of the *Commentaries* he writes:

N Qu: wt do men mean when they talk of one Body's touching another. I say you never saw one Body touch. or (rather) I say I never saw one Body that I could say touch' d this or that other. for that if my optiques were improv' d I should see intervalls & other bodies . . . betwixt those wch now seem to touch.

Between any two of my ideas, then, there is a bit of duration which can itself be divided into an infinite number of bits or moments. The situation can be pictured as in Figure 2.

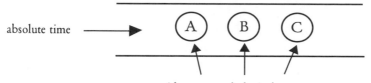

absolute time

ideas or psychological moments

Fig. 2. Time

Hence, since I am not thinking in those infinite number of moments between A and B, etc., I 'pass innumerable ages with-out a thought'. This is theoretically possible for Locke, since for him our minds can and do exist without thinking (see *Essay*, II. i). Here then we have one side of the dilemma.

It is harder to see what or who Berkeley was getting at in the other side of the dilemma or *reductio ad absurdum*. He may have been attacking those philosophers who combined the infinite divisibility of time with the Cartesian conception of mind as something that cannot exist without thoughts. Thus if our thoughts exist in absolute time, then, as we have seen above, between any two thoughts there will be some bit or length of absolute time, how-ever minuscule, which is thoughtless. But if the mind moves through such thoughtless moments, then given Descartes's view of mind as an essentially thinking thing, it must 'be annihilated every moment of life'. We are, that is, annihilated in the non-thinking moments between A, B, C and every thought.

Berkeley's subjective theory of time, since it denies that time is absolute and infinitely divisible, evades these absurdities. It also, as I have been suggesting, supplied him with an argument for immortality. In short, if there is no public time, then there would seem to be no time in which I could cease to exist. I cannot con-ceive an end to my train of ideas. It would make no more sense to say that (my) time can end than that (my) space can end, or that I can come to the end of it. Yet while I do not seem able to conceive my annihilation, I can conceive my eternal existence, given a negative definition of eternity as unending succession or indefinite continuance. This, as we have seen in Chapter 1, was Berkeley's view of infinity in his early 'Of Infinites' essay, of November 1707, where (with Locke) he rejects the (positive) concept of a completed infinite. That Berkeley was pursuing this line of argument on immortality is supported by entry 14 of the *Commentaries*:

+ Eternity is onely a train of innumerable ideas. hence the immortality of ye Soul easily conceiv'd. or rather the immortality of the person, yt of ye soul not being necessary for ought we can see.

Of course, in this key note Berkeley does not say that immortality is proved, but that it is 'easily conceiv'd'. Yet elsewhere he does explicate other important truths, which he does argue for, in this way: they are truths 'so near and obvious to the mind that a man need only open his eyes to see 'em' (see *PHK*, sects. 6 and 149). So once one clearly sees that a 'train of innumerable ideas' defines both a person and eternity, one immediately realizes that the person is immortal.

Berkeley's novel theory of time also, I suggest, enabled him to overcome certain theological difficulties which were raised by the once notorious William Coward (1657–1725), whose books of 1702–6 attracted fierce clerical criticism; indeed some of them were condemned by Parliament and burned by the public hangman. For Coward the soul was neither a substantial being, nor was it naturally immortal. Neither doctrine was part of authentic Christianity, he maintained; they were artificial grafts derived from pagan philosophy. For him, when we die our living, breathing bodies are extinguished, although they will be resurrected at the Last Judgement. Coward claimed to be restoring Christianity to its original, biblical purity by excising the graft of pagan philosophy.

Coward has a number of interesting criticisms of the (then) orthodox view, which, according to him, combines pagan philosophy and divine revelation. Here are two from his *Farther Thoughts concerning Human Soul* (London, 1703).

1. If our souls are naturally immortal, then they must go somewhere after death—presumably either to Heaven, Hell, or

(perhaps) Purgatory or Limbo. But that would mean that all souls who die before the Day of Judgement have either been sentenced without a trial, or have been pre-judged—either of which possibilities is unjust and makes a farce out of the Last Judgement (*Farther Thoughts*, 150).

2. The conjunction of the biblical and philosophical conceptions of immortality also leads to absurdities such as the following. If the souls of men go to Heaven or Hell after death, then plainly the soul of the first murderer, Cain, went to Hell after he died. Hence Cain's soul has been in Hell some 6,000 years. But suppose that some other man murders his brother and dies this year. He will receive 6,000 years less punishment than Cain, although, by hypothesis, he has committed exactly the same crime. This, too, casts doubt on God's justice (ibid. 153–4)

Now a Roman Catholic theologian could in some measure blunt the force of these difficulties by the doctrine of Purgatory or Limbo, since it might provide a neutral place to which the deceased soul could go before being judged and punished or rewarded. But this was not open to Anglican theologians like Berkeley. However, Berkeley can offer an answer to Coward's problems that is consistent with Anglicanism, by means of his novel theory of time. For since time is subjective, Cain need not suffer more time in Hell than the more recent murderer. God can slow down the flow of Cain's ideas, or accelerate the time of the recent brother-murderer, thereby bringing the extent of their punishments into line. The Anglican can also dissolve the problem of where departed souls reside before the Last Judgement and that of pre-judgement, if he accepts Berkeley's theory of time. He need not agree with Coward that we are extinguished at death, because he can say with Berkeley that 'the Resurrection follows the next moment to death'.

Another theological problem for which Berkeley seems to have a solution is alluded to in *Philosophical Commentaries*, no. 127, 'Question put by Mr Deering touching the thief in paradise'. That this relates to time is clear from its marginal sign 'T' which, as we know from Berkeley's key, means Time. The problem, I take it, refers to the apparent conflict between Luke 23: 43 and

24: 46; for in the first text Jesus says to the thief 'Today shalt thou be with me in Paradise', whereas in the second he tells his disciples that he rose from the dead 'on the third day'. But, then, how was he able to be with the thief in Paradise two or three days earlier? To this Berkeley could have answered that if Jesus had no ideas in the three days, then no time passed, at least for him; nor need any time have passed for the thief, until his emergence in Paradise. But three days of time did pass for the disciples; hence Jesus might have been assuming their sense of time when he spoke to them of three days.

Why did Berkeley not publish in the *Principles* his distinctive argument for immortality, which also provided answers to serious theological difficulties? One possibility is that, in line with his strategy of gradual or phased presentation, he intended to do so in Part II of the *Principles*. On this interpretation, the theory of time, as presented in *Principles*, Part I, sect. 98, was to set the stage for its theological exploitation in (the unhappily lost) Part II. This was his strategy with the optic-language argument, and it was also, as we shall see in Chapter 6, his strategy with the emotive theory of religious terms. Berkeley had developed the theological application of the emotive theory in his 1708 *Manuscript Introduction*, but while he published the theory in 1710 he did not publish its theological application until *Alciphron* in 1732.

Now there is some positive evidence that Berkeley did have (at least early on) a strategic intention for section 98. For in the *Commentaries*, no. 185, he advises himself 'to allow' (strategically) the 'existence' of 'persons not thinking', even though he thinks it is a mistaken opinion. In the event, he did not make use of this prudent accommodation, since in section 98 he openly states that 'the soul always thinks'.

However, there is probably more to it than the losing of the manuscript of Part II in Italy, since Berkeley might well have published his novel time-theory of immortality, and his criticisms of Coward, in *Alciphron* or the revised 1734 edition of the *Principles*. In the 1730 letter to Johnson he says that he did not 'think fit or necessary to publish' the 'several Paradoxes' (*Works*, ii. 293). He may have felt that it was no longer 'necessary' to publish them in 1730 since the Coward debate had by then died down. Yet there were, I suspect, deeper, theoretical reasons why it was not 'fit' to publish his 'several Paradoxes'.

Very briefly and speculatively, Berkeley's novel theory of immortality seems to lead to the conclusion that the soul is an eternal being which cannot be created or destroyed, 'even by the infinite power' of God. For how could God create or destroy the soul except at a particular time? But this seems to generate a number of perplexities, for example, that at a given moment in (God's) time he created (my) time. But what sense can be given to talk of the beginning or end of (my) time? Similarly, if God creates human times in his own time, then does not his Divine Time encompass them and become absolute time under another name? But this should be no more acceptable to Berkeley than the Newtonian–Lockean theory of absolute time. In both cases, there would be a real, absolute time 'participated in by all beings' (sect. 98). So Berkeley's novel theory seems logically to tend towards the opinion, repudiated by him in *Principles*, sect. 141, that the soul 'is absolutely incapable of annihilation'. And this opinion in turn tends towards transmigration of the soul, an even more unacceptable doctrine for a Christian philosopher. For if my soul has existed eternally, then my present embodiment, as David Berman, is unlikely to be its only one.

There is another reason, too, closer to Berkeley's philosophy, which may have turned him away from the distinctive argument for immortality, hinted at in the *Philosophical Commentaries*, no. 14. We know that before publishing his *Principles* Berkeley debated with himself long and hard about the correct concept of mind. At one time he seems to have accepted something like a Humean, non-substance concept of mind. This is particularly clear from the striking entries 579–81 in the *Commentaries*, where he writes:

+ Consult, ransack yr Understanding wt find you there besides several perceptions or thoughts ...

+ Mind is a congeries of Perceptions. Take away Perceptions & you take away the Mind ...

+ Say you the Mind is not the Perceptions. but that wch perceives. I answer you are abus'd by the words that & thing these are vague empty words wthout a meaning.

Each of these entries has the plus mark, +, in the margin, which Berkeley often used as a mark of rejection. And in the *Principles* he did reject this Humean, congeries notion of mind or person; and he rejected it for a substance theory of mind, according to which mind is distinguished from the ideas it perceives. Indeed, it is this substance theory which forms the basis of his official proof of immortality in section 141. Now *Commentaries*, entry 14, also has the plus sign in the margin, and it is possible that it, too, was rejected because it implied a Humean view of mind as a 'train of (innumerable) ideas', rather than as that (substance) which has ideas.

Either of these reasons could explain why Berkeley never pub⁄ lished what I have taken to be his novel account of immortality or any criticisms of Coward derived from it. The chief difficulty with my general reconstruction is that there is no statement of the theory or clear reference to Coward in the *Philosophical Commentaries* (although nos. 127 and 390 may allude to him). This absence is worrying; yet it would not be exceptional. For we should also expect to find in the *Commentaries* some reference to, or statement of, other notable theories, such as that vision is God's language; but we do not find it.[17] Supporting my thesis is the fact that Coward's fame or infamy reached its height around the same time (about 1705) as Berkeley's 'earliest inquiries about time' (about 1707).

[17] Berkeley's confident statement of this theory in *Principles*, sect. 44, strongly suggests that he had held it in 1709 and earlier.

4

The Middle Years
(1713–1721)

I

Berkeley's varied career seems to fall naturally into three periods, each marked by an idealistic cause or crusade. In the previous three chapters I examined the first period, in which he developed his immaterialist philosophy, a philosophy which he hoped would reform philosophy and lead men to a radically theistic or spiri-tualistic view of the world. This period, of philosophical idealism, began while Berkeley was still a student and was effectively com-pleted with the publication of the *Three Dialogues* in 1713, when he was a young man of twenty-eight. The third and final period spans the years 1735 to 1753, his later middle and old age, when, as Bishop of Cloyne, he advocated a medicine called tar-water, which he believed would cure or alleviate all physical ills. I shall be examining this final period, of medical idealism, in Chapter 7. From an outward point of view, both the first and third periods were largely uneventful. This is in sharp contrast to the middle period, 1714–34, which is the subject of this and the next chapter. Whereas the first and last periods were spent in Ireland, in Counties Kilkenny, Dublin, and Cork, the second, outgoing period sees Berkeley in, among other places, London, Oxford, Paris, Turin, Naples, Rome, Florence, Newport, Rhode Island, Boston, and then back to London and Dublin. This is by far the most colourful phase of Berkeley's life, when he meets many of the leading figures of his day and is seen most clearly on the world stage. It is also his great period of social idealism.

Berkeley left Ireland in early 1713. Arriving in London, he soon became acquainted with the literary élite: with Richard Steele (1672–1729), the editor of the *Tatler*, Joseph Addison (1672–1719), Alexander Pope, and John Arbuthnot (1667–1735)—the creator of John Bull and Berkeley's 'first proselyte'. His introduction to some of these men was through his writings, to others he was introduced by Swift, with whom he had probably become friendly in Ireland. The two men had much in common: they both attended the same school and university; they were both Anglican clergymen and great writers. They both wrote against the freethinkers; indeed, in *Alciphron* ii. 26, Berkeley took over one of Swift's conspiracy theories: that the freethinkers were really disguised Popish missionaries.[1] Swift, who was then at the height of his political power, also, as we shall see, rendered Berkeley more substantial services. In his 'Journal to Stella' of 12 April 1713, Swift writes:

I went to Court today on purpose to present Mr Berkeley, one of your Fellows of Dublin College to Lord Berkeley of Stratton. That Mr Berkeley is a very ingenious man, and a great philosopher, and I have mentioned him to all the ministers, and have given them some of his writings; and I will favour him as much as I can.[2]

Berkeley came to London partly with the intention of publishing his *Three Dialogues*, which he did in May 1713, by which time he was involved in another literary venture. Following the demise of the *Tatler*, Steele had started a new periodical, called *The Guardian*, for which he had enlisted Berkeley's help. In the first collected edition, published in 1714, the publisher (Steele) states that 'Mr Berkeley of TrinityCollege in Dublin has embellished [the work] with many excellent arguments in honour of religion and virtue' (*Works*, vii. 173). Among the topics Berkeley discusses in his *Guardian* essays are the afterlife (no. 27), the distinction between natural and artificial pleasures (no. 49), the utility of religion (nos. 55 and 126), education and religion (no. 62), how religion enlarges and irreligion narrows the mind (nos. 70 and 83), and the Christian idea of God (no. 88).

[1] See below, Ch. 6. § VIII, and my 'The Culmination and Causation', 269–70.
[2] *Works of Jonathan Swift*, iii. 147.

There has been some dispute about exactly which of the 175 *Guardian* papers Berkeley wrote, since nearly all the papers were either anonymous or pseudonymous. By all accounts, Berkeley was the third biggest contributor—Steele and Addison being the first and second. The authorship question is important, since the *Guardian* contains some of Berkeley's earliest published views on religious issues. However, those readers who may not wish to go into this difficult yet intriguing question can omit the next section.

II

There have been five notable attempts at determining Berkeley's share of the *Guardian*. The first was in a 1765 letter by Berkeley's son, George, to Bishop Percy; the most recent in J. C. Stephens's 1982 edition of the *Guardian*, which draws heavily on Luce's scholarly work on the subject. In Figure 3 we can see the state of play after more than two centuries.

Attribution	*Guardian* numbers													
George Berkeley, *fils* (1765 letter)	3	27	35	39	49	55		62		70	77				126
John Nichols (1789 edn. of *Guardian*)	3	27	35	39	49	55		62	69	70	77	83	88	89	126
A. C. Fraser (1871 edn. of *Works*)	3	27	35	39	49	55		62	69	70	77	83	88	89	126
A. A. Luce (1955 edn. of *Works*, vii)	9*	27	35	39	49	55		62		70	77	83	88	89	126
J. C. Stephens (1982 edn. of *Guardian*)	9*	27	35	39	49	55	58	62		70	77	83	88	89	126

*part of

Fig. 3. Table of *Guardian* Essays attributed to Berkeley

There are, then, nine papers which are unanimously ascribed to Berkeley: numbers 27, 35, 39, 49, 55, 62, 70, 77, and 126. In my opinion, Luce has made a convincing case for adding numbers

83, 88, 89, and omitting number 3. On the other hand, I am not persuaded by Stephens's reasons for adding 58, and I think that most of 69 must be returned to the list. The evidence for 69 is from Berkeley's friend and philosophical disciple, the American Samuel Johnson (1696–1772). In his *Elementa Philosophica* (Philadelphia, 1752), which is dedicated to Berkeley, Johnson prints, as he puts it:

A Philosophical Meditation or Prayer, of the late Archbishop of Cambray [Fénelon (1651–1715)]: In his demonstration of the existence of God, as it is expressed (nearly) by Bishop Berkeley, in the Guardian, No. 69.[3]

Johnson had many conversations with Berkeley in Rhode Island in 1729–31, and it is hard to believe that he would so confidently ascribe *Guardian* no. 69 to Berkeley without some express declaration from his friend and mentor. Once this is accepted, then it becomes almost certain that Berkeley also wrote some if not all of 81, since, as Luce has pointed out, 81 goes with 69. Certainly, the person who revised Fénelon's meditation in 69 also contributed the prayer in 81.

And there are further consequences as well. In his *Bibliography of George Berkeley* (2nd edn. 1973), T. E. Jessop discusses 'Five pieces, written by the author of the *The evidence of the existence of God* (Fénelon); supposed to be translated by Bishop Barclay' (p. 47). Now one of Jessop's reasons for regarding this work as spurious is that 'there is no evidence that Berkeley ever turned his hand to translation . . .'. But if we accept Johnson's attribution—as I think we must—then we do have evidence that Berkeley was involved in translating, or revising the translation, of the very writer in question, namely, Fénelon.

On the negative side, I think we can now be certain that Berkeley did not write the whole of 39 or—probably—27 and 35. In a 1957 article, E. J. Furlong had conjectured from biographical evidence that Berkeley did not write the concluding portion of 39. For if he penned the unpleasant remark that the writings

[3] *Samuel Johnson: his Career and Writings*, ed. H. and C. Schneider (New York, 1929), ii. 438.

of two (living) free-thinkers have 'raised our longing to see their posthumous works', then, according to Furlong, 'we should have to revise [our] opinion of him . . .'.[4] Stephens's editorial comment is that while Furlong's conjecture has 'a certain attractiveness', it leans 'heavily . . . on a reading of Berkeley's character that may be debatable' (*Guardian*, p. 639). I think it is debatable; for Berkeley was, as we shall see, extremely hostile to the free-thinkers. Indeed, according to J.S. Mill, 'the war against freethinkers was the leading purpose of Berkeley's career as a philosopher'(Mill, 465). Yet, for all that, Furlong was right: Berkeley did not write the concluding seven paragraphs of 39. For in some Steele papers recently acquired by the British Library (Add. MS 61618) a fragment of this concluding section has been discovered in Steele's hand.[5] There are a few implications of this discovery: the four-line N.B.s at the end of no. 27 and of no. 35, and the five-line introduction to 39, can no longer be confidently ascribed to Berkeley.

On a positive note, I think there is conclusive evidence, not adduced by Luce, for ascribing 27 and 89 to Berkeley; for their author misquotes 1 Corinthians 2 in precisely the way Berkeley does in his first sermon and *Manuscript Introduction*. All four texts have: 'Eye hath not seen, nor ear heard, neither hath it entered the heart of man to conceive . . .'; whereas the King James version has 'neither have entered' instead of 'neither hath it entered' and does not add 'to conceive' after 'heart of man'.[6]

One final *Guardian* paper which I shall consider is number 130. Luce rejects it, but he notes that it 'contains, I think, the nearest approach to Berkeley's style and manner, and I have sometimes wondered whether there could have been a confusion between the names which sound so similar . . . Bartlett and . . .

---

[4] Furlong, 'How much of Steele's *Guardian* 39 did Berkeley write?', *Hermathena* 89 (1957), 77.

[5] See *Berkeley Newsletter* 7 (1984), 25.

[6] Three contemporaries who have the King James version are R. Bentley and G. Stanhope in their Boyle *Lectures* of 1692 and 1701/2; *A Defence of National and Revealed Religion: Being a Collection of Sermons Preached at the Lectures founded by . . . Boyle* (3 vols.; London, 1739), i. 4 and 747; and Browne in his *Letter in Answer*, 96.

Berkeley . . .'.[7] The attribution of 130 to 'the modest and good . . . Rev. Mr. Bartlett' was made by Steele in his *Apology for Himself* (London, 1714), 45; and one may indeed wonder whether Steele had confused the names, since, as his biographer confirms, such carelessness would not have been uncharacteristic.[8] And there are also, I argue, four strong reasons linking 130 to Berkeley.

(1) Steele's description of the writer as 'modest and good' corresponds with his opinion of Berkeley as expressed in a letter in *Guardian* 90:

'Till I knew you, I thought it the Privilege of Angels only to be very knowing and very Innocent . . . Your Contempt of Pleasures, Riches and Honour, will Crown you with them all . . .'[9]

(2) The writer of *Guardian* 130 tries to debase the name 'free-thinker'; and this, as we shall see in Chapter 6 § V, was something that Berkeley was anxious to do at the time. (3) And the way in which the writer of 130 tries to discredit 'free-thinkers' coincides precisely with Berkeley's distinctive view on how we know other minds. According to the *Guardian* writer:

The Mind being itself invisible, there is no other way to discern its Existence, than by the Effects which it produceth. [But because the] modern productions of our *Free-thinkers* . . . look rather like the Effects of Chance, or at best of Mechanism, than a Thinking Principle . . . [we should] speak of *Free-thinkers* in the Neuter Gender, using the term *it* for *him*. (p. 435)

This statement is strikingly similar to what we find in section 27 of the *Principles*: 'Such is the nature of spirit or that which acts, that it cannot be of it self perceived, but only by the effects which it produceth.' Notice that the last six words here are exactly the same as in the first sentence quoted from the *Guardian*. (4) My final correspondence is more slight than (1), (2), or (3), but probably even more decisive. In his 'De Ludo Algebraico' (1707),

---

[7] 'Berkeley's Essays in the *Guardian*', *Mind* 52 (1943), 263.
[8] See Calhoun Winton, *Richard Steele, M. P.* (Baltimore, 1970) 237.
[9] *The Guardian*, ed. J. C. Stephens (Lexington, Ky., 1982), 324–5; all subsequent quotations from the *Guardian* will be from Stephens's 1982 edition.

Berkeley answers those who are contemptuous of mathematics by quoting (loosely) the testimony of Sir William Temple (1628–99), that it is mathematics 'quae[que] vos a barbaris distinguunt . . . Vide *Tentamen Anglicum de Hortis Epicuri, a Gulielmo Temple, Equite Aurato, conscriptum*' (*Works*, iv. 219). Now in *Guardian* 130 the essayist mentions the same *aperçu*: 'The Mathematics are so useful and ornamental to Human Life, that the Ingenious Sir *William Temple* acknowledges, in some part of his Writings, all those Advantages which distinguish Polite Nations from Barbarians to be derived from them' (p. 431). Berkeley does not, especially in his early works, often quote from other authors. But when he does quote, he frequently uses the same quotation more than once, as in the case of 1 Corinthians 2 and the passage in Locke's *Essay*, IV. vii. 9, about the impossible triangle (see *NTV*, sect. 125, and *PHK*, Introduction, sect. 13). But even more noteworthy in the two paraphrases of Temple's *aperçu* is that they are closer in thought and expression to each other, I think, than to the original; for Temple's statement from the 'Gardens of Epicurus' reads:

. . . I know of no Advantage Mankind has gained by the Progress of Natural Philosophy, during so many Ages it has had Vogue in the World, excepting always, and very justly, what we owe to the Mathematicks, which is in a manner all that seems valuable among the Civilized Nations, more than those we call Barbarous, whether they are so or no, or more so than ourselves.[10]

That the writer of *Guardian* 130 should adapt Temple's remark, speak about our knowledge of other minds in nearly Berkeley's own words, be so concerned to debase the name 'free-thinker', and be eulogized by Steele—all this persuades me that that writer was Berkeley.

To sum up the positive results of our examination: Berkeley wrote part of number 9, most of numbers 27, 35, 39, 69, all of 49, 55, 62, 70, 77, 83, 88, 89, 126, and, almost certainly, numbers 81 and 130.

---

[10] Temple, *Miscellanea, the Second Part* (5th edn., London, 1705), 80.

III

In the previous chapter I quoted some of Berkeley's statements from *Guardian*, no. 89, on immortality, a topic he also touches on in numbers 27 and 55. In the *Guardian* essay, we find for the first time his aggressive campaign against the free-thinkers. His principal target was Anthony Collins, whose *Discourse of Free-thinking* (London, 1713), which popularized the term 'free-thinking', had appeared about the same time Berkeley arrived in London. In a letter of 26 January 1712/13, Berkeley writes: 'There is lately published a very bold and pernicious book entitled *A Discourse of Free Thinking*. I hear the printer of it is put into Newgate...' (*Works*, viii. 58). In *Guardian*, no. 39, 'Ulysses Cosmopolita' (i.e. Berkeley) amusingly describes how having taken a marvellous 'philosophical snuff' he was able to visit Collins's pineal gland:

... I made directly to [his] Understanding ... but ... found the Place narrower than ordinary, insomuch that there was not any room for a Miracle, Prophesie, or *Separate Spirit* ... I discovered *Prejudice* in the Figure of a Woman standing in a Corner, with her Eyes close shut, and her Fore-fingers stuck in her Ears; many Words in a confused Order, but spoken with great Emphasis, issued from her Mouth. (pp. 156–7)

Berkeley's fanciful essay about spying on Collins's mind reflects a certain factual truth. For it was probably about this time that Berkeley went 'several times [into London freethinking] Clubs in quality of a learner [and] on one of these occasions ... heard Collens [*sic*] declare that he had found a demonstration against the being of a God ...'. We have this story from Berkeley's American friend, Samuel Johnson, and it is corroborated by Berkeley's Advertisement to *Alciphron* (1732).[11] I shall be saying more about this curious story when I discuss *Alciphron* in Chapter 6.

Much of the material in his *Guardian* essays Berkeley later deployed in *Alciphron*. Thus his curious depiction of prejudice as a woman with 'her Fore-fingers stuck in her ears' featured in the title-page vignette for volume two of *Alciphron*. For in this vignette

---

[11] See *Samuel Johnson*, i. 26.

(see below, Figure 5) the blindfolded figure on the pedestal has her fingers stuck in her ears. It is likely that at least one passage in the Preface to the *Three Dialogues* was written in London and with Collins in mind; for here Berkeley speaks '. . . of that loose, rambling way [of thought], not altogether improperly termed freethinking by certain libertines in thought, who can no more endure the restraints of logic than those of religion, or government' (*Works*, ii. 168). Berkeley never lost his aversion for Collins, who, even as late as *Siris* (1744), sect. 354, is named with Hobbes and Spinoza as a modern atheist.

We are told that for each of his *Guardian* papers Berkeley received a dinner and a guinea from Steele. Berkeley's involvement with the *Guardian* led to another literary collaboration with Steele, on a work which has only recently been identified as by Berkeley. This is a three-volume educational anthology entitled the *Ladies Library*, published in 1714.[12] It is composed almost entirely of extracts from leading religious writers such as Archbishops John Tillotson (1630–94), Jeremy Taylor (1630–94), Fénelon. Its main interest is in the light it throws on Berkeley's choice of authors and reading at this early period. We know he was responsible for assembling the extracts from a contract discovered by Mr Stephen Parks, of Yale University; it begins: 'Whereas the Reverend Mr George Berkeley Hath made a Commonplace or Collection out of the best English Authors wch He hath agreed to print with Jacob Tonson Junr in two or more Vols . . . to be Intituled the Ladys Library . . .'. The contract is signed by Steele, who agreed to (and did) write prefaces for the three volumes. The *Ladies Library* seems to have sold well, passing through eight impressions by 1772.

IV

Steele signed the contract for the *Ladies Library* on 15 October 1713. Perhaps it is no coincidence that on the same day Berkeley writes

[12] S. Parks, 'George Berkeley, Sir Richard Steele and the *Ladies Library*', *The Scriblerian* 12 (1980), 1–2; and E. J. Furlong and D. Berman, 'George Berkeley and the *Ladies Library*', *Berkeley Newsletter* 4 (1980), 4–13.

from London: 'I am on the point of going to Sicily, [as] chaplain to Lord Peterborough, who is ambassador extraordinary', for the coronation of the new king (*Works*, viii. 73). When the *Ladies Library* was published Berkeley was probably in either France or Italy. His appointment as Peterborough's chaplain, which had been brought about by Swift, lasted about ten months. It developed Berkeley's taste for travel. After a few months in France, where he may well have met and had philosophical conversations with Malebranche, he travelled to Italy (*Life*, 70–1). On New Year's day 1714 he crossed a treacherous part of the Alps. He describes the crossing in a lively letter to his friend Thomas Prior (1680?–1751):

We were carried in open chairs by men used to scale these rocks and precipices, which in this season are more slippery and dangerous than at other times, and at the best are high, craggy, and steep . . . My life often depended upon a single step . . . I am now hardened against wind and weather, earth and sea, frost and snow; can gallop all day long, and sleep but three or four hours at night. (*Works*, viii. 78)

In Italy Berkeley spent some time in Turin and Genoa, and also at Leghorn, which had an English colony and was then the only place in Italy where the Anglican service was tolerated. It was here that he preached a number of sermons, following one of which, as Stock amusingly tells us, he had some anxious moments. For as he was sitting in his chamber the next day—

. . . a procession of priests in surplices, and with all other formalities, entered the room, and without taking the least notice of the wondering inhabitant, marched round it, muttering certain prayers. [Berkeley's] fears immediately suggested to him that this could be no other than a visit from the Inquisition, who had heard of his officiating before heretics without licence, the day before. As soon as they were gone, he ventured with much caution to enquire into the cause of this extraordinary appearance, and was happily informed, that this was the season appointed by the Romish calendar for solemnly blessing the houses of all good catholics from rats and other vermin; a piece of intelligence which changed his terror into mirth. (Stock, 7–8)

As two of Berkeley's ten extant sermons were preached at the English church at Leghorn, this might be an appropriate place to comment briefly on his preaching. Judged by the evidence of the extant sermons, and some sermon notes, his preaching was not distinguished; which is perhaps surprising, given his admirable prose style and the brilliance and originality of his philosophical and theological writings. (A similarly moderate judgment might be passed on his correspondence: in an age of great letter writers, Berkeley's letters are—with about thirty exceptions—rather ordinary.) Luce has suggested that his 'sermons probably sounded better than they read' (*Works*, vii. 4). And there is some evidence that the sermons he delivered in America made an impact. In one of these he is reported as saying 'Give the devil his due, John Calvin was a great man' (ibid. 3). One person who heard Berkeley preach in Boston on 12 September 1731 wrote in his diary: 'In ye morn Dean George Berkeley preacht in ye (King's) Chapel, from ye 1st Epistle to Timothy, ye 3rd chap. verse 16, a fine sermon; according to my opinion I never heard such a one. A very great auditory.'[13]

Apart, perhaps, from the two sermons which I touched on in Chapters 1 and 3, and *Passive Obedience*, which is really not a sermon or sermons (as we have it), the extant sermons have little or no direct bearing on his distinctive philosophy or theology. Their content, writes Luce,

... is almost entirely devotional and hortatory ... The churchmanship and the doctrine are those of the high-church, tory tradition, taking the *via media* between Rome and dissent; apostolic teaching, the sacraments of the Gospel, the creeds and the apostolic succession are defended; a narrow, barren or exclusive orthodoxy is condemned ... (*Works*, vii. 4)

V

Berkeley returned from the Continent to London in late 1714, during stirring times. The death of Queen Anne had plunged Britain into political turmoil and uncertainty. It was not clear whether an attempt would be made to bring back the exiled Stuart Pretender, or whether the Act of Succession would be honoured. We now

[13]   B. Rand, *Berkeley's American Sojourn* (Cambridge, Mass., 1932), 45.

know that the Tory leader, Henry St John (1678–1751), with whom Berkeley was acquainted, was conspiring with the Stuarts. At this stage, however, Berkeley had little or no sympathy for the Jacobites, for he issued a vigorous pamphlet, *Advice to the Tories who have taken the Oath* (London, 1715), in which he called upon the Tories to honour their Oath of Allegiance to King George I.

Whether Berkeley was sympathetic to the Jacobite cause earlier, when he wrote *Passive Obedience*, is (as we shall see) another matter. For Berkeley, personally, the issue came to a head a year later, in 1716, when he sought the modest church preferment of St Paul's in Dublin.[14] His eagerness for St Paul's is shown in two letters to Percival, written in England, where Berkeley was still on leave from Trinity College. In the first letter, of May 1716, he tells Percival that the Prince of Wales has recommended him:

The letter from the Prince is enclosed and seconded by Mr. Secretary Stanhope, so that I think it cannot fail of success. The living is reakoned to be worth about a hundred a year, but I put the greater value on it because it is consistent with my [Trinity College] Fellowship. (*Works*, viii. 98)

By the end of May, however, Berkeley's confidence had been shattered. In a letter of 26 May 1716 he implores Percival to write to the Duke of Grafton, the Lord Lieutenant of Ireland, telling him that Berkeley is 'well affected to his Majesty's Government'; for, Berkeley continues, 'I cannot but be solicitous to have my character cleared to the Lords Justices and others there [in Ireland], who are probably misled by the calumny of interested persons who are strangers to me' (*Works*, viii. 99). That Berkeley's efforts were in vain, we learn from a letter Percival received a few days later from Charles Dering: 'I did hear some time ago that Mr Berkeley was to succeed Charles Carr in his living of St Paul's, but I doubt he will not succeed, the Lords Justices having made a strong representation against him, and they say one Tirrel [*sic*] is to have that living.'[15]

---

[14] St Paul's Church is on North King Street, on the north side of Dublin. The church was rebuilt in the 19th cent.

[15] Rand, *Berkeley and Percival*, 159.

Why did the Lord Justices make a strong representation against Berkeley? According to Joseph Stock, Berkeley's early biographer, Lord Galway (a Lord Justice in 1716) represented Berkeley as a Jacobite, and hence unworthy of the living of St Paul's (Stock, 4). From the beginning, *Passive Obedience* was rumoured to be politically heterodox. Thus in the preface, 'To the Reader', Berkeley says that he felt compelled to publish his 'three discourses [delivered] not many months since in the [Trinity] College-chapel' because 'the false accounts that are gone abroad concerning them have made it necessary' (*Works*, vi. 15).

In the event, the published discourses seem to have done Berkeley more harm than good. Mr. Duke Tyrrell (b. 1680) did obtain the living of St Paul's, and in November 1716, marking his triumph, he preached two sermons which were published with the title *The Established Church Vindicated* (Dublin, 1716). More interesting still, Tyrrell wrote a detailed letter to Robert (later Lord) Molesworth denouncing his rival and asking for Molesworth's help.[16] Written in Dublin on 14 May 1716, Tyrrell's letter contains a number of minor revelations. Thus we learn that the man who recommended Tyrrell for St Paul's and 'laboured to serve [him] with unusual zeal' was none other than the father of Berkeley's (future) wife, Anne Forster (1700–86). Tyrrell then informs Molesworth that 'a recommendation is come . . . from the prince [of Wales] his secretary and Mr Secretary Stanhope in favour of Mr Berkly [*sic*] which if complyd with will fix him [not only] in St Pauls [but also in the sinecure of] St Nicholas without . . .'—a fact which neither Berkeley nor his biographers mentions. Having set the stage, the interested Tyrrell now begins his character assassination of Berkeley with a eulogy on Molesworth:

Mr Molesworth who has been and ever will be a patron of public liberty, who has defended it so warmly and successfully with his pen will I am persuaded obstruct the promotion of a person who appeared publicly nay printed a book in defence of the slavish doctrine of passive obedience & can go to as great a height as any that went before him.

[16] State Papers, Ireland 63/374, pp. 185–8. Tyrrell's letter has not been noticed by Berkeley's biographers.

this treatise came out at a time when a dangerous attaque was made not only on the libertys of the kingdom in general but of this city [Dublin] in particular[17] by the late ministry [of Harley and Henry St John] for which piece of service he [Berkeley] has been ever since highly esteemed by all the Jacobites in this kingdom. the book may be bought in London but in case you have not seen it & cannot meet with it there I shall send you one whenever you will please to command me. he travelled [from Oct. 1713 to Aug. 1714] with the late Lord Peterborrow [*sic*] in the late times has been & is still a creature of Dean Swift & is reakond here as much in the Tory interest as the highest Church man of them all. his preferment will be very unpopular create much uneasiness & give a general discontent.

Although Berkeley's *Passive Obedience* passed through three editions in two years, Tyrrell's hostile remarks would seem to be the only surviving contemporary criticism of the book. Tyrrell also castigates Berkeley both for his three-year absence 'from his duty and business' at Trinity College and for his continuing 'in the measures & esteem of the late [Tory] ministry as long as they continued in power'. (Perhaps *Passive Obedience* was one of 'his writings' which Swift mentions that he gave to 'all the [government] ministers'.)

Tyrrell then expresses his confidence that Molesworth has 'interest and weight enough to sink a representation grounded on misinformation and that his representation of Mr Berkeley's character as a tory will have influence enough with the prince and induce his royal highness . . . to recoil from what has been done in his favour'. The account by Stock fits in here, although, according to Stock, it was Lord Galway rather than Molesworth who represented Berkeley as a Jacobite, 'an impression which Mr. [Samuel] Molyneux [(1689–1728) the prince's secretary and Berkeley's friend], as soon as he was apprized of it, took care to remove from the minds of their highnesses by producing the work in question [*Passive Obedience*], and showing them that it contained nothing but principles of loyalty to the present happy establishment'(Stock, 4).

---

[17] This presumably refers to the disputes over the succession to the mayoralty in 1711–13, in which the Tory administrator overruled the choice of the Aldermen.

Tyrrell concludes his letter by describing his own political and religious principles, particularly his anti-clerical and pro-deistic sympathies, which would have been congenial to Molesworth, as Tyrrell no doubt knew, and disdained by Berkeley, as we know from his *Guardian* essays and *Alciphron*.[18] Molesworth was closely identified with Lord Shaftesbury (1671–1713), whose cordial letters to Molesworth were published in 1721 by John Toland, Molesworth's protégé. The fact that Tyrrell's letter is among the State Papers (in London) is important, because it indicates that Molesworth did use it in government circles. The description of Berkeley as 'a creature of Dean Swift' would probably have been effective for Tyrrell's purposes in 1716. Later, however, Swift and Molesworth drew closer together as fellow colonial nationalists; indeed, in 1724 Swift dedicated his most famous *Drapier Letter* to Molesworth.

VI

Was Berkeley, as Tyrrell suggests, a Jacobite favourer of the 'slavish' doctrine of passive obedience? The question cannot, I think, be accurately answered unless *Passive Obedience* is examined in its specific historical and Irish context. For Berkeley's three discourses were, after all, directed at an Irish audience; thus in the preface 'To the Reader' Berkeley says that the aim of his discourses was 'to arm the youth of our university' against the 'pernicious' view 'that subjects may lawfully resist the Supreme authority, in those cases where the public good shall plainly seem to require it' (*Works*, vi. 15). Among the Irish thinkers who championed this 'pernicious' view was Molesworth himself. In the Preface to his influential *Account of Denmark as it was in the Year 1692*, first published in

---

18 Tyrrell writes: 'I have always declared myself against the independency of the Church on the civil powers . . . I thought every man ought to judge for himself in matters of religion & that no synods of ecclesiasticks have any authority to make creeds or articles of faith for their brethern . . . every honest man can make as good a collection for himself of articles necessary to be believed out of the bible as any made for him by general councils. I never was for persecution on any account nor for making the Sacrament . . . the test of a particular church or party. All this I say in confidence to you . . .' (State Papers, Ireland 63/374).

1694, Molesworth defends 'public liberty' (to use Tyrrell's phrase) and castigates the 'slavish' doctrine of 'passive' or 'blind obedience' (1745 edn., p. xiii). He associates passive obedience with priest craft and kingcraft; he also—unfortunately for Berkeley—especially objects to its being taught by clergymen in universities (ibid., pp. xv–xvi). For Molesworth, the people have a right to rebel. Neither a rightful king nor even a legally elected parliament can oblige the people to accept a government 'which shall afterwards tend to the detriment of the universality' (pp. xviii–xix). Molesworth also briefly opposes the claim that there is biblical support for 'those unintelligible doctrines of passive obedience' (p. xvii).

On the whole, however, Molesworth is rhetorical and suggestive rather than a sustained champion of rebellion or the Glorious Revolution. For that we must look to Berkeley's former antagonist, Archbishop King, particularly to his *Europe's Deliverance: a Sermon* (Dublin, 1691), his *State of the Protestants* (4th edn., 1692) and—on a more theoretical level—to his *De Origine Mali* (1702). Although deeply conservative, King was the leading Irish ideologue of the Glorious Revolution. His principles are reflected in Tyrrell's 1716 sermon and even in Francis Hutcheson's Dublin writings, especially the *Inquiry into the Original of our Ideas of Beauty and Virtue* (London, 1725), a work which (as we shall see below) unites the influence of Molesworth and King.

In cases of 'extream necessity', says King in the *State of the Protestants*, resistance must be acceptable (Introduction, sect. 3). And since 'King James designed to destroy and utterly ruin . . . the Liberty and Property of the Subjects in general . . . there remained no other prospect, or human possibility, of avoiding this slavery and destruction designed against the Kingdom and Protestants of Ireland, but by accepting the Protection, and submit ting to the Government of their present Majesties [William and Mary]' (ibid. sect. 4). Furthermore, King argues, God shows us when the ordinance against resisting the supreme power may be suspended by sending providential signs; and in his 1691 *Sermon* King records eighteen such signs which attended William's victory over James. Thus, for King there are what we might call internal criteria which justify rebellion (enslavement and imminent ruin) and external ones (providential signs).

Consider now sections 38 and 39 of *Passive Obedience*, where Berkeley examines a 'fourth . . . prejudice which influenceth the impugners of non-resistance . . .' (*Works*, vi. 15). Although, as usual, Berkeley does not name his opponents, his comments clearly show his opposition to Molesworth's general position and to what I have called the Kingean internal criteria. Against the 'prejudice' which 'arises from the natural dread of slavery', Berkeley writes: 'But how harsh soever the sentence may appear, yet it is most true, that our appetites, even the most natural, as of ease, plenty, or life itself, must be chained and fettered by the [moral] laws of nature and reason.' Neither loss of life, nor slavery, nor 'great sufferings and hardships', nor any 'temporal calamities', can justify violating the moral law against rebellion, according to Berkeley. This is a strong absolutist position, which the pragmatic King and the liberty-loving Molesworth would have regarded as little short of vicious or insane. For Molesworth and King think that we can and must judge whether a particular situation justifies rebellion, whereas Berkeley thinks that such 'situational ethics' would lead to 'the most horrible confusion of vice and virtue, sin and duty' (sect. 10).

Put in another way, Berkeley is a strong rule-utilitarian, whereas King and Molesworth are implicit act-utilitarians. According to Berkeley, we are neither intelligent enough nor honest enough to determine by our 'own private disinterested opinion . . . what makes most for the public good at [a certain] juncture' (sect. 9). The public good will suffer if we are prepared to transgress negative moral laws, such as 'thou shalt not resist the supreme power', even in what seems to be extreme cases. Because God wills 'the general well-being of all men' (sect. 7), he wishes us to obey unconditionally these crucial negative principles even if they bring upon us 'poverty, death and disgrace'. For, if necessary, he will compensate us in the afterlife. 'And therefore, the least degree of rebellion is, with the utmost strictness and propriety, a sin' (sect. 16).

Rebellion is doing what God wills that we should never do. But can God, in certain extreme cases, make rebellion morally acceptable? Berkeley does not directly address this question, but it is not difficult to work out what he would say. He would not dismiss the possibility out of hand, since, according to him, God does not—as Shaftesbury, Hutcheson, and presumably Molesworth thought—will something because it is moral. Rather, it is the will of God, he holds, that makes an action moral (sect. 31). Thus God could, according to Berkeley, make rebellion justifiable in certain extreme cases. But he will not, and he knows that we can know that he will not. For if we thought there were, or could actually be, exceptions, then moral chaos would ensue. The 'well-being of mankind' (sect. 8) demands 'fixed unalterable standards of good and evil' (sect. 13). And although we have judgement enough to determine these in advance, *a priori*, we do not have judgement enough to obey them selectively or situationally. The act-utilitarian may officially and even sincerely renounce any selfish or sectarian point of view; but in practice his position will collapse, Berkeley is in effect arguing, into some form of egoism or sectarian act-utilitarianism. At times, Berkeley seems to be saying that if there were no unconditional moral maxims and if we did not believe and act as if there were, then morality itself would be impossible. So in section 54 he writes: '. . . if there were no inflexible rules, but all negative as well as positive duties might be dispensed with . . . there would be an end of all morality.'

Berkeley does not explicitly apply his absolutist, rule-utilitarian theory to the Glorious Revolution, but the application would have been crystal clear, I believe, especially, as Tyrrell indicates, in 1712. Those who rebelled against James II had sinned. So William King and Robert Molesworth, two of King William's leading Irish supporters, had sinned. And as the Revolution which ousted the Stuarts had been founded on sin, so the present establishment was by implication, it would seem, sinful. Hence it is not surprising that Berkeley was represented by Tyrrell (and apparently Molesworth) as disloyal to the present Hanoverian government, and that this representation blocked him from obtaining St Paul's. And yet there is a cruel irony in this, since, according to Berkeley's moral principles, it is always wrong to be an active enemy of the present government.

Archbishop King would not accept this principle. In the Appendix to his *Origin of Evil*, he brings together miracles and morality to form what seems to be his theoretical basis:

'tis certain that God, who is the Author of Nature and establish'd the Laws of it, can either alter them or add to them when he sees it proper. Neither does he want Means, whenever he pleases, to assure Mankind that he will do it. When therefore we find any Alteration in the Laws of Nature, we may from hence conclude that God demands our Attention. And hereupon we esteem the Promulgation of a new Law recommended to us by this Token to be an authentic Declaration of the Will of God. In this manner were the *Mosaic* and *Evangelic* Laws establish'd; *viz* by *Miracles*.[19]

King's position, to put it crudely, is that in 1688–9 God sus-pended the moral law against rebellion in England and Ireland and showed that he had done so by eighteen providential signs or tokens which attended William's triumph over James. In this 'miraculous chain of Providences' King mentions that the Pope fell out with the King of France at just the right time; that Mary's consort, William, was a great leader, and had an interest in England; that the pretended birth of an heir to James was badly managed, and so on. (Curiously, King does not mention the most famous 'providence', the so-called 'Protestant wind' which assisted William's fleet as it distressed James's.) In short, 'such a mirac-ulous chain of providences' show, King argues in his sermon (p. 23), that God favoured William, and thus sanctioned rebellion against James. The Glorious Revolution was, King might have said, a moral miracle.

For Berkeley, however, God will not suspend either a natural or a moral law for the good of an individual or a nation. God can do it, but he will not, because his actions are not directed to 'par-ticular views' (sect. 14). For 'Suppose a prince, on whose life the welfare of a kingdom depends to fall down a precipice: we have

19   *Origin of Evil*, trans. E. Law (3rd edn., Cambridge, 1739), 494.

no reason to think that the universal law of gravitation would be suspended in that case' (sect. 27). For King, on the contrary, God had manifestly intervened in eighteen near-miraculous ways for William and the welfare of Great Britain and Ireland.

In section 14 Berkeley seems to admit that 'the natural good' of a 'nation' might 'be better promoted by a particular suspension' of a law of nature. 'Yet for all that,' he answers, 'nature still takes its course'; God 'will not change or deviate . . . how wise or benevolent soever it may be thought by foolish men to do so'. If King heard this preached in the College Chapel, he could hardly have been pleased with Berkeley. Nor, as we have seen in Chapter 1, would it have been the first time that the young Fellow had antagonized his Archbishop.

The Glorious Revolution created a moral dilemma: it was a test-case for moral and political theory, especially in the early part of the eighteenth century. For nearly everyone it was regrettable that the lawful sovereign of Britain and Ireland had to be overthrown. For King, whose autobiography shows that he was personally agonized, the revolution was pragmatically and theologically justified.[20] For Berkeley, we may infer, it was simply wrong. King is more of an Occasionalist here; Berkeley more of a Leibnitzian. For King, God does intercede in the moral world; for Berkeley, he does not; since he has from the beginning designed certain moral principles which should not, and need not, ever be tampered with by God or man.

King's justification of the Glorious Revolution is an odd mixture of the medieval and the modern, the providential and the pragmatic. This is in keeping with his general theological stand-point (as we shall see in Chapter 6), which may be described as old-fashioned negative theology reinterpreted representationally. King was adept at putting old wine in new bottles. He did not accept the (then emerging) Lockean or natural-right justification for revolution. Possibly he recognized that if the Lockean theory were accepted, it could be used by the Catholic Irish against the Protestant Ascendancy. For if everyone had a natural right to lib-

[20] See *A Great Archbishop . . . William King*, ed. C. S. King (London, 1906), esp. 22–23.

erty, then why should the downtrodden native Irish not rebel against their Anglican overlords? Against the pragmatic form of this challenge, King could have replied that God has not shown by any providential signs that he approved of rebellion against the Ascendancy.

One eminent Irish philosopher who did employ the rights justification and an explicit form of act-utilitarianism, was Francis Hutcheson, a son of Irish philosophy who left Ireland in 1730 to become father of Scottish philosophy. In his *Inquiry into ... our Ideas of Beauty and Virtue* (1725; 3rd edn., 1729), which was published 'owing to [Molesworth's] approbation' (p. xviii), Hutcheson maintains that 'wherever any Invasion is made upon *unalienable Rights* [such as life], there must arise a ... *Right* to *Resistance*' (pp. 294–5). Yet rights seem to have for Hutcheson a utilitarian basis; for as the 'Tendency to the *publick Good* is *greater* or *less*, the *Right* is *greater* or *less*' (p. 278); hence 'there can be no *Right*, or *Limitation* of Right, inconsistent with, or opposite to, the greatest publick Good' (p. 298). Hutcheson then concludes in a Kingean fashion: 'And therefore in Cases of *extreme Necessity*, when the State cannot otherwise be preserv'd from Ruin, it must certainly be *Just* and *Good* ... [for] Persons who can do it, to use the Force of the State for its own Preservation ... in some *transitory Acts* ...' (p. 298). Hutcheson, I suggest, is presenting a more explicit, progressive and secular version of King's defence of resistance: it is more explicit in its act-utilitarianism, more progressive in its use of natural rights theory (appropriate for a legally disadvantaged Dissenter), and more secular in not using any providential argument. Ultimately, however, King and Hutcheson, who were on friendly terms, agree that a defence of resistance depends on something like the public good.[21]

While a concept of the public good is largely implicit in King and Molesworth, it is explicitly used by Hutcheson and Berkeley.

---

[21] See W. R. Scott, *Francis Hutcheson: His Life, Teaching and Position in the History of Philosophy* (Cambridge, 1900), 49–50. In 1725 Hutcheson sent his *Inquiry* to King, with a letter in which he mentions 'the great pleasure he has lately received by reading ... De Origine Mali'. Scott, who prints this letter (p. 49), wrongly ascribes it to Hutcheson's friend, Charles Moore.

For Berkeley, though, the public good can never, ultimately, be advanced by rebellion, whereas for Hutcheson it can. The two Irish philosophers go in different ways. Hutcheson has a more naturalistic conception of the public good, Berkeley a more theological one. A condition that 'would make life intolerable' would, for Hutcheson, justify rebellion; whereas, for Berkeley, such a 'temporal calamity' would not, since God could compensate us in the next life. Because Hutcheson's God does the good rather than creating it (pp. 274–6), he would approve of an action such as rebellion if it were demanded by the public good. Berkeley would reject this, first, because it is God's will, not the public good or will, that makes something morally good, and, secondly, because we could never be sure that the public good would be served by rebellion. In short, Berkeley is a theological ruleutilitarian, Hutcheson a secular actutilitarian. In Berkeley and Hutcheson we see the difference between what I have called the Irish right wing and left wing.[22] King in this instance holds a middle position which combines a pragmatic situational ethics with an extreme supernaturalism.

King's apology for the Glorious Revolution was most influential in Ireland, as we can tell from *The Established Church Vindicated*, the triumphant sermons published in late 1716 by Duke Tyrrell, Berkeley's successful rival for St Paul's, Dublin. Thus Tyrrell says that the Revolution 'was accomplished by such an immediate Interposition of Providence . . . it was so much the Lord's doing . . .' (p. 1). Nor was it only providential; it was also practically necessary, for, as Tyrrell urges, we were 'within a few Weeks of Ruin' (p. 40). As Tyrrell's providential and pragmatic defence of the Glorious Revolution was probably derived from King, so his opposition to the 'independence of the Church on the State' was probably drawn from Molesworth's friend Matthew Tindal, whom Berkeley singles out in *Passive Obedience*, sect. 50, for particular vilification.

Tyrrell also criticizes certain unnamed active 'antirevolution churchmen' (p. 15). 'The Revolution', he writes, 'tho' it carries

---

[22] See above, Ch. 1, and my 'Enlightenment and CounterEnlightenment in Irish Philosophy', *Archiv für Geschichte der Philosophie* 64 (1982), 148–65.

so many plain tokens of Divine Approbation in it, and is so visibly God's Handy-work, is nicely [cleverly] censured and exam-ined by . . . Anti-Revolutioners' (pp. 42–3). 'The enemies of our Constitution . . . furiously assaulted [its foundation with] learning and subtilty . . . [and] . . . arguments . . . founded on religion' (p. 2). Tyrrell must surely be alluding here to what in his letter to Molesworth he had called Berkeley's 'dangerous attaque' in *Passive Obedience*.

The Kingian point of view is also noticeable in such Irish works as William Hamilton's *The Dangers of Popery and Blessings Arising from the Late Revolution* (Dublin, 1723). Thus Hamilton, who was Archdeacon of Armagh, refers to King's 'excellent *State of the Protestants*' (p. 15), and succinctly combines its providential and pragmatic approaches. King William's life is composed, Hamilton states, of a 'series of actions hardly to be paralle'd in story' (p. 13), and 'nothing but the utmost terror could have induced the Protestants of Ireland to rise up in arms'. So the Protestants just had to rebel against James, and William's provi-dential life showed that God approved.

It is not difficult to see philosophy emerging from political expedience in King's works. It is also understandable that Archbishop King would gather support from Irish writers on this issue. King was the ideologue *par excellence*, the practical man who put his practice into theory. On the other hand, it is by no means easy to see what ideological purpose Berkeley's *Passive Obedience* may have been serving. For those like Tyrrell, of course, there was nothing particularly puzzling in this: Berkeley wrote as a crypto-Jacobite, and had the Stuarts returned after Queen Anne's death (as they had after Cromwell's), Berkeley would have expected a reward. While the Jacobite construction was plausible in Berkeley's day, it has since seemed much less so. All Berkeley scholars have, I think, dismissed it, usually pointing out that Berkeley expressed anti-Jacobite sentiments privately in a letter of 1709 and publicly in his *Advice to the Tories* (1715).[23]

[23] See Berkeley's letter of 21 Oct. 1709 to Percival (*Works*, viii. 22–3). Although the *Advice to the Tories* was published anonymously, Berkeley's authorship was known to Percival (see *Works*, vi. 49) and, it now appears, to Richard Steele; see British

And yet the motivation for *Passive Obedience* remains puzzling. As my sketch of the Irish scene shows, I think, *Passive Obedience* could hardly have failed to arouse the hostility of powerful figures such as Molesworth and King. Given the continuing agitation of the Sacheverell controversy, the precarious state of Queen Anne's health, her Stuart sympathies and the growing fears that the Tory ministry wished to bring back the Stuarts, the publication of *Passive Obedience* in 1712 could only have been 'highly esteemed by . . . the Jacobites . . .' as Tyrrell put it.[24] How could a perceptive man like Berkeley publish a work, whose very title contained the emotive words 'Passive Obedience', without recognizing that it would be construed as Jacobital?

Now one way of resolving this puzzle is to suppose that Berkeley was a Jacobite sympathizer in 1712, but not one in 1715 or thereafter. The following developments in late 1713 and 1714 might well have marked a turning point for Berkeley: the Pretender solemnly refused to renounce Roman Catholicism; George, the Elector of Hanover, 'came to the crown [in 1714] without force or artifice', as Berkeley emphasizes in the *Advice to the Tories* (*Works*, vi. 57); and, perhaps even more important, by 1715 both Whigs and Tories had taken the Oath of Allegiance to George, which was, Berkeley argues, morally binding (ibid.). Indeed, in *Passive Obedience* Berkeley takes the negative precept 'Thou shalt not forswear oneself' to be of the same absolute order as 'Thou shalt not resist the supreme power' (sects. 3 and 15). In short, any of these three developments might have changed his (possible) 1712 sympathies for the Stuarts. What I am suggesting is that when Berkeley issued *Passive Obedience* in 1712 he had an ulterior aim—to encourage a Stuart return after Anne's death.[25] Such a return would erase in

Library, Add. MS 61688, fo. 99. Until recently, scholars have known of only one edition—printed in London—of the *Advice*; see *Works*, vi. 44–50, and G. Keynes's *A Bibliography of George Berkeley* (Oxford, 1976), 207–8. There is, however, a Dublin edition, published in the same year by James Carson of Fishamble Street, a copy of which is in the Huntington Library, California.

[24] See W. E. Lecky, *History of England in the Eighteenth Century* (1892), i. 164–76. In 1713 an abstract of King's *State of the Protestants* was issued in London; the whole work was reprinted in Dublin in the same year.

[25] For a different view, see Clark, pp. xxii–xxiii.

some measure the moral blot of rebellion in 1688–9. It would also resolve the problem of the Non-Jurors, whose scrupulosity about oaths Berkeley must surely have admired.

Once, however, George had taken possession of the crown and had received the Oath of Allegiance, then Berkeley would, consistently, lose his Jacobite sympathies. My interpretation coheres reasonably well with Berkeley's supposedly anti-Jacobite letter of 21 October 1709. For while it would be 'wickedness in anyone', he says in the letter, 'to attempt to disturb the public peace, by introducing the family of the Stuarts', when there was a *de facto* sovereign (*Works*, viii. 22), he might also have said that imme-diately after the death of Anne there would be no clear-cut British sovereign. The Elector of Hanover would not then have 'the crown in possession' (*Works*, viii. 22). Where my interpre-tation does not fit so well, however, is with Berkeley's other criterion for kingship, namely, the concurrence of 'the people or their representatives, i.e. Lords and Commons' (ibid.). For by 1712 the Lords and Commons had established the Elector's right to the throne by the Act of Succession. On the other hand, as Parliament had passed the Act, it could also have changed its mind; and to many in 1712 it looked as though both people and Parliament favoured a change in the succession. It seems plausible to me, therefore, that Berkeley preached his three sermons and published *Passive Obedience* to encourage such a change of mind.[26]

There is a curious piece of negative evidence which seems to fit my interpretation. Why, in short, did Berkeley sanction three editions of *Passive Obedience* between 1712 and 1713 but did not reprint it in his 1752 *Miscellany, containing several Tracts*? Surely the most complete statement of his moral and political philosophy would have been an admirable companion to his *Essay towards*

---

[26] In fact, I am not sure how seriously we should take this 1709 letter. It was, after all, written to Percival at an early stage in the relationship; it also appears to be in conflict with *Passive Obedience*, since in the letter Berkeley says that he disapproves of Higden because 'he seems to be against all resistance whatsoever to the king *de facto* ... Now by this it appears his principles do not favour the late Revolution, though indeed he is now for submission to the government established' (*Works*, viii. 23). Yet what Berkeley says here about Higden seems no less appropriate to his own position in 1712.

Preventing the Ruine of Great Britain and the *Discourse Addressed to the Magistrates*, originally published in 1721 and 1738. According to my interpretation, he omitted *Passive Obedience* because after 1715 he no longer approved of its implicit Jacobite message.[27] Of course, strictly speaking (as Samuel Molyneux may have pointed out to the Prince of Wales in 1716) Berkeley's book could not be used to justify rebellion against any *de facto* king. Yet even in 1752, Berkeley might have feared that such subtlety could easily be overlooked. The memory of the 1745 Stuart rising in Scotland, and his efforts to counteract it in Ireland, may still have been fresh in his mind.

On the other hand, Berkeley's motivation in 1712 might have been purely rationalistic, as befits a believer in *a priori* deductive ethics. On this view, Berkeley would appear to be an almost caricature philosopher—deducing eternal moral truths with almost complete indifference to his own time, particularly to what happened in 1688 or what would happen at the death of Queen Anne.

What is clear is that, whether Berkeley wrote as a crypto-Jacobite or as a pure *a priori* moralist, he suffered for his political statements. He failed to obtain the living of St Paul's, Dublin, which he very much wanted. The bitter experience may help to explain—supposing Berkeley came to know of Molesworth's involvement—Berkeley's absence from the Molesworth circle (which flourished in Dublin in the 1720s) and also his notorious hostility to Molesworth's friend, Lord Shaftesbury, particularly in the third dialogue of *Alciphron*.[28] The experience would also, I suggest, have encouraged Berkeley to look outside Ireland for his future, especially given the influence of Molesworth, King, and their followers in Ireland.

[27] Another possible explanation for the omission is that by 1752 Berkeley had abandoned his strong (1712) defence of passive obedience for a more moderate position. This is suggested by the (recently discovered) statement of his wife: 'I have heard the Bp [Berkeley] say that his Idea of passive Obedience, was *obedience to the lawful powers*. There must be lawful powers *somewhere*; and *passive obedience* to *that power* is *a duty*, when nothing is required *contrary* to duty.' The concluding qualification is not, I think, to be found anywhere in *Passive Obedience*, where nothing is allowed to supersede the duty of passive obedience. See my 'Mrs Berkeley's Annotations', 18.

[28] See Scott, *Francis Hutcheson*, 28–30, 96–9, and *Works*, iii. 10–12.

In the event, as we shall see in the next chapter, Berkeley turned towards America and his Bermuda college project. Was it a coincidence that he decided to call his projected college St Paul's? My suspicion, to put it somewhat dramatically, is that Berkeley hoped to make up for losing the Irish St Paul's by the far more ambitious St Paul's Bermuda. In 1729 he left England for America. He had obtained the lucrative Deanery of Derry in 1724, but by then he had, as he wrote to Percival in the previous year, 'determined . . . to spend the residue of my days in the Island of Bermuda' (*Works*, viii. 127). Yet the Bermudean St Paul's also failed. However, on his return from America Berkeley did salvage something from the failure. In 1734 he was appointed Bishop of Cloyne. He was consecrated in Dublin in May 1734. Where? Where else but St Paul's?[29]

---

[29] According to Stock, he was 'consecrated at St Paul's church in Dublin on the 19th May' (p. 28).

5

The Bermuda Project
(1722–1731)

I

Shortly after failing to obtain St Paul's, Dublin, in 1716, Berkeley left Britain on his second Continental tour. He went as tutor or travelling companion to St George Ashe, the son of the prelate whose ordination of him six years earlier had provoked the ire of Archbishop King. This tour was to be more extensive and adventurous than his first. It lasted some four years, during which Berkeley gained a wide appreciation of the arts. He apparently took little delight in music at the time, having, as he said, 'eyes but no ears' (*Life*, 76). Most of his time was spent in Italy: first in Turin, then in Rome viewing the galleries and antiquities, then touring in Apulia, and visiting the island of Ischia. It also now appears (from the evidence of his signature in the visitor's book of the University of Padua) that he was in the north of Italy and spent much of 1719 in the Republic of Venice.[1]

Berkeley may have intended to publish an account of his Italian travels, since he kept detailed journals, four of which have been preserved (see *Works*, vii. 231–3). In the event, the only item he had published was his firsthand description of an eruption of Mount Vesuvius in 1717, which he communicated to the Royal Society through his friend John Arbuthnot. This paper, his journals, and the letters he wrote to Pope, among others, show him to be an intrepid traveller and a careful observer. Berkeley's main enthusiasm in the arts was in the area of architecture, an interest

---

[1] See E. Chaney, 'George Berkeley in the Veneto', *Bolletino de CIRVI*, I. ii (1980), 83–5.

which would show itself theoretically in the third dialogue of *Alciphron* and practically in, among other things, the house he would build in Rhode Island.[2]

Before returning to Britain in 1720 Berkeley wrote an essay on motion, the subject proposed by the French Academy for a prize dissertation. Berkeley's *De Motu* did not win the prize, but he published his Latin essay some time after his return to London in 1721. This was Berkeley's first theoretical publication since the *Three Dialogues* (1713). During the intervening time he had been working on the second (lost) part of the *Principles*, some small portion of which he perhaps incorporated in *De Motu*. In this 'highly original and in many ways unique essay', as Karl Popper has called it, Berkeley anticipated important ideas in modern physics.[3] His critique of absolute motion and space, briefly stated in *Principles*, sects. 110–17, is here more fully and technically developed.

Immaterialism is implicit but not stated or argued for in *De Motu*. Berkeley does, however, clearly reaffirm his commitment to dualism. Mind is active, body is entirely passive:

There are two supreme classes of things, body and soul. By the help of sense we know the extended thing, solid, mobile, figured, and endowed with other qualities which meet the senses, but the sentient, percipient, thinking thing we know by a certain internal consciousness. Further we see that those things are plainly different from one another, and quite heterogenous. (sect. 21)

Berkeley immediately adds, in words that may for some recall those of Ludwig Wittgenstein, 'I speak of things known; for of the unknown it is profitless to speak.'[4] Berkeley argues that there is no active force, or principle of motion, in bodies. Thus in section 27 he contends that the resistance we feel in stopping a body in

[2] For a useful assessment of Berkeley's aesthetic development in Italy and its impact on his later work, see E. Chaney, 'Architectural Taste and the Grand Tour: George Berkeley's Evolving Canon', *Journal of Anglo-Italian Studies* 1 (1991), 74–91. Chaney describes Berkeley as 'a highly gifted amateur with a rare degree of precision' (p. 78).

[3] Popper, 'A Note on Berkeley as Precursor of Mach and Einstein', in Armstrong, Engle, and Turbayne.

[4] *Works*, iv. 36; compare the final sentence of Wittgenstein's *Tractatus Logico-Philosophicus*.

motion does not prove that the body acts, but only that we are having certain (muscular) sensations; and 'it is quite certain that we should be affected in the same way, whether that body were to be moved by itself, or impelled by another principle' (*Works*, iv. 38). The argument here is similar to that which he deploys in the *Principles* against matter: that 'we might be affected with all the ideas we have now, though no bodies existed without, resembling them' (sect. 18); and if there were no external bodies 'we might have the very same reasons to think there were that we have now' (sect. 20). In *De Motu*, Berkeley is also concerned to demarcate physics and mechanics from metaphysics and theology. Whereas the former sciences are concerned with the series of sensible objects and the laws which connect them, metaphysics and theology reveal the real, spiritual causes of these sensible appearances.

In 1721 Berkeley also published *An Essay towards Preventing the Ruine of Great Britain*, a civic sermon, as it were, on the moral, social, and religious corruption of Britain. Although the *Essay* has much in common with his *Guardian* essays, it contains a note of urgency lacking in the earlier essays. Berkeley's attack on the free-thinkers is continued here, but with even greater harshness. Thus he writes: '. . . the public safety requireth that the avowed contemners of all religion should be severely chastised; and perhaps it may be no easy matter to assign a good reason why blasphemy against God should not be . . . punished with the same rigour as treason against the king' (*Works*, vi. 70–1). The new tone is, no doubt, partly to be explained by the 'miseries the nation was plunged into by the fatal South Sea scheme in 1720' (Stock, 11).

For whatever reason, Berkeley seems to have lost confidence in the Old World and was looking hopefully to America. For it was probably in the early months of 1722 that he conceived his plan for a missionary and arts college in Bermuda, which was to engage him for the next decade. We first learn of the project from his letter to Percival of 4 March 1723. The letter opens: 'It is now about ten months since I have determined with myself to spend the residue of my days in the Island of Bermuda, where I trust in Providence I may be the mean instrument of doing some good to mankind' (*Works*, viii. 127). Berkeley then outlines his plan for the college or seminary, stating its aims, rationale, and prospects. Most of the points made here are presented more elaborately in his *Proposal for the better Supplying of Churches in our Foreign Plantations* (London, 1724). But the plan, as we have it, was disarmingly simple, and can be briefly described. The proposed college—to be called St Paul's—was to train colonial youth and native Indians. They were all to be become clergymen. The former were to man the understaffed churches; the latter were to become missionaries to their heathen brethren.

The novelty of Berkeley's plan was in the the use of local talent, so to speak. The clergy who were then employed in colonial churches were both few in number and poor in quality. They were mostly men from England and Ireland who were unable to find employment in the Old World. Missionaries to the Indians were also in short supply, and those that offered themselves were handicapped by ignorance of the Indian languages. Yet why, we might ask, was Berkeley so enthusiastic about—to quote the *Proposal*'s subtitle—'converting the Savage Americans to Christianity'? Why not, as he says himself, convert the 'infidels, papists, and dissenters . . . at home'? One answer he gives is that the Indians are 'fitter to receive' truth, because they are 'unimʼ proved by education . . . and unincumbered with all that Rubbish of Superstition and Prejudice'.[5]

Berkeley chose Bermuda as the location of his college for the following reasons. Bermuda was equidistant from most of the important colonies; it had a good climate, and also a rocky coastʼ line that would protect the college from pirates; and, although there was a good supply of necessary provisions, the island produced no enriching commodity: hence the teachers of St Paul's would not be tempted to become traders.

When Berkeley broached his ambitious plan to Percival in 1723, he was in Dublin, where he had resumed his academic duties at

---

[5] *Works*, vii. 356. Being without prejudice, the Indians would also stand in less need of Berkeley's persuasive strategy, about which he may have lost confidence, given the poor reception of his philosophy (at least by that time).

Trinity College. By then he was canvassing support for his own projected college. He enlisted some Fellows of Trinity College to become fellows of the Bermudean college, chief among whom was Robert Clayton, the future heterodox Bishop of Clogher. After obtaining considerable support in Ireland—Dean Swift was one of his advocates—Berkeley spent five hectic years from 1723 to 1728, mostly in England, lobbying and campaigning for his projected college.

Fate seemed to be smiling on the venture. On the death of Esther Vanhomrigh—Swift's Vanessa—Berkeley found himself her co-heir, much to his surprise, since he was scarcely acquainted with her. He regarded the bequest as a 'providential' sign in favour of his Bermuda Project (*Works*, viii. 130). In the following year his financial position was again enhanced by his appointment on 4 May 1724 as Dean of Derry, one of the more valuable livings in Ireland. Following this appointment, Berkeley resigned as Senior Fellow, thereby severing his official connection with Trinity College.

In London—after a brief visit to his northern Deanery— Berkeley went from strength to strength. Against considerable odds, he obtained for his college a charter, private contributions, and the promise of a grant of £20,000 from the British Parliament. In September 1728, with his bride, Anne, he set sail for America. Just before departing, he explained his plans in a letter of 5 September:

> ... tomorrow with the blessing of God I shall set sail to Rhode Island ... where I design to purchase a piece of land with my own mony in order to supply our college with such necessaries as are not the product of Bermuda ... The mony contributed by Subscribers is ... made payable to Dr Clayton with whom I have left the patent for receiving the 20,000£ ... I propose to continue at Rhode Island till such time as Dr Clayton hath received that mony and is come to Bermuda with the rest of my associates where I intend to join them.[6]

Berkeley then spent nearly three years in Rhode Island, waiting payment of the grant. Near Newport, he bought a farm on which

---

[6]   The letter is printed in the *Berkeley Newsletter* 4 (1980), 14.

he built a house, which he called Whitehall. The house, still standing, gives some evidence in 'its striking Ionic doorcase' of his architectural interests.[7] Berkeley preached often at Trinity Church in Newport and 'sometimes in the adjacent parts of the continent', where he seems to have observed the conditions of the Indians. Some of his sermon notes of this period are still extant. His sermons seem to have been popular not only with his fellow Anglicans, but with 'many Quakers and other sectaries' (*Works*, viii. 202). Berkeley also made contact with some leading American intellectuals, in particular, Samuel Johnson, with whom he discussed his immaterialist philosophy.[8] Probably the bulk of his time was spent writing his biggest book, *Alciphron*, in which he defends Christianity against the free-thinkers. *Alciphron* consists of seven dialogues; and most of its setting, and perhaps some of its characters, are drawn from Berkeley's experience in Rhode Island.

After months of anxious waiting, Berkeley finally received a decisive letter in early 1731 from Edmund Gibson (1669–1748), Bishop of London, informing him that the promised grant would never be paid. The details are provided by Stock:

After having received various excuses, Bishop Gibson ... (in whose diocese all the West Indies are included) applying to Sir Robert Walpole [1676–1745], then at the head of the treasury, was favoured at length with the following very honest [?] answer: 'If you put this question to me', says Sir Robert, 'as a minister, I must and can assure you that the money shall most undoubtedly be paid as soon as suits with public convenience: but if you ask me as a friend, whether Dean Berkeley should continue in America expecting the payment ... I advise him by all means to return home to Europe, and to give up his present expectations. (Stock, 23)

After receiving Bishop Gibson's letter, by which he was 'informed of this conference', Berkeley replied early in 1731, thanking the Bishop for sending him

---

[7] See Chaney, 'Architectural Taste', 91. The house is illustrated in *Life*, opposite p. 181 and in *Images*, 63.

[8] See Luce, 'The Philosophical Correspondence between Berkeley and Johnson', *Hermathena* 56 (1940), 93–112.

... Sir Robert Walpole's answer which leaves no room to deliberate what I have to do. I shall therefore prepare to get back as soon as possible. I was prepared for this event by advices from other hands particularly some from Ireland which informed me that all my associates to a man had absolutely abandoned the design upon which I came and betaken themselves to other views having been tired out with discouragement and delay which hath proved as fatal to our College as an absolute refusal.[9]

II

Berkeley returned to London in October 1731 dejected but by no means beaten. Indeed, his return signalled a new creative period of authorship rivalling that of the heroic years 1709–1713. Over the next four years he issued the following six works:

A Sermon before the Society for the Propagation of the Gospel in Foreign Parts (delivered in 1731, published in 1732)

Alciphron: or the Minute Philosopher ... containing an Apology for the Christian Religion (1732)

The Theory of Vision or Visual Language shewing the immediate Presence ... of a Deity Vindicated and Explained (1733)

The Analyst; or, a Discourse Addressed to an Infidel Mathematician (London, 1734)

A Defence of Free-Thinking in Mathematics (London, 1735)

Reasons for not Replying to Mr Walton's Full Answer (Dublin, 1735).

These works, and particularly *Alciphron*, will be the subject of the following chapter. However, a good deal more remains to be said about the Bermuda project, which, for many of Berkeley's contemporaries (and probably for Berkeley himself), was the centre-piece of his career. Thus one anonymous author, writing shortly after Berkeley became Bishop of Cloyne, and alluding to his philo-

---

[9] Berman, 'Some New Bermuda Berkeleiana', *Hermathena* 110 (1970), 27. For a detailed and sympathetic account of Berkeley's Bermuda project and his period in America, see *Life*, chs. vii–ix, or E. S. Gaustad, *George Berkeley in America* (New Haven, Conn., 1979).

sophical contributions and his missionary endeavours, made the following prediction about Berkeley's fame: 'His eminent Talents, by which he shines in the learned World, will not give him so much Lustre and Distinction in the annals of future Times, as that Apostolic Zeal which he is so confessedly endowed'.[10] This prediction has not been fulfilled; nor are we likely to accept Stock's judgement that Berkeley's 'benevolent project . . . alone entitles him to as much honour as all his learned labours have procured for him . . .' (Stock, 16). Stock certainly regarded the missionary scheme as the most important episode in Berkeley's life, and he devotes one third of his biography to it. Stock's judgement seems to have been shared by Dr Johnson (1709–84), who wished to write a life of Berkeley.[11] Although no admirer of Berkeley's immaterialism, Johnson was impressed with Berkeley's project, which he called a 'pious and beneficient design'. And in a conversation on the subject in 1754 Johnson is quoted as saying that Berkeley's son, George, 'might be vain, as well he may, of such a father . . .'.[12]

The importance of the Bermuda project is also reflected in Berkeley's writings of 1732–5. Most of them, as we shall see, were aimed against free-thinking in religion, which Berkeley believed had undermined his projected college. Thus in a letter of 2 March 1731 he writes: 'What they foolishly call free thinking seems to me the principal root or source not only of opposition to our College but of most other evils in this age' (*Works*, viii. 212). Berkeley alludes to his disappointment in the first section of *Alciphron*, where he speaks of the 'miscarriage' of an affair which brought him into a 'remote corner of the country', an affair that cost him 'a great loss of time, pains, and expense'. When he exclaimed later in *Alciphron* v. 2 that 'this present world is not designed or adapted to make rational souls happy', he probably felt it

---

[10] *Gentleman's Magazine*, iii (London, 1734), 443.
[11] According to Berkeley's son, George, Johnson 'had a wish to be my father's biographer; but when applied to . . . I declined to furnish him with materials for that purpose . . .'; see my 'Some New Bermuda Berkeleiana', 28.
[12] 'Some New Bermuda Berkeleiana', 29; for Johnson's famous stone-kicking 'refutation' of Berkeley's immaterialism, see Boswell's *Life of Samuel Johnson* (Dublin, 1992), i. 397.

personally. The failure of his projected College, as he wrote in March 1731, 'lay heavy upon my spirits' (*Works*, viii. 212).

The significance of the project for Berkeley can also be seen, almost literally, in the two title-pages of *Alciphron* (present in the 1732 editions), each of which has a vignette. In the first-volume vignette (see Figure 4) Berkeley links the abandonment of his project with the abandonment of God. He does this by means of an open, spouting fountain, to the right of which there are three labourers digging a cistern. The meaning of the vignette is made clearer by one of the mottos beneath it, a quotation from Jeremiah 2: 13 'They have forsaken me the Fountain of living waters, and hewed them out cisterns, broken cisterns that can hold no water.' On one level, the vignette symbolizes the rejection of God and religion by the free-thinkers or, as Berkeley prefers to call them, following Cicero, 'minute philosophers', against whom *Alciphron* was written. This message is enforced by the vignette's other motto, taken from Cicero's *De Senectute* 85: 'But if when dead I shall be without sensation, as some minute philosophers think, then I have no fear that these philosophers, when they are dead, will have the laugh on me'—a quotation that Berkeley exploits in dialogue 1, section x.

Yet at another and more esoteric level the fountain vignette symbolizes the abandonment of Berkeley's project by the English Government as well as by Berkeley's associates. But why suppose that he had his defeated project in mind here? The answer is to be found in a key passage in his 1724 *Proposal*, which also enables us to make sense—as I have elsewhere argued—of other puzzles in Berkeley's life and work:

. . . to any Man, who considers the divine Power of Religion, the innate Force of Reason and Virtue, and the mighty Effects often wrought by the constant regular Operation even of a weak and small Cause; it will seem natural and reasonable to suppose, that Rivulets perpetually issuing forth from a Fountain, or Reservoir of Learning and Religion, and streaming through all Parts of *America*, must in due time have a great Effect, in purging away the ill manners and Irreligion of our Colonies, as well as the Blindness and Barbarity of the Nations round them:

Especially, if the Reservoir be in a clean and private Place, where its Waters, out of the Way of any Thing that may corrupt them, remain clear and pure; otherwise they are more likely to pollute than purify the Places through which they flow. (*Works*, vii. 358)

Clearly, then, Berkeley identified his hopeful missionary college with 'a Fountain, or Reservoir of Learning and Religion'. The identification can also be seen, I believe, in the best-known painting of Berkeley, generally called 'The Bermuda Group' (see Figure 7), painted by Berkeley's friend, John Smibert (1684– 1751). This famous conversation piece shows Berkeley, his wife, child, and associates (Smibert is on the extreme left). The picture also contains in the background 'rivulets . . . issuing from a fountain or reservoir . . .', which must surely stand for Berkeley's project. What makes this interpretation especially cogent is the gesture of the central figure in the painting, a Miss Handcock, companion to Berkeley's wife. It is clear that Miss Handcock is pointing at something. It is also reasonably clear that her gesture was intended to be symbolical, rather than merely naturalistic; for as H. W. Foote comments in his *John Smibert, Painter* (Cambridge, Mass., 1950), her 'left arm and hand [are] held rather awk-wardly . . .'.[13]

So the 'fountain or reservoir' lies, in more than one sense, in the background of the painting. In pointing to the background Miss Handcock is pointing to the purpose or goal which drew the Dean and his associates to America. That she seems to be looking intently at Berkeley—who is himself looking heaven-wards—confirms this. The picture (of which there is another less-polished version) is supposed to have been painted in America in 1729/30, when the American project was still a pregnant possibility and the fountain of St Paul's might (under Berkeley's management) have produced 'mighty effects'. Thus the background to Smibert's conversation piece depicts the *Proposal*'s extended water-image, and both convey Berkeley's hope for the spiritual and moral cleansing of the New World.

[13] H.W. Foote, *John Smibert, Painter* (Cambridge, Mass., 1950), 46.

But by 1732 the fountain of religion and learning, which was to purify the colonies, had been defeated; Berkeley's pious project had been 'absolutely abandoned' and forsaken, not only by Walpole and the English government, but also by the Dean's former associates, among them Robert Clayton, who had become an Irish bishop.[14] So in the defeat of St Paul's College Berkeley saw his own abandonment and that of God, which he graphically expressed on the first title-page (Figure 4) of his main theological work.

The second vignette (see Figure 5) should be read, I suggest, in a similar way. Here again we have two mottoes printed below the engraving—one quotation from Scripture, the other from a pagan writer.[15] The first is from Hosea 12: 7: 'The balances of deceit are in his hand'; the second is from Plato's *Cratylus* 428 D: 'The worst of all deceptions is self-deception.' As I pointed out in Chapter 4, the standing figure depicts irreligious prejudice (as described in *Guardian* 39), which Berkeley took to be a principal source of opposition to his project (*Works*, viii. 212). Hence, as the first vignette symbolizes the abandonment of Berkeley's missionary project, the second depicts the force which defeated it; and both vignettes identify the target of *Alciphron*—the free-thinkers, whose infidelity Berkeley describes as 'an effect of narrowness and prejudice' (*Alc*. vi. 11).

As to the seated figure in the second vignette, I suggest that it is Robert Walpole. By refusing to pay the £20,000 granted by Parliament, he was chiefly responsible for defeating Berkeley's project. While ostensibly supporting the scheme—indeed, he gave it money from own pocket—he really opposed it, although (as we have seen from Stock's account above) not in a straightforward

---

[14] In a letter of 2 March 1730/1 Berkeley speaks of 'this long continued delay' which has 'made those persons who engaged with me entirely give up all thoughts of the College . . . So that I am absolutely abandoned by every one of them' (*Works*, viii. 212).

[15] Nicholas Barker has suggested to me that this underlines the message of Berkeley's text that reason can demonstrate the folly of unbelief as effectively as revelation; see his 'Typography and the Meaning of Words: the Revolution in Layout of Books in the Eighteenth Century', in G. Barber and F. Bernhard (eds.), *Buch und Buchhandel in Europa im 18. Jahrhundert* (Hamburg, 1981), 127–65.

They have forsaken me the Fountain of living waters, and hewed them out cisterns, broken cisterns that can hold no water. Jerem. ii. 13.

Sin mortuus, ut quidam minuti Philosophi censent, nihil sentiam, non vereor ne hunc errorem meum mortui Philosophi irrideant.

Cicero

Fig. 4. Vignette from title page of *Alciphron*, vol. 1 (1732)

The Balances of Deceit are in his Hand. Hosea xii. 7.

Τὸ Ἐξαπατᾶωϛ αὐτὸν ὑφ' αὑτε̃, πάνϳων χαλεπώτατον. Plato.

Fig. 5. Vignette from title page of *Alciphron*, vol. 2 (1732)

way. Hence Berkeley may well be alluding to Walpole's dissembling in the quotation from Hosea. This is supported, too, by
the context; for in Hosea 12: 7 it is a merchant who is said to be
holding the balances of deceit. Given Walpole's position as head
of the Treasury and his close connection with the City, the parallel
would be appropriate. Walpole also seems to have been known
as a sceptic in religion, so that he is suitably represented as resting
on the plinth of irreligious prejudice, which is blocking his view
of the (living) waters in the background.[16]

That Berkeley took the defeat of his missionary college very
much to heart is clear from the fountain motif. Not only does it
appear on the first title-page of *Alciphron*, but it recurs in the
background of at least one contemporary portrait of Berkeley by
John Vanderbank (1694?–1739), best known from the 1800
engraving by Skelton. In this engraving (Figure 8) the fountain
motif, based on that in *Alciphron*, is nearly as prominent as the
Bishop himself. Water symbolism also appeared earlier in the
background of the John Smibert portrait of Berkeley (Figure 6),
executed in 1728, which shows the Dean pointing at a rocky
coast across an expanse of calm blue water, which clearly symbolizes the Bermuda enterprise. Finally in the portrait of Berkeley as
bishop (Figure 9), we see in the background a ship in full sail
on a rough sea. This, together with the Bishop's holding a book
inscribed 'Voyage to the Indies', suggests a retrospective view of
Berkeley's stormy project. Thus in the background of these contemporary portraits we have, in effect, a fourfold view of Berkeley's
great project. We are able to see it (i) in distant prospect (Figure 6),
(ii) as hopeful actuality (Figure 7), (iii) as failure (Figure 8),
and (iv) in stormy retrospect (Figure 9).

The fountain imagery enables us to glimpse the grandeur of
Berkeley's project. The project was bolder and more far-reaching
than his *Proposal* would alone suggest. For example, Berkeley's

---

[16] See McCabe, *A Rationalist Encyclopedia* (London, 1984), 613. Not surprisingly,
Alciphron was attacked by two of Walpole's close associates: Lord Hervey, in *Some
Remarks on the Minute-Philosopher* (1732), and Bishop Hoadley, in an essay in the *London
Journal*, 10 and 17 June 1732 (both repr. in Garland, i. 1, 135–6, 187–252).

Fig. 6. Portrait of Dean Berkeley by John Smibert, *c.*1728. Oil on canvas, 100.5 × 75 cm.

Proposal gives no indication that he intended to build not only a college but also a city in Bermuda. But, by chance, his carefully and classically conceived plan for the city has been preserved.[17]

---

[17] It was first published in *The Works of George Berkeley* (Dublin, 1784), ii, facing p. 419; see *Images*, 45.

Fig. 7. The Bermuda Group—Dean Berkeley and his entourage—by John Smibert, c.1729/30.

Fig. 8. Engraving of Bishop Berkeley, 1800, after portrait by J. Vanderbank, *c*.1734, 26.0 × 33.2 cm.

Fig. 9. Portrait of Bishop Berkeley, May 1733. Oil on canvas, 124 × 99 cm.

He also, according to his daughter-in-law, had it clearly in mind to introduce episcopacy in America. Berkeley is supposed to have said that unless this was done,

that noblest, grandest part of the British Empire of the WHOLE world will be lost; they [the Colonies] will shake off the Mother Country in a few years. Nothing but introducing Bishops amongst them *can* keep them together, can keep them loyal. Church and State, in every country, must stand and fall together.[18]

It is in his famous poem, 'On the prospect of Planting Arts and Learning in America', that Berkeley allows the boldness of his design to emerge most clearly. The poem was written in 1726, at a high-point of the project, but not published until 1752. Here are the three last stanzas:

> There shall be sung another golden Age,
> The rise of Empire and of Arts,
> The Good and Great inspiring epic Rage,
> The wisest Heads and noblest Hearts.
>
> Not such as *Europe* breeds in her decay;
> Such as she bred when fresh and young,
> When heav'nly Flame did animate her Clay,
> By future Poets shall be sung.
>
> Westward the Course of Empire takes its Way;
> The four first Acts already past,
> A fifth shall close the Drama with the Day;
> Time's noblest Offspring is the last.   (*Works*, vii. 373)

These concluding lines, among the best known and most inspiring Berkeley ever published, are also among his most enigmatic. Taken with the preceding stanzas, the lines suggest that the American project was to play a significant part in some world-historical

---

[18] *Poems by George Monck Berkeley*, pp. ccccxlix–ccccl. In the *Proposal* Berkeley seems to be cautiously hinting at this plan to introduce bishoprics. The missionaries, he says, will receive 'Holy orders in England (till such time as Episcopacy be introduced in those Parts) . . .' (*Works*, vi. 348). It may be noted that Berkeley's son George was active in the movement which led to the first American bishop being consecrated—in 1784.

development. But what are the 'four first Acts already past'? Berkeley gives us little help either in the poem, or in his Bermuda publications, or in his letters of the period. Indeed, in the one letter (of 1726) in which we learn of the poem (and which contains an early version entitled 'America or the Muse's Refuge: A Prophecy'), he is secretive, even to the extent of denying his authorship (*Works*, viii. 152).

Shortly after his return from America Berkeley delivered the annual *Sermon before the Society for the Propagation of the Gospel*, published in February 1732, in which we might expect some slight gloss on his poem. There is none. Yet we have a clue, curiously enough, in the Society's annual sermon delivered two years earlier by Zachery Pearce (1690–1774), who was personally involved in the Bermuda project as one of those appointed to collect 'contributions and subscriptions' (*Works*, vii, 361). Pearce's sermon reveals, I suggest, the eschatological aspect of Berkeley's poem and project. His text is Isaiah 49:6, which proclaims 'salvation unto the end of the earth'. Pearce argues that this 'prophecy' is to be fulfilled in America:

It is observable, that this so lately discover'd World lies in the very Route and Road, which Christianity seems to have all along taken: in the East, we know, it first appear'd; and, as it spread itself, it shaped its Course* with that of the Sun, the Emblem of its Light and Glory: to the Westward* it travell'd, and in length of time took possession of those *European* Countries, which are now called *Christendom*; and ever since this more Western Tract of *America* has been known, [Christianity] has continued by degrees to gain ground . . . (p. 26)

Pearce goes on to say (p. 27) that this may well be 'the time for the conversion of the Americans' and the realization of God's designs. For 'we know that this Time will come, and, for ought we know, this day* of the Lord may now be at hand'.

The similarity in wording between Berkeley's poem and Pearce's sermon—to which I have called attention by asterisks— is unlikely to be accidental. And Pearce's comment on the ancient use of the term 'Empire' makes that even less likely; for he explains that 'in the Language of Sacred and profane Authors, every great Empire is called the whole World' (p. 16). Thus, if Pearce is following Berkeley, the Westward course of Empire should mean the Westward course of the whole world. It is a curious idea, but one which was certainly in Berkeley's mind when he first penned his last stanza; for the final line originally read, 'The world's great effort is the last' (*Works*, viii. 153).

If we use Pearce's sermon as a gloss or key, we can see that the 'Acts' mentioned in the poem are the different phases in the spread of Christianity. Thus Pearce tells us that Christianity 'was published at first in Judaea, from whence it spread to Samaria, and other Parts where the Jews dwelt . . . till at last . . . St Paul, by the Direction of the Holy Spirit, began to apply himself to the Gentiles . . .'(p. 16). Here we seem to have three Acts, and a fourth would be the establishment of Christendom in Europe (of which Pearce speaks in the long quotation above). The fifth Act, then, and the close of the religious Drama, was to be the general conversion of America.

I am not, however, claiming that this is the only plausible inter-pretation of the last stanza. Some commentators have held that the four acts of Empire refer to the four ancient Kingdoms of Babylon, Medo-Persia, Greece, and Rome, alluded to in Daniel 2: 36–45, and the fifth and final act is that which 'shall stand for ever'. Dr Johnson seems to have held this, and it has been supported more recently by Donald Greene and Harry Bracken.[19] Yet I think that this interpretation from Daniel is less cogent than that from Isaiah *via* Pearce. For one thing, Berkeley speaks not of four Empires but of four Acts of (presumably one) Empire, which I take to be the four phases in the spread of Christianity, God's 'spiritual Empire' (as Pearce writes on p. 23). Moreover, the Daniel interpretation would thematically sever the final, escha-tological stanza from the rest of the poem; whereas if we suppose, following Pearce, that the fourth Act of Empire was Christianity's 'possession of the European Countries', then the prophecy

---

[19] Greene, 'More on Berkeley's Prophecy', *The Scriblerian* 14 (1981), 58; Bracken, 'Bishop Berkeley's Messianism', in R. H. Popkin (ed.), *Millenarianism and Messianism* (Leiden, 1988), 71–3.

develops naturally from the penultimate stanza, in which Berkeley describes Europe's spiritual decadence.

While Greene and Bracken are certainly correct in holding that Daniel's prophecy of the five Kingdoms was widely known, the interpretation I have taken from Pearce was also available in Berkeley's time. Thus as early as 1634 a correspondent of Joseph Mede (1586–1638) had written: 'And then considering our English Plantations of late, and the opinion of many grave Divines concerning the Gospel's fleeting Westward; sometimes I have had such Thoughts, Why may not that be the place of New Jerusalem?'[20] Similarly, George Herbert (1593–1633) in 'The Church Militant' also emphasizes the westward movement of religion and Christianity:

> The course was westward, that the Sun might light
> As well our understanding as our sight.

Herbert also significantly observes:

> Religion stands on tip-toe in our land,
> Readie to pass to the American strand.[21]

Of course, Berkeley might have had both the Isaiah and the Daniel prophecies in mind and wished his readers to have both as well. In whichever case, it should be evident that his poem is apoc-alyptic or eschatological. However, this is denied by E. L. Tuveson, who argues in his book *Redeemer Nation: The Idea of America's Millennial Role* (Chicago, 1968) that Berkeley's poem contains

no expectation of a universal millennium. The golden age is to be in the Western Hemisphere only, and there is no hint that a renovating influence will go forth to the world. Again, no apocalyptic commentator would characterize the millennium merely as 'Time's noblest offspring', implying that it is only one, albeit the best, product of natural historical process. (p. 94)

But when in 1726 the poem was called 'A prophecy' its last line read, as we have seen, 'The world's great effort is the last'. In

---

[20] Mede, *His Works, Corrected and Enlarged* (London, 1664), 979.
[21] *The Temple: Sacred Poems* (London, 1674), 184 and 190.

1752 Berkeley toned down (understandably enough) this unfulfilled eschatological prophecy, but he did not suppress it.

Although Berkeley's grand scheme was abortive, his visit to America had positive results. The many towns and institutions named after Berkeley in America—most notably, Berkeley in California—are eloquent witnesses to his impact there. His presence in America also generated interest in his philosophy; thus the first indigenous philosophy textbook, the *Elementa Philosophica* (Philadelphia, 1752), was deeply indebted to Berkeley, and was in fact dedicated to him. The book was written by his Connecticut friend, Samuel Johnson, and was printed by Benjamin Franklin (1706–90). Berkeley also gave large and much needed collections of books to Harvard and Yale; and to the latter he gave his Rhode Island farm. Berkeley may justly be regarded as the first, or one of the first, great Irish-Americans.

III

American education benefited from Berkeley's visit, but so, too, did Berkeley's philosophical fortunes. The first two decades in the reception of Berkeley's immaterialism were grim indeed, as Harry Bracken has shown in his *Early Reception of Berkeley's Immaterialism*. Yet these early years were not 'doldrum years', as most scholars had thought before Bracken's valuable work. For Berkeley's philosophy was the object 'of repeated and concerted attacks', Bracken shows, and by the early 1730s 'the patterns of insult, ridicule and distortion were well established in the Republic of Letters . . .' (p. 38). We find, Bracken concludes, 'that Berkeley already has a reputation—he has already been called a sceptic, atheist, idealist, egomist [i.e. solipsist] and fool' (p. 84). Bracken has persuasively argued that this early reputation has distorted the understanding of Berkeley's philosophy even up to our own day. By making us aware of the formative but forgotten influences of our philosophical ancestors, Bracken has done much to free us from their infantile views of Berkeley's immaterialism.

My aim here is to continue (what might be called) Bracken's psycho-historical analysis of the infancy and childhood of Berkeley's philosophical reception. Yet my perspective will be somewhat different. Instead of asking why Berkeley's philosophy was rejected and abused, I shall be asking why it was now embraced and praised. For by this time a new note can also be heard. Amidst the abuse there is now some praise. A philosophy cannot live on criti-cism alone. And after Berkeley's return from America in 1731 his writings begin to attract friends as well as foes. Why? Plainly, part of the answer is: on account of their intrinsic merits. But just as there were, as Bracken shows, extra-philosophical causes for the ear-lier detraction and vilification, so there were extra-philosophical causes for the later positive developments. The most important, I shall argue, was Berkeley's involvement in the Bermuda project. It estab-lished his reputation for piety and high moral character, and made his name almost a byword for virtue and benevolence. It gave sub-stance to Pope's tribute, 'To Berkeley, ev'ry virtue under heav'n'.[22]

But why, it might be asked, should this reputation for virtue have affected his philosophical fortunes? One answer is that in Berkeley's time there was still a strong belief in the connection between moral practice and philosophical theory.[23] Hence, if a man were known to be wicked, his philosophical theories were dis-credited. Conversely, if he was known to be virtuous, his theories would be taken more seriously; and the latter, I suggest, is what happened in Berkeley's case. Thus, in 1738 even Voltaire defended Berkeley's doctrines by pointing out that he was formerly a missionary in America, and Thémiseul de Saint-Hyacinthe did the same five years later.[24] 'Aligned with no side, he was attacked by all sides'—this was true before the 'benevolent project', as Stock called it, but not after. After, Berkeley's name became increasingly aligned with virtue, and this alignment both blunted criticism of his philosophy and attracted support for it.

I should, however, make some clarifications and qualifications. In the first place, there is some evidence that Berkeley's moral

---

[22] Pope, 'Epilogue to the Satires', Dialogue II (1738), in *Pope: Poetical Works*, ed. by H. Davis (London, 1966), 417.

[23] See my *History of Atheism*, 154–9.

[24] Bracken, 2–3.

character had been eulogized before the Bermuda project—by, for example, Richard Steele and Bishop Atterbury.[25] But their praise would hardly have been well known. It was, above all, the Bermuda project that gave their remarks prominence and substance. Thus it is significant that Berkeley's name is first explicitly linked with Virtue in Swift's poem, 'The Storm: Minerva's Petition', which was written around 1722 or 1723, because in 'The Storm' Swift associates Berkeley with the Bermuda project:

> And if you [Pallas] must have your petition
> There's Berkeley in the same condition;
>
> .   .   .   .   .   .
>
> But if you'll leave us B——p Judas,
> We'll give you Berkeley for Bermudas.

The poem closes with the well-known lines:

> Believed it best to condescend
> To spare a foe, to save a friend;
> But fearing Berkeley might be scared,
> She left him Virtue for a guard.[26]

Were it not for the 'benevolent project', the earlier eulogies might never have entered into the public consciousness. They were mere streams; Bermuda was the river that powered Berkeley's moral reputation.

It is also the case that various events following on the Bermuda scheme did much to enhance and consolidate Berkeley's public image. First of all, there was the publication of his powerful writings in support of theism and Christianity. Appearing in 1732–5, in the wake of the project, they won for Berkeley the reputation of champion of the faith. Before that, as Bracken has shown, the theistic dimension of his philosophy had been played down by early commentators.[27] No doubt, Berkeley's opposition to free-thinking and his defence of religion would, alone, have helped

---

[25] See below, Ch. 8 § III.

[26] See *The Poems of Jonathan Swift*, ed. Harold Williams (Oxford, 1958), i. 304–5. Williams dates the poem 1722, but 1723 seems more likely since Berkeley's first reference to his project is in a letter of 4 Mar. 1723.

[27] See above, Ch. 3 n. 3.

his philosophical reputation. What I wish to point out is that it also enhanced his moral reputation. Just as his benevolent project reflected positively on his previous philosophical theorizing, so his strong-minded commitment to Christianity confirmed his moral character.

The benevolent Bermuda project of 1724–31 and the theo-logical writings of 1732–5 fit and support each other perfectly, especially if one subscribes—as most of Berkeley's contemporaries did—to the orthodox view on the connection between religion and morality. Finally, the fact that Berkeley himself was one of the most zealous adherents of this position helped to complete the picture. Dean Berkeley could therefore be seen as an almost perfect instan-tiation of the orthodox position. As Marcus Aurelius is often seen as the exemplification of the ideal Stoic sage, so Berkeley came to be seen as a paradigmatic Christian: perfectly moral and religious.

The next important event in Berkeley's life sealed this asso-ciation of high moral character and deep religious commitment. In 1734 he became Bishop of Cloyne. This gave institutional recognition to his fame for virtue and religion. He now became the good and great bishop. But the goodness existed prior to and independent of his episcopal character, as is clear from the opening of Pope's famous tribute of 1738: '*Ev'n* in a *bishop* I can spy desert' [my italics].

IV

Thus a number of events and circumstances combined to produce Berkeley's extraordinary reputation for virtue—not the least of which was that his moral character was sung by some of the most gifted poets of the time. After 1735, therefore, even his most determined opponents would find it difficult to dismiss his views in the pre-1730 cavalier way.

I am willing to allow the Right Reverend author of the Ideal Philosophy every virtue under heaven, (as the celebrated Mr Pope has ascribed to him) . . .

I very much esteem the Bishop of Cloyne; he is a great and worthy man: but great men are not infallible, and his ideal philosophy, I assure you, sir, will be exploded . . .

These two polite quotations are from a correspondent of the *Gentleman's Magazine*, who, in a number of essays written between 1750 and 1752, tries to show the utter falsity of Berkeley's imma-terialism.[28] It is indicative of Berkeley's growing philosophical fortunes that there should be a serious debate about his philosophy in a popular magazine. But equally noteworthy is the tribute that opponents feel obliged to pay his moral character. This comes out also in Andrew Ramsay's *Philosophical Principles of Natural and Revealed Religion* (Glasgow, 1748):

The learned Doctor Berkeley . . . from a sincere and pious zeal against the absurd system of the Materialists . . . has ventured to deny not only the real existence of bodies, but even the possibility of their creation. (p. 239)

No doubt the great and good Doctor did not perceive those fatal [Spinozistic] consequences of his Scheme. (p. 245)

The importance of Ramsay's comments is that they link Berkeley's benevolence with his theological theories: the 'good' doctor's immaterialism was directed against pernicious atheism.

This plausible picture of Berkeley's character and intentions became the dominant one. Thus Thomas Reid, in his *Enquiry into the Human Mind* (1764), speaks of 'the good Bishop', who 'had that warm concern for religious and moral principles which became his order' (p. 23). Like Ramsay, Reid celebrates Berkeley's benevolence and intentions. Reid also thought that Berkeley's principles led, logically, to dire results—of a Humean, however, rather than of a Spinozistic kind. A more whimsical, but substan-tially the same, picture was painted by another Scottish philosopher, James Oswald, in his *Appeal to Common Sense* (Edinburgh, 1766):

It is probable that the design of disproving the reality of matter, was first entertained by the Bishop of Cloyne, in the gayety of his heart, with a

---

[28] The quotations are from letters signed T. D., in the *Gentleman's Magazine* 20 (1750), 156, and 21 (1751), 358.

view to burlesque the refinements of infidels. But the good Bishop was caught in his own trap; and, like the infidels themselves, became the dupe of his own subtility.   (p. 96).

James Beattie, Berkeley's most vociferous Scottish antagonist, also found it necessary to express his admiration for the Bishop's moral character. In his *Essay on the Nature . . . of Truth* (3rd edn., Dublin, 1773), Beattie says:

Still, I shall be told, that Berkeley was a good man, and that his principles did him no hurt. I allow it; he was indeed a most excellent person; none can revere his memory more than I. But does it appear that he ever acted upon his principles . . . ?   (p. 204)

Similarly, the belligerent William Warburton states that, although Berkeley persisted in the 'most outrageous whimsery that ever entered into the head of any ancient or modern madman', he was 'a good man, a good Christian, a good citizen, and all in an eminent degree'.[29]

Probably the most famous eighteenth-century instance of this eulogizing tendency is enshrined in the *Critique of Pure Reason* (1781), where Kant says: 'we cannot blame the good Berkeley for degrading bodies to mere illusion'.[30] Nor has this glowing picture of the good bishop lost any of its extraordinary attraction in our century.[31]

V

The Bermuda project was thus not in vain. It proved to be providential—for Berkeley's philosophical reputation. Hence, as John Brown expressed it, only 'coxcombs [would] vanquish Berkeley by a grin'.[32] Yet I would not wish to claim that the image of the virtuous dean and good bishop shielded Berkeley's philosophy against all derisive attacks. There were still coxcombs,

[29] See *Berkeley's Complete Works*, ed. A. C. Fraser (Oxford, 1901), iii. 400.

[30] See *Critique of Pure Reason*, trans. N. K. Smith (London, 1968), 89.

[31] After a highly critical study of Berkeley's thought, George Pitcher launches into an enthusiastic eulogy of his moral character, in *Berkeley*, 252–4.

[32] John Brown, 'Essay on Satire, occasioned by the Death of Mr. Pope' (1745); repr. in *A Collection of Poems* (London, 1770), iii; see p. 328.

as is plain from the following quatrain in the *London Magazine* of 1740:

> Dean *Berkley* says the world's not *real*,
> That all things but *deceive* him:
> His scheme, tis certain, is *ideal*;
> And who, but must believe him?   (p. 397)

There were also sober critics, such as Andrew Baxter and Philip Doddridge, who were not deflected from serious criticism by Berkeley's moral fame.[33] Nor would I wish to claim that the Bishop's reputation for benevolence was entirely derived from the Bermuda project, the subsequent theological writings and the bishopric. Berkeley's advocacy of tar-water in 1744 helped, as did such social writings as the *Querist* (1735–7) and the *Word to the Wise* (1749). My thesis is that the Bermuda project formed the nucleus of Berkeley's moral reputation, and that this reputation tempered the more rancorous critics and encouraged a more serious and sympathetic reading of his philosophical works.

In surveying the philosophical reception I have almost entirely considered the critics. I now turn to Berkeley's philosophical friends, who appeared in print none too soon; for, once again, a philosophy cannot live on criticism alone.

Probably the first important friendly gesture was made in 1728, with the publication of Ephraim Chambers's imposing *Cyclopaedia, or a Universal Dictionary of the Arts and Sciences* (London). The *Cyclopaedia* contains large extracts from Berkeley's *Principles*, particularly in the articles 'Abstraction', 'Body', 'External,' and 'Matter'. Chambers did not quite endorse Berkeley's theories, but by giving them extensive coverage, he undoubtedly encouraged the serious study of Berkeley's immaterialism. Moreover, in the context of the earlier history of abuse and misrepresentation, the fair play given by Chambers to Berkeley might have been (and indeed was) seen as tacit endorsement. Since the *Cyclopaedia* reached a fifth edition by 1743, it also made Berkeley's views accessible to a wide readership.

---

[33] See Bracken, *Early Reception,* ch. 5, and Doddridge (1702–51), *Course of Lectures* (London, 1763), Appendix, repr. in Garland, vol. i. II, 362–3.

The *Cyclopaedia* appeared at what was probably the high-point of the Bermuda episode, although there is no concrete evidence that the Bermuda publicity influenced Chambers. However, the next friendly gesture was certainly influenced by the American venture. It was made by Berkeley's friend Samuel Johnson in an essay in the *Present State of the Republic of Letters* of 1731. Like Chambers's articles, it is not very committal. Johnson's essay is entitled: 'An Introduction to the study of Philosophy . . .'; it begins with two mottoes: one from Cicero, the other from Berkeley's *De Motu*. The influence of the latter work is especially apparent on page 387, much of which is taken from *De Motu*, sects. 22 and 24. In his general metaphysical position Johnson is definitely, though implicitly, Berkeleian. Thus he writes:

Now there are two general heads to which all things may be referred, that we can come to the knowledge of, viz. bodies and spirits: by bodies I mean all sensible things, as consisting of certain fixed combinations of sensible qualities, such as extension, figure . . . sounds, tastes . . . even whatever we perceive by our senses.   (pp. 381–2)

Johnson's support for Berkeley could hardly be called bold; indeed the essay itself was anonymous. But from this humble beginning he was to offer, as we shall see, stronger and stronger backing for Berkeley's philosophy.

In 1732 an essay was published by a seemingly bolder adherent of Berkeley's immaterialism. It is entitled 'Body exists in the mind only', and it appeared in the *Touchstone; or Paradoxes brought to the Test . . .* (London), a work which contained four other essays, also anonymous. Our fourteen-page essay is composed of (unac-knowledged) extracts from Berkeley's *Principles* and *New Theory of Vision*. It also contains one passage from *Clavis Universalis* (London, 1713), the work of Berkeley's fellow immaterialist, Arthur Collier.[34]

Another appreciative gesture was made in a long review of 1735, in the *Present State of the Republic of Letters*. Although the anonymous reviewer is not a Berkeleian, he is clearly sympathetic

[34] See my 'An Early Essay concerning Berkeley's Immaterialism', *Hermathena* 109 (1969), 38–9.

to Berkeley's immaterialism (especially to its treatment of substance) and characterizes it soberly and with respect (pp. 102–3). Immaterialism was winning converts. In 1737 a series of letters was published between John Jackson and William Dudgeon, in which the latter defends both immaterialism and the rejection of abstract general ideas. Dudgeon, a Scotsman, does not mention Berkeley, but an early reviewer saw Berkeley as his source and inspiration.[35]

A year later, another Scotsman entered the lists—Berkeley's greatest philosophical contemporary, David Hume. In his *Treatise of Human Nature* (1739) Hume praises Berkeley as a 'great philosopher' on account of his rejection of abstract general ideas (see part 1, sect. vii). Hume's references to Berkeley in the recently uncovered *Letter from a Gentleman* (Edinburgh, 1745) are of considerable interest. Protecting himself against the charge of atheism, Hume shelters behind the reputation of the good bishop: 'Our author [i.e. Hume himself] indeed asserts, after the present pious and learned Bishop of Cloyne, that we have no abstract or general ideas, properly speaking...'. Later in the pamphlet, Hume defends his agnostic treatment of substance by noting that 'This opinion [that we have no idea of substance] may be found everywhere in Mr *Locke*, as well as in Bishop *Berkeley*.'[36]

A work that draws heavily on Berkeley's arguments for the existence of God is Samuel Johnson's *A Short System of Morality* (1746). Referring to the *Three Dialogues*, Johnson infers an almighty and intelligent cause from the passivity and orderliness of sensible things. He also deploys Berkeley's novel optic-language argument (which I shall be discussing in the next chapter), although Johnson's statement of it is more guarded than that of his mentor. It is by means of vision, says Johnson, that 'the great Author of nature appears to be continually present with me, discovering his mind and will... and, *as it were*, speaking to me'.[37]

[35] See *Several Letters to ... Jackson from William Dudgeon* (London, 1737), esp. 18–20, 26–8; see also the *History of the Works of the Learned* (April 1737), article 26, 318.

[36] *A Letter...*, ed. E. C. Mossner and J. V. Price, 26 and 30.

[37] See *Samuel Johnson: His Career and Writings*, ed. H. and C. Schneider (1929), ii. 482, my italics. All references to Johnson's writings are to this work.

This cautiousness is typical of Johnson. In 1752 he published his *Elementa Philosophica*, which incorporated a revised version of his *Short System of Morality*. The *Elementa* contains Johnson's most whole-hearted support of Berkeley's philosophy, and it is the first general book on philosophy by a professed Berkeleian. Johnson endorses Berkeley's views on representationalism (Schneider, p. 375), the heterogeneity of sight and touch (p. 376), and the Molyneux problem (p. 423), and refers to nearly all of Berkeley's published works. When a new edition of the *Elementa* was published in London in 1754, Johnson had a copy sent to Berkeley's friend, Bishop Secker, whose acknowledgement of 19 March 1754 contains the astute remark: 'You have taken very proper care to keep those who do not enter into all the philosophy of the good and great man [Berkeley] from being shocked at it.'[38] One indication of Johnson's cautiousness and eclecticism is to be found in the section 'Of Signs, Metaphors and Analogy', where he refers approvingly to *Alciphron* vii, but also to the *Procedure, Extent and Limits of Human Understanding* (London, 1728) of Berkeley's antagonist, Peter Browne (pp. 403–4). Still, the *Elementa* represented a major victory for Berkeley's philosophy, especially in America where it was used as a textbook.

It is sometimes thought that Berkeley's fame dates from the nineteenth century; in fact, it reached a high point in the 1750s. Thus in *An Essay on the Existence of Matter* (London, 1751), the first separately published critique of Berkeley's immaterialism, the anonymous writer points out that, although the bishop's 'system was probably at first regarded more on account of the high reputation of its author', many have been impressed, subsequently, by its plausible arguments.[39] He continues:

In effect, Mr *Chambers*, in the *Cyclopaedia*, speaks very favourably of this opinion; and by what has been published in the *Gentleman's Magazine*, it appears that many gentlemen of good understanding, and unquestionable abilities, have been persuaded of its truth. (p. 5)

---

[38] *Samuel Johnson*, ii. 331.
[39] See *An Essay on the Existence of Matter*, 4–5, in Garland, vol. i, II, 89–123.

The writer's attempt to refute Berkeley's philosophy testifies, in fact, to the growing power of that philosophy. Not only does he treat Berkeley courteously, he also candidly admits that the Bishop's philosophy 'has never been effectively confuted' (p. 4).

No doubt the clearest proof of the growing popularity of Berkeley's philosophy was the lively debate in the *Gentleman's Magazine* between 1748 and 1752, which must have given him considerable satisfaction, since both in quality and quantity his adherents have (in my opinion) the upper hand.[40] One final testimony to the success of Berkeleianism should be mentioned, as it rounds off this survey and also brings us to the year of Berkeley's death. In 1753 a large two-volume *Supplement* to Chambers's *Cyclopaedia* was published in Dublin, containing much additional material on Berkeley's views, especially in the articles on 'Distance', 'Extension', and 'Philosophy'. The compilers of the work were plainly interested in Berkeley's earlier thought, but also in its later developments. Thus there is a sympathetic account of tar-water in the article 'Tar'; and Berkeley's defence of Christian mysteries by parity of reasoning with mathematical mysteries is given attention in the articles 'Mystery' and 'Paradox'. Also interesting are the articles on 'Idea' and 'Notion', which contain lengthy quotations from the second edition of the *Principles* (London, 1734), in which Berkeley introduced changes in his use of the terms notion and idea.

By the time Berkeley died he had become a 'great name', even to opponents such as Robert Clayton. To friends such as Secker, he was 'the great and good man'.[41]

---

[40] All the contributions are in the form of letters, most of which are initialled. The progress of the debate was as follows (the figures are page nos.):

(1747) R. M., 439, for Berkeley's philosophy; Verax, 573–4, against.

(1748) R.M. 14–15, for; Colin Clout, 205, facetious; T. J., 500–1, sympathetic; S. T., 501, for.

(1749) T. K., 105–6, sympathetic; T. I., 268–9, sympathetic; T. J., 277–8, for.

(1750) ABC, 499, unsympathetic; R. M., 541, sympathetic; T. D., 540–1, against.

(1751) W. W., 13, for; B., 56, against; Convexo, 59–60, critical of both sides; T. D., 155–6, against; W. W., 204–5, for; T. D., 252–4, against; W. W., 309–11, for; T. D., 357–8, against; W. W., 609, for.

(1752) Anti Berkeley, 11–12, against; 64–5, the debate grows tedious; W. W., 128–9, for; 214, mediator.

[41] See below, Ch. 7. § VII; for tributes similar to Secker's, see Fraser, 352–5.

VI

Having argued that Berkeley's philanthropic Bermuda project played a crucial role in the reception and acceptance of his philos-ophy, I now want to take a final, critical look at this project. For although it was and continues to be the object of great admiration, it had two doubtful elements which need to be examined. Let us first look at Berkeley's views on negro slavery, a subject which in the *Proposal* he discusses with that of the shortage of clergy in America:

To this [shortage, he writes,] may be imputed the small Care, that hath been taken to convert the Negroes of our Plantations, who, to the Infamy of England, and Scandal of the World, continue Heathen under Christian Masters, and in Christian Countries. Which could never be, if our Planters were rightly instructed and made sensible, that they disappointed their own Baptism by denying it to those who belong to them: That it would be of Advantage to their Affairs, to have Slaves who should *obey in all Things their Masters according to the Flesh, not with Eye-service as Men-Pleasers, but in Singleness of Heart as fearing God*: That Gospel Liberty consists with temporal Servitude; and that their Slaves would only become better Slaves by being Christians.   (*Works*, vii. 346)

There is much in the latter part of this passage which a reader, particularly a modern reader, may find shocking. Berkeley objects to the West Indian planters not because they keep slaves, or even because they mistreat them; his grievance is that they do not baptize them. He then moves to a pragmatic criticism: quoting from Ephesians 6:5, he points out that the planters's 'slaves would only become better slaves' by becoming Christians—better slaves, not better persons.

The *Proposal* is not the only place in which Berkeley mentions slavery; it is briefly touched upon in his S.P.G. sermon of 1732, where he again castigates the planters, this time for having 'an irra-tional contempt of the Blacks, as creatures of another species, who have no right to be instructed or admitted to the Sacraments . . .' (*Works*, vii. 122). Now some historians—W. E. H. Lecky[42], for

---

[42] *History of England in the Eighteenth Century* (London, 1892), ii. 248 .

instance—quote this remark as redounding to Berkeley's credit; and in many respects it does, since it shows, that he was no racist. But it also makes his endorsement of slavery even more puzzling. For since Berkeley did not hold, as Edward Long and other eighteenth-century writers did, that blacks 'should be classed with orang-outangs as a "different species of the same genus"', we may wonder what his justification was.[43] If blacks do not differ sub-stantially from whites, then what right have whites to enslave them?

Now another popular justification of slavery at the time was that a black was thought liable to be a slave because he was a heathen.[44] But this rationale was not open to Berkeley, because, as we have seen, he insists that the negroes should be baptized and that this will make no difference to their status as slaves. They would, he says, only become 'better slaves by being Christians'. But then what *was* Berkeley's justification for slavery? One tenable answer is that he thought the Bible sanctioned slavery. This inter-pretation is supported by his *Querist* (1735–7), where he concludes his defence of 'temporary slavery' with the question: 'What [does] the word "servant" signify in the New Testament?' The answer is provided by Jessop in his editorial note to this query: 'The Greek term (δοῦλος) means "slave"' (*Works*, vi. 137).

A limited defence of Berkeley's views on slavery has been offered by Edwin Gaustad in *George Berkeley in America*:

While to a later age it may seem no great service to blacks to argue that they could lawfully be both Christians and slaves at the same time, the case is otherwise. For if Christianity were a genuine option, then neither blackness on the one hand nor slavery on the other meant a spiritual inferiority or separation. At an irreducible minimum, this meant that black slaves, too, had souls. That Christianity did not eliminate attitudes

---

[43] See R. Coupland, *The British Anti-Slavery Movement* (London, 1964), 28.

[44] The legal basis of this justification was a decision by the court of common pleas in the reign of William and Mary; but this decision was overruled by Yorke and Talbot in a pronouncement of 1729; see F. Klingberg, *The Anti-Slavery Movement in England* (New Haven, Conn., 1926), 37. In his 1732 sermon Berkeley alludes to this pronouncement when he castigates the 'erroneous Notion, that the being baptised is inconsistent with a state of slavery . . . To undeceive [the planters] in this particular, it seemed a proper step, if the opinion of his Majesty's Attorney and Solicitor-General could be procured' (*Works*, vii. 122).

of racial inferiority and physical degradation is a circumstance too familiar and depressing to require elaboration. But history, like nature, knows no sudden jump. Berkeley took a step, however tentative and tiny, when he argued for greater intensity and responsibility in trying to Christianize blacks. (p. 91)

Gaustad seems to assume the benignity of Berkeley's Christian stand on slavery; his question is: to what extent did it serve the right cause? But suppose that Berkeley, like some Quakers, had said the opposite of what he did say: that the Gospel was *inconsistent* with slavery. Would that have been a 'step' in the wrong direction? By suggesting that the Bible sanctioned slavery Berkeley would seem to have strengthened the cause of slavery in this world. That he may have helped the slaves in the next world is, of course, entirely possible; but surely that is not the issue—unless we sup- pose that the 'step' Gaustad had in mind was in spiritual rather than temporal history.

Advantages in the spiritual and temporal realms must be dis- tinguished if the argument is not to be confused. Thus Berkeley calls attention to the temporal advantage to the slave-owners, not to the slaves, if the blacks become Christians. Similar things can be said of his views on passive obedience, which we examined in the previous chapter. Berkeley is quite clear that compliance with the moral absolute of passive obedience may lead to 'great suffering and . . . temporal calamities'; but still the sovereign must not be resisted, however tyrannical; for God will compensate the compliant sufferer in the next life for suffering or death in this' (*Works*, vi. 37–8).

This distinction also seems to be pertinent to the second topic. As I noted above, one of the imaginative parts of Berkeley's American plan was in the use of native Indian missionaries to convert their fellow Indians to Christianity. But how were these natives to be obtained? Berkeley's answer is rather chilling: 'The young Americans necessary for this purpose, may in the beginning be procured, either by peaceable methods from those savage nations, which border on our colonies, and are in friendship with us, or by taking captive the children of our enemies' (*Works*, vii. 347). The

Indian children are to be kidnapped. Why? No doubt, for their spiritual advantage. Of course, in fairness to Berkeley, it should be pointed out that similar practices, involving aboriginals and gypsies, have occurred even in our own time. Yet it is not clear that such contextualizing, although valid, removes that much of the chill from Berkeley's proposal. Thus Harry Bracken, who is sympathetic to Berkeley's moral views, regards his plan to kidnap Indian children as an 'extraordinary proposal' that stands in need of explanation. Bracken's own explanation is also religious. The 'key', he suggests,

is that Berkeley accepts the [then] popular view that the American Indians are the Lost Tribes of Israel. As Jews, their conversion is especially dear to God and each conversion promises, as Paul tell us in Romans xi, to bring closer the Second Coming.

Bracken does, however, note that 'Unfortunately for my sugges, tion, Berkeley does not mention the widely-held Jewish–Indian thesis. But I submit that an explanation of this sort is required to make sense of the incredible and totally out-of-character savagery recommended in his American prophetic dream.'[45]

A. C. Fraser has also, I think, captured something of Berkeley's deep messianism, when he says that St Paul's College, Bermuda, was to be the centre 'from which Christian civilization might radiate over the Utopia of a New World, with its magnificent possibil, ities in the future of the human race'.[46] But, for better or worse, it was not to be.

---

[45] 'Bishop Berkeley's Messianism', 73.
[46] *Berkeley's Complete Works* (1901), iv. 343.

6

Philosophical Theology
(1732–1735)

I

Alciphron is Berkeley's longest book and his most comprehensive statement on religion. It was composed while he was in Rhode Island and published in 1732, soon after his return to London. During the next three years he issued four shorter works which have a bearing on his theological system. The unity and strength of this system has not been appreciated, probably because commen-tators have concentrated on Berkeley's better-known philosophical writings of 1709–13. *Alciphron* has also suffered from dismissive judgments, even from admirers of Berkeley, like J. S. Mill and Leslie Stephen. Thus Stephen calls it 'the least admirable perfor-mance of that admirable writer'. And Mill is even more damning: 'were it not the production of so eminent a man, it would have little claim to serious attention.'[1] That these judgements are very far from the mark, I now hope to show.

Religion, Berkeley clearly recognized, consists of more than natural or rational theology. Christianity is concerned with grace, original sin, the doctrine of the Trinity, and an afterlife; these matters of faith and mystery are discussed in *Alciphron*, dialogue vii. Yet in order to believe sensibly in mysteries such as the Holy Trinity and the grace of God we must, according to Berkeley, first believe that there is a God. If the God of theism—a good, wise, provident creator of the world—did not exist then there

---

[1] Stephen, *History of English Thought in the Eighteenth Century* (London, 1876), ch. IX. 59; Mill, 465. For a recent challenge to the traditional belittlement of *Alciphron*, see Clark, p. xxi, and my *Berkeley's Alciphron in Focus* (London, 1993).

would hardly be much point in speaking about his grace or his three-in-one nature. Hence in *Alciphron*, dialogue iv, Berkeley carefully presents his proof that there is such a God. Unlike his earlier proof or proofs, which we examined in Chapter 3, this demonstration does not involve the denial of matter. It moves as follows:

1. There are some things that we know directly or immediately, such as the objects of sense: colours, odours, etc. However, there are also things which we know, or infer, only by their effects. Berkeley mentions animal spirits and force, but the most crucial inferred entities for his argument are other human minds (*Alc.* iv, sects. 4–5).

2. The human mind is different from its physical embodiment, and we can know that there are other intelligent and wise minds only from the bodily effects that minds 'actuate'. For 'By the person . . . is meant an individual thinking thing, and not the hair, skin, or visible surface, or any part of the outward form, colour, or shape of [that person; hence we do not see] that individual thinking thing, but only such visible signs and tokens, as suggest and infer the being of that invisible thinking principle or soul.' (sect. 5).

3. But there are innumerable intelligent and wise effects in nature which are not assignable to human agents: 'a man with his hand can make nothing so admirable as the hand' (sect. 5); and the vegetable, animal, and solar systems also show extra-ordinary unity and connection. Consequently, if we are justified in inferring other (finite) human minds, we must also, *a fortiori*, infer a divine (infinite) mind from those (non-human) effects. Up to this point Berkeley's proof is largely a reworking, from an epistemological point of view, of the traditional cosmological and teleological proofs for a Deity. Berkeley had largely formulated this line of argument in his *Principles* (1710), sects 145–8. It is essentially the passivity argument, outlined in Chapter 3, although without its immaterialistic components.

One novelty of Berkeley's procedure is that it clearly brings to the fore, possibly for the first time in the history of philosophy, the problem of other minds. Descartes had glanced at this problem in the *Meditations*, but Berkeley places it in centre-stage. For Berkeley forces his reader to choose between God and solipsism: between having the company of other minds, which must include God, or being entirely alone (apart from one's ideas) in the universe. If one insists on strict demonstration, then one must be a solipsist.

The next phase of the demonstration is even more distinctively Berkeleian. It is based on his *Essay towards a New Theory of Vision*, originally published in 1709, but revised and republished with the first three editions of *Alciphron* (all printed in 1732).

4. What most compels us to believe that there are other minds is that they talk to us. Hearing a man speak convinces us that he is 'a thinking and reasonable' mind (*Alc.* iv. 7). Berkeley is here suggesting that it is man's ability for language that distinguishes him from other living creatures, rather than (as Locke apparently thought) the capacity to form abstract general ideas.

5. Now, if our knowledge of God is really on the same level as our knowledge of other minds, then it must be shown that God, too, speaks to us. And this is precisely what Berkeley tries to do in sections 7 to 15. The most effective way of seeing the force of his argument that vision is a language—sometimes called the optic-language argument—is by listing the correspondences he provides between God's visual language and a language such as English or Hebrew. In this way we shall also be able to see the main lines of his *New Theory of Vision*—a work which Adam Smith described as 'one of the finest examples of philosophical analysis that is to be found, either in our own, or in any other language'.[2]

5.1. Just as there is no necessary connection or resemblance between a spoken or written word and the thing that it signifies, so there is no necessary connection or resemblance between visual data and the tangible objects they stand for. Berkeley's justification of this fundamental doctrine draws on (i) direct experience, (ii) conceptual argument, and (iii) experimental evidence.

---

[2] *Essays on Philosophical Subjects* (Dublin, 1795); in Garland, vol. 1. II, 434.

(i) He thinks that we can become aware that what we immediately experience by sight are ' light and colours, with their several shades and degrees' (*Alc.* iv. 10 and *TVV*, sect. 42), and that these are altogether different from what we touch. In the *Theory of Vision*, sects. 79–85, Berkeley describes our visual world more technically, as a field (or fields) of minimum visual points— his version of the (dubious but then generally accepted) theory that what we immediately see are points on the retina (see above, Ch. 2 § II). Thus if we could put ourselves into the position of a person born blind and made to see, we should recognize that upon first sight our visual experience would tell us nothing about tangible objects. It is only when we have correlated our experiences of sight with those of touch that the former are able to tell us anything about the latter (*Alc.* iv. 11).

(ii) Berkeley also argues that heterogeneity of sight and touch is shown in the impossibility of combining or quantifying a visual datum with a tactile datum. Thus (in *NTV*, sect. 131) he writes: '. . . A blue and red line I can conceive added together into one sum and making one continued line: but to make, in my thoughts, one continued line of a visible and tangible line added together is, I find, a task . . . insurmountable'. But if two things cannot be added then they must be qualitatively different.

(iii) Finally, Berkeley appeals in *Alciphron*, iv. 15 n., and in the *Theory of Vision, Vindicated and Explained* (1733) to William Cheselden's recent (1728) report in the *Philosophical Transactions* of a boy blind from infancy and made to see. In the latter work, section 71, Berkeley quotes Cheselden:

When he [the boy] first saw, he was so far from making any judgment about distances that he thought all objects whatever touched his eyes (as he expressed it) as what he felt did his skin . . . He knew not the shape of anything, nor any one thing from another, however different in shape or magnitude.

This suggests that the boy had no understanding of what he immediately saw. He did not connect the new visual data with the objects he knew by touch.

5.2. The collection or system of arbitrary signs both in English and in vision is orderly and coherent. An innumerable combination of signs can make known to us an endless variety of things. For example, a certain roundish green shape generally stands for a tangible apple; the smaller the patch of green, the further away (kinesthetically) the tactile object is likely to be; and similar things can be said about the information with which visible signs supply us concerning the size and texture of tangible objects.

5.3. As there is a grammar and syntax in English, so there are the laws of nature which contingently govern the orderly appearance of visual (as well as other) sense-data. According to Berkeley, our best understanding of this grammar of nature is provided by Newton's *Principia*. Moreover, we can use the two languages— English and vision—even though we are ignorant of their grammars (see *Principles*, sects. 108–10).

5.4. We must learn both languages. We are less aware of learning the visual language because (i) it is a language which all people—apart from those who are blind—learn; (ii) we start learning it at an age when we are barely able to reflect; and (iii) it is practised constantly (*Alc.* iv. 2).

5.5. In using both languages we are concerned primarily with what the signs signify; hence when 'we hear the words in a familiar language', we 'act as if we heard the very thoughts themselves' (*NTV*, sect. 51). Similarly we act as though we see the tangible object, when all we in fact immediately see are light and colours. It is hard in both languages to see the characters as mere characters, or marks on a paper, rather than as words or signs having meaning. We are insensibly carried to what the signs signify; and this movement is more powerful in the optic language because it is virtually a universal language. But once we succeed in mentally putting ourselves in the position of someone born blind and made to see (as described in Molyneux's famous problem and more empirically in the Cheselden experiment), we shall then realize that such a person is like a Chinaman who hears English words for the first time (*Alc.* iv. 11).

5.6. There are 'tricky' elements in both languages: as there are puns and homonyms in English, so there are visual illusions. The illusion that Berkeley examines in detail is the so-called harvest moon, that is, when the moon on the horizon appears much larger than at the meridian (*NTV*, sects. 67–78). These tricky signs show, too, that there is no necessary connection in either language between sign and thing signified. The large moon seen on the horizon does not mean that it (the tangible moon) is more than usually large—any more, that is, than the word 'bank' must signify the place where money is kept and dispensed, rather than the ground near a river.

5.7. Both languages usefully direct our actions, attitudes, and emotions; the visual language teaches us 'how to act in respect of things distant from us, as well in time as place' (*Alc.* iv. 7). Seeing a visual precipice before us is like hearing someone shouting out: 'Don't come any further; it's dangerous!'

5.8. In both cases, context is important, and the actual meaning and import of a sign can be affected by contextual and extra-linguistic factors, such as emphasis and tone with English words and the positioning of visible signs. 'Now, it is known', writes Berkeley in section 73 of the *Theory of Vision*, that

a word pronounced with certain circumstances, or in a certain context with other words, hath not always the same import and signification that it hath when pronounced in some other circumstances or different context of words. [Similarly] The very same visible appearance [of the moon] as to faintness and all other respects, if placed on high, shall not suggest the same magnitude that it would if it were seen at an equal distance on a level with the eye.

5.9. Both languages may afford amusement and exaltation as well as instruction; here one can compare the delight in the natural beauty of a sunset with the delight in a poem (see *Principles*, sect. 109).

II

I have now listed some nine correspondences laid down by Berkeley between the conventional language of English and the divine language of vision. His conclusion is: 'Upon the whole, I think we may fairly conclude that the proper objects of vision constitute an universal language of the author of nature . . .' (*NTV*, 3rd. edn., sect. 147). That is, we have 'as much reason to think, the universal Agent or God speaks to [our] eyes, as [we] have for thinking any particular person speaks to [our] ears'. And '. . . this visual language proves, not a Creator merely, but a providential governor actually and intimately present and attentive to our interests . . .' (*Alc.* iv. 14). Of course, if the optic language was not literally or 'really' (*Alc.* iv. 12) a language, then Berkeley's conclusion would not follow. A visual language, in a sense, could prove only a God, in a sense. Berkeley stresses that the optic language proves more than a distant deistic God, or God in some attenuated sense. This is an important point, and it provides the transition to the second part of dialogue four, where he criticizes certain non-literal accounts of God, particularly those offered by his former Archbishop and Provost, William King and Bishop Browne.

In his 1709 *Sermon on Predestination* King had tried to defend the theistic conception of God from charges of incoherence—for example, that God's perfection is incompatible with evil in the world; that his prescience is incompatible with man's free will—by arguing that we have no literal knowledge of God's attributes. For if we have no proper knowledge of God's prescience or perfection, King holds, then we cannot know that it is in conflict with human freedom or evil in the world.[3] Of course, this was a debate that went back many hundreds of years, both pro and con. Thus the charge of incoherence or contradiction can be found in Epicurus; and negative theology goes back to Denys the Areopagite (about AD 500) and to Plotinus (about AD 205–70). But Bayle had in his *Dictionary, Historical and Critical* (1697) revived these disconcerting Epicurean charges; and King and Browne had given the defence by negative theology a new turn by drawing on Descartes and Locke, among others, particularly on their theories of representation, substance, and the primary/

---

[3] See my introduction to King's *Sermon on Predestination*, 8–9.

secondary quality distinction. King's position can be described, I have elsewhere argued, as theological representationalism, a theory that became dominant in eighteenth-century Ireland, as it was held by Browne, Synge, Skelton, Ellis, and even Edmund Burke.[4] But it was forcibly opposed by Berkeley, who first expressed his opposition to it privately in a letter of 1 March 1709/10, then publicly in *Alciphron* iv. 16–22.

The theory of King and Browne amounted, as Berkeley saw it, to saying that God is an 'unknown subject of attributes absolutely unknown' (*Alc.* iv. 17). Now in the *Principles*, sect. 77, Berkeley had driven the materialists to admit that their conception of matter amounted to an 'unknown support of unknown qualities'. Clearly, these two positions employ virtually the same (objectionable) theory of substance. Berkeley also opposed representationalism in its theological form in *Alciphron* for essentially the same reasons as those which led him to attack it in its materialistic form in the *Principles*. In short, our supposedly representative notions either do or do not resemble their objects. If they do, then they give us proper knowledge. If they do not, then it is absurd to say that the one is like the other. There is no medium, Berkeley urges, between likeness and non-likeness.

Consider, too, this stratagem of the materialist, which Berkeley outlines in the *Principles*, sect. 80:

In the last place, you will say, what if we give up the cause of material substance, and assert, that matter is an unknown *somewhat*, neither substance nor accident, spirit nor idea, inert, thoughtless, indivisible... For, say you, whatever may be urged against... any... positive notion of matter, hath no place at all as long as this *negative* definition of matter is adhered to.

Now compare this defensive action of materialism with another such action, this time in theology, which Berkeley sums up in *Alciphron* iv. 17: 'hence whatever objections might be made against the attributes of God they [e.g., King and Browne] easily solved, by denying those attributes belonged to God in this, or

---

[4] See my 'Enlightenment and Counter-Enlightenment', sects. II and III, and 'Culmination and Causation', sect. II.

that, or any known sense or notion.' Berkeley then proceeds to show that both negative theology and negative materialism are untenable. If the words 'God' and 'matter' are taken in no proper sense, then they are empty. This is his answer to the negative materialist:

. . . you may . . . use the word *matter* in the same sense, that other men use *nothing*, and so make those terms convertible in your style. For after all, this is what appears to me to be the result of that definition, the parts whereof when I consider with attention, either collectively, or separate from each other, I do not find that there is any kind of effect or impression made upon my mind, different from what is excited by the term *nothing*. (*PHK*, sect. 80)

Berkeley has essentially the same answer in *Alciphron* iv. 17 to negative theologians, such as Browne and King; for to say that all of the divine attributes are unknown and unknowable in this life is

the same thing as to deny they belonged to Him at all. And thus denying the attributes of God, they in effect denied His being, though perhaps they were not aware of it. . . . For how are things reconciled with the divine attributes when these attributes themselves are in every intelligible sense denied, and, consequently, the very notion of God taken away, and nothing left but the name without any meaning annexed to it?

Berkeley was, in short, aware of the unintelligibility and inutility of both conceptions. As he emphatically puts it *Alciphron* iv. 18:

. . . if this [conception of God] could once make its way, and obtain in the world, there would be an end of all natural or rational religion, which is the basis both of the Jewish and Christian: for he who comes to God . . . must first believe that there is a God, in some intelligible sense: and not only that there is something in general, without any proper notion, though never so inadequate, of any of its qualities or attributes: for this may be fate, or chaos, or plastic nature, or anything else as well as God.

Thus we have 'God' without religion; and in the parallel conception in *Principles*, sect. 77, we have 'matter' without materialism. It is important to see the close similarity in Berkeley's attacks on materialistic and theological representationalism, if only as an antidote to the simplistic and often-expressed criticism that Berkeley was strong-minded against matter, but weak-minded and uncritical about spirit; that he failed to see that the same arguments which he had deployed against matter could be used as effectively against spirit and God.

Berkeley took up the theological issue again in the *Theory of Vision Vindicated* (1733), sect. 6, where he asks 'incautious friends [of religion] . . . to return to speak of God and his attributes in the style of other Christians, allowing that knowledge and wisdom do, in the proper sense of the words, belong to God . . .'. At about the same time, Browne issued his *Things Divine and Supernatural Conceived by Analogy* (London, 1733). Believing that *Alciphron* iv was aimed at his earlier *Procedure, Extent and Limits of Human Understanding* (London, 1728), Browne added a long chapter to the later work (pp. 374–554), which contains an extensive attack on *Alciphron* dialogue iv and, to a lesser extent, dialogue vii. Browne criticized Berkeley's natural theology (in *Alciphron* iv) for being too literal and cognitive, and his emotive account of mysteries (in *Alciphron* vii) for not being literal and cognitive enough. Berkeley responded to the first charge in a letter to Browne (recently identified as by Berkeley) in which he pressed his former Provost to admit that God is either literally wise or not wise at all. 'Between these, there is no medium; God has ends in view, or he has not . . .'.[5] For Berkeley the issue was fundamental.

The Berkeley–Browne debate highlights Berkeley's commitment to rationalism in theology. Hence it shows the absurdity of statements such as the following:

In the first half of the eighteenth century rationalism achieved its greatest popularity . . . But by the middle of the century philosophy had found a new direction. Bishop Berkeley and William Law [1686–1761] had demonstrated the invalidity of natural reason and shown man's need of revelation . . .[6]

[5] J.-P. Pittion, D. Berman, A. A. Luce, 'A New Letter by Berkeley to Browne on Divine Analogy', *Mind* 78 (1969), 389.

[6] R. Grant and D. Tracy, *A Short History of the Interpretation of the Bible* (2nd edn., London, 1984), 109; see also J. Downey, *The Eighteenth-Century Pulpit* (1969), 64.

It is hard to imagine a more wrong-headed judgement about Berkeley, although one which could make sense if Browne is substituted for Berkeley. The fideist, Law, and the theological representationalist, Browne, were natural allies, as indeed Law himself testifies; for in his *Case of Reason*, Part I (London, 1731), Law pays this tribute to Browne:

The justness and certainty of this kind of [negative theological] reasoning, is, with great perspicuity and judgement, asserted and proved, in a late excellent *treatise* [Browne's *Procedure*] and I hope the worthy author will not be long, before he gratifies the world, in their eager expectation of those *tracts*, which, he has promised, should follow it.   (pp. 45–6)

Browne did issue one of these tracts, the *Divine Analogy* (1733), which, as I noted above, attacks *Alciphron*, often abusively. Berkeley's strong commitment to rational theology, so clearly expressed in *Alciphron*, iv. 18, puts him poles apart from Law and Browne. Since God is at the basis of religion, for Berkeley, any uncertainty or vagueness in our conception of God must affect the stability of the rest of religion. One 'cannot prove, that God is to be loved for His goodness, or feared for His justice, or respected for His knowledge . . . [if these] attributes [are] admitted in no particular sense, or in a sense which no one can understand' (*Alc*. iv. 18). Our knowledge of God is for Berkeley essentially scientific knowledge: from the optic language he knows that God is wise, since 'this optic language hath a necessary connexion with knowledge, wisdom and goodness' (*Alc*. iv. 14). 'The being of a God', he states in the penultimate section of *Alciphron*, 'is capable of clear proof, and a proper object of human reason'. But this is not to say that all religious doctrines are like scientific judgements.

III

Berkeley was the first modern philosopher to formulate and support the theory that words have legitimate uses which do not involve informing or standing for ideas. In Chapter 1 we looked at the genesis of this theory—particularly its negative, non-cognitive aspect—in Berkeley's first sermon and entry 720 of the *Commentaries*. It is, however, in the *Manuscript Introduction* to the *Principles* that the whole theory is first clearly presented; for here he also (more positively) describes the three non-cognitive functions of language:

... the Communicating of Ideas marked by Words is not the chief and only End of Language, as is commonly suppos'd. There are other Ends as [1] the raising of some Passion [2] the exciting to or deterring from an Action, [3] the putting the Mind in some particular Disposition. To which the former is in many cases barely subservient and some-times omitted.   (pp. 110–11)

In some respects the *Manuscript* account of emotive language is Berkeley's most complete, since it is here that he applies the theory in detail to a religious mystery—the afterlife—and also suggests a mechanism—association or customary connection—whereby the non-cognitive words concerning the afterlife can evoke emotions, actions, and dispositions. Berkeley's account centres on his favourite Pauline proposition, from I Corinthians 9, which he had used in his first sermon and would use again in *Guardian* 27 and *Alciphron*, vii. 10. In the *Manuscript Introduction*, however, a few words from the Common Prayer Book are added, thereby issuing in this formulation: 'the Good Things which God hath prepared for them that love him are such as Eye hath not seen nor Ear heard nor hath it enter'd into the Heart of Man to conceive.' Berkeley takes these words to be cognitively empty; for 'who is there that can say they bring into his Mind clear and determinate Ideas or in Truth any Ideas at all of the Good Things in store for them that love God?' (p. 105). Yet neither are 'those words of the Apostle ... utter'd without all meaning and design whatsoever'. They have a use and purpose, namely, 'to beget in us a Chearfulness and Zeal and Perserverance in Well Doing', and these emotive results can be achieved if an association develops between the non-cognitive Pauline utterance and the desired actions and dispositions. For, asks Berkeley:

What is it that Hinders why a Man may not be stirr'd up to diligence and zeal in his Duty by being told he shall have a good Thing for his Reward, tho' at the same time there be excited in his Mind no other Idea than barely those Sounds or Characters? When he was a Child he had frequently heard those Words used to him to create in him an obedience to the Commands of those that spoke them. And as he grew up he has found by experience that upon the mentioning of those Words by an honest Man it has been his Interest to have doubled his Zeal and Activity for the service of that Person. Thus there having grown up in his Mind a Customary Connexion betwixt the hearing the Proposition and being dispos'd to obey with chearfulness the Injunctions that accompany it . . .   (p. 107)

Berkeley first published the emotive theory in the *Principles*, Introduction, sect. 20, which greatly condenses his account in the *Manuscript* and contains no mention of association or a possible application to religion. It is in *Alciphron*, vii. 7–10, that Berkeley first publicly used his fruitful theory to explain the import and force of religious mysteries. His characterization of the three non-cognitive functions of language—the evoking of (1) emotions, (2) dispositions, and (3) actions—changed little between 1708, 1710, and 1732. Thus in *Alciphron*, vii. 14, he says that words or signs '. . . have other uses besides barely standing for and exhibiting ideas, such as raising proper emotions, producing certain dispositions or habits of mind, and directing our actions'. He then discusses four specific mysteries: grace in section 7, the Holy Trinity in section 8, and original sin and a future state, both in section 10, where he also expressly identifies faith with the three non-cognitive functions of language: 'Faith, I say, is not an indolent perception, but an operative persuasion of the mind, which ever worketh some suitable action, disposition or emotion in those who have it . . .'.

Consider, for example, the doctrine of the Trinity. Although a man may form no distinct idea of trinity, substance, or personality, this does not imply, Berkeley maintains, that the mystery is meaningless; because it may well produce in his mind 'love, hope, gratitude, and obedience, and thereby become a lively operative principle influencing his life and actions . . .' (sect. 8). Berkeley deals in a similar way with grace, original sin, and a future state. He admits that they have little or no cognitive content, but this does not prevent their meaningful use. Thus talk of grace has the tendency to produce good habits and piety; original sin can deter people from committing an evil deed, and a future state is likely to produce good habits and a salutary sense of one's unworthiness. Religious mysteries are pragmatic; they are justified by their utility.

Because we know from the optic language that God is good, wise, knowing, and just, we must also realize that we ought to act and feel in certain ways. Because God is just, it is right to be fearful of doing the wrong thing; and it is imperative to develop such moral habits. Because God is good, it is right to love him; because he is wise and knowing, it is appropriate to respect him (*Alc.* iv. 18). Now, in Berkeley's view, belief in the Christian mysteries is an excellent way of bringing about these desirable ends. Nothing will so effectively make people fear God's justice as the mystery of a future state. Similarly, the best way of bringing people to love God is by means of the symbolism embodied in the Holy Trinity.

Of course, if we did not believe that God was good and just, or if we had only an analogical and distant idea of these attributes—as King and Browne believed—then there would be little point in talking about the Holy Trinity or a future state. For why should a bad man fear a being that is not literally just? Hence Berkeley's emotive account of mysteries rests squarely on his cognitive account of theology: dialogue vii of *Alciphron* rests on dialogue iv. It would be misleading, however, to give the impression that these two dialogues comprise all that Berkeley had to say about religion. In dialogues v and vi he also argues for the truth of the Christian revelation. Here he makes use of the usual arguments. He tries to show that Jesus Christ did rise from the dead, that he did perform miracles, and that the Old Testament prophecies were fulfilled by him. In this way, Berkeley has an additional reason for holding that the Christian mysteries in the

Scriptures reveal the right and desirable symbology. Not only do these mysteries flow pragmatically from a scientifically proven theology, but they also follow from the authenticity of the Scriptures. I have made less of this second string to Berkeley's bow for two reasons: (1) because it is not distinctively Berkeleian, and (2) because it has been subverted, in my opinion, by the so-called higher criticism.

Basic to Berkeley's distinctive theology is the linguistic distinction which he was the first to draw: between cognitive statements which inform—such as 'That cow is brown'—and emotive utterances which produce emotions, dispositions, and actions—for example: 'Cheer up!', 'Life's a bore', and 'Get out!'. Statements of rational theology, particularly 'God exists and is wise', are for Berkeley cognitive statements; and they support emotive utterances such as those concerning grace and Holy Trinity.[7] Berkeley's commitment to the primacy and regulative role of cognitive theology over emotive mysteries appears several times in *Alciphron*. In § II (above), I have quoted one such statement (from iv. 18), and Berkeley makes the point also in *Alciphron*, v. 27 and 29, as well as in some of his other writings, such as in his letter to Sir John James:

Light and heat are both found in a religious mind duly disposed. Light in due order goes first. It is dangerous to begin with heat, that is with the affections . . . our affections shou'd grow from inquiry and deliberation . . . (*Works*, vii. 146–7)

IV

Berkeley's discovery of the emotive theory and its application to religious mysteries did not occur in a historical vacuum. It was occasioned by the destructive use to which Toland, in particular, had put Locke's astringent theory of meaning and meaninglessness: that if a word does not signify a distinct idea, then it is

---

[7] For a somewhat different view of Berkeley's innovative theory of language, see Antony Flew's 'Was Berkeley a Precursor of Wittgenstein?', in W. B. Todd (ed.), *Hume and the Enlightenment* (Edinburgh, 1974), 153–65.

meaningless; and that since Christian mysteries do not stand for ideas, they must be as meaningless as 'Blictri'.

Now Berkeley accepted part of Toland's claim, namely, that religious mysteries do not signify distinct ideas; but this does not imply, Berkeley urged, that they are meaningless. That conclusion only follows if one accepts the Lockean *either/or*—which until 19 November 1707 Berkeley did accept, but which in *Alciphron*, vii. 1, he calls 'the primary motive to infidelity'—that words either communicate ideas and are meaningful, or do not signify ideas and are meaningless. Once one realizes the false restrictiveness of the Lockean *either/or*, one is no longer forced into the onerous, unnecessary, and absurd position of trying to provide ideas and reasons for things which, by one's own hypothesis, are above reason and beyond any human ideas. Then one can admit, with a good intellectual conscience, that the Holy Trinity, original sin, grace, and the future state are all emotive and not cognitive.

Berkeley's emotive accommodation of mysteries depends, there-fore, on his expanded theory of meaning; but this is not to say that the theory came before the application. In my view, as I have suggested in Chapter 1 § III, he discovered the theory while trying to find some way around Toland's irreligious but consistent exploitation of Locke's cognitive theory of meaning, an exploita-tion that was brought to his notice by King and Browne at the November 1707 meeting. Theory followed or went with practice. My reconstruction of the genesis of Berkeley's theory is strongly supported by the first eight sections of dialogue vii, where Alciphron (the free-thinker) does indeed apply Locke's semantic *either/or* to religious mysteries in the manner of Toland.[8] Here, working from the Lockean theory of meaning, Alciphron confi-dently asserts: 'by all the rules of right reason, it is absolutely impossible that any mystery, and least of all the Trinity, should be really the object of man's faith'. Berkeley's answer to this

[8] This is not to say that Toland was the only free-thinker who argued in this way. Thus Toland was followed by A. Collins, *An Essay concerning the Use of Reason* (London, 1707), and John Trenchard, *Cato's Letters* (5th edn., London, 1748), vol. iv, letter of 16 Mar. 1722/3; see my introduction to *Berkeley's Alciphron in Focus* (forthcoming).

(through his champion Euphranor) is, in effect, an indictment of Locke-become-Toland: 'I do not wonder you thought so, as long as you maintained that no man could assent to a proposition without perceiving or framing in his mind distinct ideas marked by the terms of it' (*Alc*. vii. 8).

V

Berkeley employed his revolutionary emotive theory more destructively in the realm of philosophy. In *Alciphron*, vii. 8, he considers a 'fine gentleman [and] lady of fashion' who may have no 'determinate idea whatever, either of fate or of chance'. Yet if they converse with 'men of depth and genius, who have often declared it to be their opinion, the world is governed either by fate or by chance', they may not only assent to one of these cognitively empty propositions, but their 'persuasion' may operate emotively, showing itself in the 'conduct and tenor of their lives, freeing them from the fears of superstition, and giving them [Berkeley ironically adds] a true relish of the world, with a noble indolence or indifference about what comes after'. Berkeley had earlier used his emotive theory to explain a crucial mystery of metaphysics, namely, how people seemed to believe in something—matter—which 'involves a contradiction, or has no meaning in it'. His solution is in section 54 of the *Principles*:

Strictly speaking, to believe that which involves a contradiction, or has no meaning in it, is impossible . . . [But] In one sense indeed, men may be said to believe that matter exists, that is, they act as if the immediate cause of their sensations, which affect them every moment and is so nearly present to them, were some senseless unthinking being.

In short, the actual meaning of the word 'matter' is emotive: it makes certain men act as if the cause of their sensations were material rather than spiritual.

Like 'fate' or 'chance', but unlike 'grace', the non-cognitive word 'matter' has a pernicious or dangerous tendency. It encourages undesirable emotions, habits, and actions—which, in *Principles*, sects. 86–94, Berkeley associates with scepticism, atheism, and idolatry. Hence the word should, he suggests in the *Three Dialogues*, be omitted at least from philosophical discourse. Towards the end of the third dialogue, Philonous had convinced Hylas that 'matter' was an empty word masquerading as a cognitive one. Hylas, however, is fondly attached to it: 'I have been so long accustomed to the term *matter*, that I know not how to part with it.' It continues to have emotive force for him: 'To say, there is no *matter* in the world, is still shocking to me', says Hylas, who then asks Philonous: 'What think you therefore of retaining the name *matter*, and applying it to sensible things? This may be done without any change in your sentiments . . .'. To this sug׳ gestion Philonous answers:

With all my heart: retain the word *matter*, and apply it to the objects of sense, if you please, provided you do not attribute to them any sub׳ sistence distinct from their being perceived. I shall never quarrel with you for an expression.

Yet, having said that, Philonous then goes on to explain why the term 'matter' should not be used, and ends his speech with these weighty words:

. . . in philosophical discourses it seems the best way to leave it ['matter'] quite out; since there is not perhaps any one thing that hath more favoured or strengthened the depraved bent of the mind towards *atheism*, than the use of that general confused term.' (p. 261)

Turn now and compare this important passage with another discussion in the fourth dialogue of *Alciphron*. Here Lysicles, who speaks for Berkeley's free׳thinking opponents, is also worried by a word: 'I could wish indeed the word God were quite omitted, because in most minds it is coupled with a sort of superstitious awe, the very root of religion' (sect. 16). Just as Philonous (Berkeley's spokesman) wishes the word 'matter' to be left 'quite out', so Lysicles, the free׳thinker, wants the word 'God' to be 'quite omitted'. Why? Because each of them objects to the unde׳ sirable emotive effects which the respective words are likely to produce: 'the depraved bent of the mind', in the one case, 'super׳ stitious awe', in the other.

Both Philonous and Lysicles believe that these emotive effects are not only undesirable but unjustifiable. Philonous, of course, argues this at great length, pursuing his materialistic opponent through many theories, stratagems, etc., to the conclusion that matter is either contradictory or meaningless. Lysicles, on the other hand, exploits more easily the King/Browne theory in order to reach virtually the same conclusion about God. Yet, like Philonous, he is also prepared to allow the use of the objectionable word, but on certain conditions: 'I shall not, nonetheless, be much disturbed, though the name be retained, and the being of God allowed in any sense but in that of a Mind, which knows all things, and beholds human actions, like some judge or magistrate, with infinite obser-vation and intelligence' (sect. 16). And so Lysicles concludes:

And, now we have granted you that there is God in this indefinite sense, I would fain see what use you can make of this concession. You cannot argue from . . . unknown attributes in an unknown sense. You cannot prove that God is to be loved for His goodness, or feared for His justice . . . (sect. 18)

The resemblance between this line of argument and that quoted above from the *Three Dialogues* is striking. The words 'matter' and 'God' are retained, but their new meanings preclude their old uses and effects. 'Matter', understood as Philonous understands it, cannot help materialists, nor should it have its former evo-cative force. 'God', as Lysicles understands the word, cannot be of any service to theists; nor can it provide a basis for religious mysteries. In each case, the argument moves as follows: (1) the ordinary usages of the words 'matter' and 'God' have been found to be unacceptable or untenable; (2) but one feels that the words themselves should not, or need not, be discarded; (3) therefore they are redefined, given a new sense; (4) but the new sense will not—for better or worse—allow the words to function in their old ways. (5) There is also the suggestion—made by Lysicles at the beginning, Philonous at the end—that it would be preferable simply to discard the objectionable word.

Berkeley's precocious insight into the emotive power of certain words is also evident in the first dialogue of *Alciphron*, sect. 10.

Berkeley was annoyed that the free-thinkers, particularly Anthony Collins, had appropriated the name 'free-thinker', since it is charged with commendatory force. As Berkeley has Euphranor say: 'I cannot bear to argue against free-thinking and freethinkers' (*Alc.* i. 10). To do so would be like arguing against, say, patrio-tism in our own time. Both free-thinking and patriotism are, *prima facie*, praiseworthy. But different persons or parties have read different meanings into these words. Both terms are vague enough to allow this, while still retaining their commendatory force. What Berkeley says about 'free-thinker' could, with minor modification, be said about 'patriot': that the

. . . name being too general and indefinite, inasmuch as it comprehends all those who think for themselves, whether they agree in opinion with these gentlemen [the free-thinkers] or no—it should not seem amiss to assign them a specific appellation or peculiar name, whereby to distin-guish them from other philosophers . . . (Alc. i. 10)

To this suggestion Alciphron, the free-thinker, obligingly but unwarily agrees: 'In the eyes of a wise man words are of small moment. We do not think truth attaches to a name.' Neither did Berkeley think that truth attached to a name, but he did think that certain names have an emotive power, as Euphranor's response shows: 'If you please then, to avoid confusion, let us call your sect by the same name that Tully (who understood the force of lan-guage) bestowed upon them.' 'With all my heart', says Alciphron, 'Pray what may that name be?' 'Why', replies Euphranor, 'he calls them *minute philosophers*.'

When Philonous answered Hylas' suggestion about retaining the term 'matter', 'With all my heart: retain the word *matter* . . .', he surely had less heart in it than when Alciphron answered Euphranor's similar request 'With all my heart'. For 'matter' carries the wrong sort of suggestion, whereas 'minute philosopher' carries just the right one—for Berkeley's purpose, that is. This title, he says, '. . . admirably suits them, they [the free-thinkers] being a sect which diminish all the most valuable things . . .'. The sub-title of *Alciphron* itself hints that Berkeley intended to challenge the name 'free-thinker': 'an Apology for the Christian Religion, against those who are *called* Free-thinkers' (my emphasis). And in two letters, of 1731 and 1732, he uses the same locution: 'called free-thinkers' (*Works*, viii. 214 and 312).

However, Berkeley did not always dispute the propriety of the name. Earlier, in 1713, he largely accepted the name, but then he tried to change its emotive force from positive to negative. We can see him trying to do this in two passages, one from the Preface to the *Three Dialogues*, the other from *Guardian* 130. In the former— part of which I quoted in Chapter 4—he remarks:

> And, to an impartial reader, I hope, it will be manifest, that the sub-lime notion of a God, and the comfortable expectation of immortality, do naturally arise from a close and methodical application of thought: whatever may be the result of that loose, rambling way, not altogether improperly termed *free-thinking*, by certain libertines in thought, who can no more endure the restraints of *logic*, than those of *religion*, or *government*.

This is more than a casual reflection on the term 'free-thinking'. Berkeley draws attention to a blameworthy aspect of freedom— that it may be unbridled or undisciplined—which he enforces both by a contrast with 'close and methodical' and also with a legal theme: free-thinkers not only break the laws of reason, but also laws enacted by government. The phrase 'libertine in thought' nicely unites the two themes; and the general effect is to cast the term 'free-thinker' in a decidedly unattractive light.

In *Guardian* 130 Berkeley ironically agrees with the free-thinkers that they are not actuated by an incorporeal spirit, but proceed only 'from the Collision of certain Corpuscles'; and this is evident, too, from their writings, which 'look rather like Effects of Chance, or . . . Mechanism'. Hence, Berkeley requests 'all Christians, that hereafter they speak of *Free-Thinkers* in the Neuter Gender, using the Term *it* for *him*'.[9] But eventually, when he came to write *Alciphron*, he altered his approach. Rather than try to change the emotive force of 'free-thinker', he decided to use a new name, derived from Cicero, 'minute philosopher'.

*

9   *The Guardian* (1982 edn.), 435.

Berkeley has not generally been given credit for being the first to develop the emotive theory, and the first to apply it to religion, metaphysics, and—as we shall see in the next chapter—economics. But there can be no doubt that he anticipates the emotive analysis of metaphysical and religious language offered by such (former) Logical Positivists as A. J. Ayer, in *Language, Truth and Logic* (London, 1936), chs. 1 and 6. The irony, of course, is that the Logical Positivists applied the emotive theory destructively to religion, whereas Berkeley used it to defend religion. It would be even more ironic if Ayer, for example, had derived his discussion of emotive language from Berkeley. However, in a private letter (of 5 May 1975) Ayer informed me:

To the best of my recollection I was not at all influenced by Berkeley's emotive theory of language when I wrote Chapter 6 of LANGUAGE TRUTH AND LOGIC. When I acknowledged the debt to Berkeley in the Preface, I am pretty sure that I was thinking only of his phenomenalism.

VI

Although a great deal more might be said about Berkeley's specific contributions in *Alciphron*, it is important to see his wider position. The general structure of his theology is represented in Figure 10.

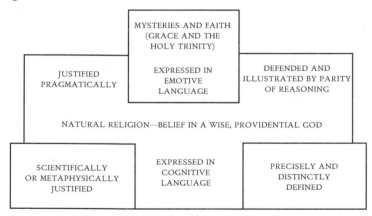

Fig. 10. Berkeley's theological position, 1732–5.

There is, however, one feature of Figure 10 that I have not as yet explained: the defence and illustration of mysteries by parity of reasoning. This line of reasoning—summed up in the proverb 'Sauce for the goose is also sauce for the gander'—constitutes an important part of Berkeley's theological strategy; he employs it in *Alciphron* and also in the *Analyst* (1734) and in the *Defence of Free-thinking in Mathematics* (1735). He outlines his approach in the penultimate, retrospective section of *Alciphron* vii. I have quoted the first part of this key passage, but it is worth quoting the whole because it provides the best single statement of his complete position:

The being of a God is capable of clear proof, and a proper object of human reason: whereas the mysteries of His nature, and indeed whatever there is of mystery in religion, to endeavour to explain and prove by reason is a vain attempt. It is sufficient if we can shew there is nothing absurd or repugnant in our belief of those points, and . . . use reason only for answering the objections brought against them. (sect. 30)

By skilfully using some of the critical results of his early work in philosophy and philosophy of science, Berkeley tries to show that there is nothing 'absurd or repugnant' in the Christian mysteries. Thus he contends that while it is hard to understand grace, it is not any harder than understanding the scientist's concept of force; although both 'grace' and 'force' are of considerable use (*Alc.* vii. 7). And while there seem to be difficulties in understanding the Athanasian doctrine of the Trinity, there are similar perplex- ities, Berkeley holds, in the widely accepted (Lockean) theory of personal identity (developed in *Essay*, II. xxvi), that personal identity consists in identity of consciousness. Berkeley's argument here runs as follows. If we divide a person's conscious life into three equal parts or periods—A, B, C—we may reasonably suppose that, although there will be many ideas in common between A and B, and B and C, there may be no ideas in com- mon between A and C. (An old man, in other words, may not remember his mental life as a child.) It will then follow, supposing the truth of the Lockean theory, that although A is the same person as B, and B is the same as C, A is not (paradoxically) the same as C. In short, Berkeley suggests, it is no less difficult to understand personal identity than how in the unity of God there can be three persons in one substance (see *Alc.* vii. 8).

Berkeley uses his work on vision, in a more positive way, to show that there is nothing absurd in prophecy. Exploiting, no doubt, section 148 of the *Theory of Vision* (and also very probably Edward Synge's 1698 critique of Toland[10]), he asks us in *Alciphron*, iv. 15, to suppose

... a nation of men blind from their infancy, among whom a stranger arrives, the only man who can see in all the country; let us suppose this stranger travelling with some of the natives ... he foretells to them that, in case they walk straight forward, in half an hour they shall meet men or cattle, or come to a house; that, if they turn to the right and proceed, they shall in a few minutes be in danger of falling down a precipice ... Must they not be infinitely surprised that one who had never been in their country before should know it so much better than themselves? And would not those predictions seem to them as unaccountable and incredible as prophecy to a minute philosopher?

In section 148 Berkeley alludes to the 'glimmering' which this subject can provide on life after death. Although he does not develop this in *Alciphron*, he probably had in mind the thought experiment he proposed in *Guardian* 27, which he hoped would offer some 'glimmering' of the afterlife and thereby enlarge the narrowness of the free-thinkers (see above, Ch. 3 § IV).

Berkeley continued his *ad hominem* defence of mysteries in the *Analyst* (1734), the tract in which he pointed out a serious flaw in Newton's method of fluxions. Berkeley addressed the *Analyst* to 'an infidel mathematician'—almost certainly the astronomer Edmund Halley (1656–1742), who had, we are told, undermined the religious faith of Berkeley's friend Dr Samuel Garth (1661–1719). According to Stock (pp. 29–30), Garth had during his last illness brushed aside thoughts of an afterlife with the remark: 'Surely ... I have good reason not to believe those trifles, since my

---

[10] See my 'Enlightenment and Counter-Enlightenment', 153–4; and 'Eighteenth-Century Irish Philosophy', in S. Deane (gen. ed.), *The Field Day Anthology of Irish Writing* (Derry, 1991), i. 770–2.

friend Dr Halley, who has dealt so much in demonstration, has assured me that the doctrines of Christianity are incomprehensible, and the religion itself an imposture.' In the *Analyst*, Berkeley tries to show that Newton's doctrine of fluxions is no more comprehensible or reasonable than religious mysteries and points of faith. Although the *Analyst* was at first angrily attacked by mathematicians, it is now generally accepted as an important contribution in the history of mathematics.[11] Theologians were immediately appreciative of the pamphlet's apologetic power in confounding the mathematicans and (as Bishop Edmund Gibson gratefully said) 'finding them work in their own quarters' (Fraser, 239 and 244). Berkeley's approach here is more sceptical than constructive, and the concluding questions appended to the *Analyst* deliver the sceptical sting. Thus he pointedly enquires:

Qu. 61 Whether it be not less exceptional to admit points above reason than contrary to reason?

Qu. 62 Whether mysteries may not with better right be allowed of in Divine Faith than in Human Science?

Qu. 63 Whether such mathematicians as cry out against mysteries have ever examined their own principles?

Qu. 64 Whether mathematicians, who are so delicate in religious points, are strictly scrupulous in their own science? Whether they do not submit to authority, take things on trust, and believe points inconceivable? Whether they have not their mysteries, and what is more, their repugnancies and contradictions?   (*Works*, iv. 102)

Berkeley had used the method of interrogatory, to a similar purpose, in *Alciphron*, vii. 7, which is composed almost entirely of questions. He was to use it again in section 50 of the *Defence of Free-thinking in Mathematics* (1735), which along with sections 3 and 7, comprise his final defence of religious mysteries by parity of reasoning with mathematics. The interrogatory form nicely suited Berkeley's strategy, which was not to establish any interpretation

---

[11] Berkeley's publication of the *Analyst* is described by F. Cajori as 'the most spectacular event of the century in the history of British mathematics. The arguments in the *Analyst* were so many bombs thrown into the mathematical camp'; see Cajori, *History of the Conception of Limits and Fluxions in Britain* (Chicago, 1919), 57.

of particular mysteries, but rather to undermine objections against mysteries. For every (alleged) difficulty and obscurity in religion, brought forward by free-thinkers, Berkeley tries to show something comparable in the supposed paradigms of knowledge: mathematics, philosophy, and science.

Berkeley's defence of religious mysteries has, broadly speaking, three prongs or components: (i) utterances about mysteries are shown to be essentially emotive; (ii) while justified pragmatically, by their effectiveness, they are also supported and evaluated by rational theology; (iii) their apparent obscurities and difficulties are shown to have parallels in the received theories of the most admired thinkers of the time, Locke and Newton. Hence one must either accept religious mysteries or reject them along with cherished philosophical, mathematical, and scientific mysteries.

Berkeley's theology, one must acknowledge, was a magnificent achievement, possibly the last great and creative theological synthesis. Its greatness lies partly in the powerful theories of which it is constituted: that of the optic language, of emotive language, of other minds, as well as those theories embodied in the various arguments by parity of reasoning. Much (although by no means all) of the strength of Berkeley's philosophical position is here superbly marshalled and displayed; and yet there is also a remarkable degree of unity, even architectonic, in this theology. Finally, it is to Berkeley's credit that he accepted and tried to meet the legitimate challenges of free-thought, rather than—as many later theologians have done—ignore them.

VII

However, there are difficulties, particularly with the optic-language argument. Thus the Humean critique of causality, which I mentioned in discussing the passivity argument in Chapter 3, is also relevant here. The crucial step (2) of the optic-language argument would also be contested by many contemporary philosophers, who hold that the human body is an essential component of personal identity. And any doubtfulness in the infrastructure of rational theology must, as Berkeley recognized, weaken the super/structure of religious mystery.

The optic/language analogue may also be contested on a number of grounds. Thus the analogue might seem to break down in that, (i) whereas with English I can hear you speak and also speak to you, this does not seem possible with God's optic/language; we cannot use visual data to speak to him. Also (ii) in English we do not create the signs or words we use, whereas God does create his (visual) signs. Yet it is not clear that these are insuperable objections. Imagine—in response to (i)—that we on earth received sounds from a distant planet which turned out to be elaborate (linguistic) messages. Suppose, too, that the messages took such a long time in coming that by the time they arrived here the distant planet had been destroyed. We should then be unable to return their messages, but it is not clear why that should mean that the messages were not expressed in language. Nor is it evident that the second objection shows an essential difference between the optic language and that of English. There are, after all, probably more striking differences between English and, say, Chinese or Hebrew.

There is, however, a more serious problem for the analogue, I think, which arises when Berkeley moves from the strategic or 'vulgar' position of the *New Theory of Vision* to the later, considered position of the *Principles* and *Theory of Vision Vindicated*. For whereas in the early semi/immaterialism there is a clear distinction between (visual) signs and (tangible) things signified, this is no longer plainly present in the later, full immaterialism, where tangible sensations are also considered to be signs (see *PHK*, sects. 66 and 108). But then it seems to follow that the tangible can be a sign of the visual. Yet is there any known language in which the signs can become the things signified and vice versa—where, for example, a cow can stand for the word 'cow'?

Another formidable challenge would be to step (5.1). Berkeley's heterogeneity thesis has been contested by many philosophers and psychologists on the grounds that there is good empirical evidence and argument that we do see and touch the same thing.[12] Yet even if the optic language breaks down as an analogue, Berkeley's theory can still be salvaged as a model or metaphor, more illuminating—as Colin Murray Turbayne has ably argued— than the rival Cartesian–Newtonian machine model. However, if vision is no longer regarded as literally a language, then it cannot prove the existence of God, in the literal sense.[13]

Berkeley's emotive theory can also be criticized. One short-coming is that he failed to see that, while non-cognitive words are able to evoke emotions, for instance, conversely emotions are able to evoke words; that is, language has an expressive function, as in 'Oh dear!' and 'Gosh!'. Berkeley's emotive account of Christian mysteries might also be disputed by those, like Friedrich Nietzsche (1844–1900), who regard piety, humility, religious awe, as emotions and dispositions that have little or no value. It should also be noted that Berkeley's general emotive account of mysteries could—with minor modification—be accepted and used by rival religions, such as Islam, as well as by such modern 'religions' as Marxism and even Nietzscheanism. However, Berkeley might well have replied to these objections that since he had established in *Alciphron* iv the truth of the Christian religion, its emotive mysteries ought to be accepted.

A more serious question is whether, on Berkeley's emotive account of mysteries, it makes sense for a Christian to believe that the Christian mysteries are really true: that, for example, grace is truly the gift of God. Certainly, a theory which could not accommodate this would be rejected by many Christians. This question seems to hinge on another question: whether, on Berkeley's scheme, statements about religious mysteries have sufficient cog-nitive content to be true, without having so much cognitive content that they fall foul of Toland's criticisms. Berkeley's answer is not clear-cut. Thus in the *Philosophical Commentaries*, entry 720, he

---

[12] See D. M. Armstrong, *Berkeley's Theory of Vision* (Melbourne, 1960), Garland, vol. 6; M. Morgan, *Molyneux's Question* (Cambridge, 1977); R. J. Brook, *Berkeley's Philosophy of Science* (The Hague, 1973); I. C. Tipton, *Berkeley: the Philosophy of Immaterialism* (London, 1974), and Garland, vol. 15; and G. Pitcher, *Berkeley*.

[13] Turbayne, *The Myth of Metaphor* (New Haven, Conn., 1962).

describes utterances about mysteries as 'propositions about things out of our reach . . . altogether above our knowledge', to which we should give our 'Humble Implicit faith'. He then compares them to words spoken in a language that we do not understand, which again suggests that they can have no cognitive content for us. And yet he concludes entry 720 by saying that when 'I shall come to plenary knowledge of the meaning of any Text then I shall yield an explicit belief', which suggests that such propositions can have cognitive content and can be true, if only in the next life.

In the *Manuscript Introduction*, however, Berkeley goes very far in the other direction. He denies that the words 'good things' 'mark out to our Understanding any Ideas' and that the utterance incorporating these words gives us any information of the pleasures of Heaven. The aim of the utterance, he holds, is to evoke appropriate dispositions; and it does this by the mechanism of 'customary connection', which is not unlike Pavlovian conditioning. However, in *Alciphron* vii Berkeley is less decided. Although he leans towards a purely emotive account of a future state (in sect. 10), he is more qualified in speaking of the doctrine of the Trinity in section 8. He describes the emotive effects it can evoke —such as hope, love, and gratitude; he also plays down its cognitive import: we cannot, he says, frame 'any abstract ideas of trinity, substance, or personality'. But he does not say that the doctrine signifies no ideas, or has no cognitive content. Nor does he say that the words 'Holy Trinity' are able to evoke emotions because a customary connection has been established between the words and the emotions.

Yet it is in his remarks on grace (in sect. 7) that Berkeley comes closest to saying that a mystery can be true. After arguing that we cannot form a distinct idea of either (physical) force or (divine) grace, he asks seven questions, one of which is: 'Ought we not therefore, by a parity of reason, to conclude there may be possibly divers true and useful propositions concerning the one as the other?' Yet he is guarded in this query. He does not say that propositions about grace are true, but that they 'may possibly' be true. Also, in the next query he stresses the emotive and non-cognitive character of the mystery: '. . . that grace may . . . influence our life and actions, as a principle destructive of evil habits and productive of good ones, although we cannot attain a distinct idea of it . . .'.

Berkeley's descriptions of grace and the Holy Trinity do appear to be less radical than his earlier, 1708, characterization of 'good things' as entirely non-cognitive and purely emotive. It is possible that his latter account, in *Alciphron*, was softened for prudential reasons. A piece of evidence in support of this reading is that Berkeley has Alciphron, the free-thinker, make the most radical statement on the issue. Under argumentative pressure, Alciphron says: 'I will allow, Euphranor, this reasoning of yours to have all the force you meant it should have. I freely own there may be mysteries; that *we may believe where we do not understand* . . .' (sect. 16, my italics). On the other hand, Berkeley may have changed his mind between 1708 and 1732; or he may never have intended to explain all mysteries in the way he explained that of the future state, as purely emotive. In some places in *Alciphron* (e.g. iv. 15 and vii. 13) Berkeley suggests that words about mysteries can function symbolically, giving us some 'glimmering' representation of what is beyond our understanding. But here again, we should like to know whether there is cognitive content in such symbolic expressions and, if so, whether it compromises Berkeley's distinctive answer to Toland. (Such symbolic representation might well run into difficulties similar to those Berkeley identifies in the King/Browne theory.) Unhappily, Berkeley says far too little on these issues for us to reach any satisfactory conclusion.

VIII

I have been concentrating in this chapter on dialogues iv and vii of *Alciphron* because they contain, in my opinion, Berkeley's most valuable contributions to philosophical theology. But there is much else in *Alciphron*: for example, Berkeley's critique in dialogue ii of Bernard Mandeville's (1677–1733) notorious doctrine that private vices make for public virtues. There is his critique of Lord Shaftesbury's ethics and aesthetics in *Alciphron* iii. There is also much traditional apologetic in dialogues v and vi. Yet in none of these areas, I think, did Berkeley shine.

While dialogues ii and iii have been extensively discussed by commentators[14], there has not been a great deal of recent interest or admiration of Berkeley's defence of revealed religion in dialogues v and vi. Yet it is worth noting that if some of his views now seem extremely weak, even naïve, they show a robust empirical grasp of what would have counted against them. Thus, in replying to the criticism that the world is really very much older than is allowed in the Ussherian or Biblical chronology, he says that, if this were so, then bits of 'pillars, vases and statues' made of hard material, 'as well as the shells and stones of the [putative] primeval world [should] be preserved [underground] down to our times'. Therefore, he asks, 'How comes it then to pass that no remains are found . . . ?' (*Alc.* vi. 23).

A final issue which I shall briefly consider before leaving *Alciphron* is Berkeley's account of the rise and nature of British free-thought. This account is to be found throughout *Alciphron*, but especially in dialogue i and in the first seven sections of the *Theory of Vision Vindicated* (1733). In my view Berkeley's is perhaps the most searching contemporary account we have of free-thought in the seventeenth and early eighteenth century. On the whole, Berkeley sees the free-thinkers, particularly Lord Shaftesbury and Anthony Collins, as more sinister and radical than a straight-forward reading of their works would suggest. He thinks that the free-thinkers disguised their real view, 'making use of hints and allusions, expressing little, insinuating much . . .' (*Alc.* i. 4). He also holds that the free-thinkers were 'accustomed to proceed gradually, beginning with those prejudices to which men have the least attachment, and thence proceeding to undermine the rest by slow and insensible degrees . . .' (*Alc.* i. 5); that they had to 'think with the learned and speak with the vulgar' (*Alc.* i. 12).

---

[14] See e.g. P. J. Olscamp, *The Moral Philosophy of George Berkeley* (The Hague, 1970).

He sums up their strategy as: 'gradual, covert, insincere' (*TVV*, sect. 5).

Why did Berkeley hold this conspiratorial view of the free-thinkers? Part of the answer, as he himself tells us in the Advertisement to *Alciphron*, is that he knew the free-thinkers not only from their printed works but from their conversation, and 'A gentleman, in private conversation, may be supposed to speak plainer than others write, to improve on their hints, and draw conclusions from their principles.' Berkeley came to know the methods and views of the free-thinkers because he 'had, as he told Mr Johnson, been several times in their Clubs in quality of a learner'; and it was 'on one of these occasions . . . that he heard Collens [*sic*] declare that he had found a demonstration against the being of a God . . .'.[15] Now I have argued elsewhere that Berkeley was right about Collins's atheism, and I also think that he was right about the general covert strategy of the free-thinkers.[16] But his analysis raises serious questions, since it should be clear that his own strategy, which I examined in Chapters 2 and 3, is very close to that which he ascribed to the free-thinkers.[17]

One obvious question is: was he projecting his own strategy on the free-thinkers? This must be considered a serious possibility. A writer who uses covert techniques may well be inclined to believe that others are (conspiratorially) using them as well. We may also recall Berkeley's description of himself in the *Commentaries*, entry 266, as 'distrustful at 8' years old. On the other hand, his distrustfulness and 'turn' for strategy may have made him sensitive to their presence in others. The question is complicated and can only be answered by looking at his particular interpretations and the evidence he adduces, which I have elsewhere tried to do. Although I am inclined to accept most of Berkeley's conspiratorial interpretations, I would not accept them all, particularly not his claim that the free-thinkers were disguised 'emissaries . . . of Rome'

[15] See *Samuel Johnson*, i. 26; also see above, Ch. 4 § III.

[16] See my *History of Atheism*, ch. 3.

[17] Of course, whereas the free-thinkers dissembled strategically to undermine religion, Berkeley (perhaps uniquely) did so to advance religion; whereas their radical goal was irreligious, his (as I have suggested in Ch. 3 § II) was profoundly religious.

(*Alc.* ii. 26). In this instance, however, Berkeley does not say that he has direct evidence, as he does in the case of Collins's atheism.

The story of his going into the free-thinkers' clubs as a learner seems to be in character with his 'unaccountable turn', that is, with his capacity to harmonize with opinions (and people) with which he did not agree (see above, Chap. 2 § I). For unless he had such a gift it would surely have been hard for him to pretend to be an irreligious 'learner'. It is not every Anglican priest who could spy on the leading free-thinkers of his day.

7

The Good Bishop
(1735–1753)

I

Returning from America, Berkeley and his family remained in London from late 1731 until early 1734. While this was for Berkeley a prolific period of writing and publication, rivalling that of 1709–13, it was also, as Luce notes, 'a second period of waiting, of waiting for a mark of Royal favour'; for without some mark of favour, Berkeley's 'position would have been difficult, if not intolerable', given the failure of his American project (*Life*, 153). The necessary preferment came in January 1734, when he was appointed Bishop of Cloyne. In February he resigned as Dean of Derry. Three months later he was back in Ireland, where in St Paul's Church, Dublin, on 19 May, he was consecrated Bishop of Cloyne.

Berkeley then travelled to Cloyne, the seat of his bishopric, a small town twenty miles from Cork. With two brief exceptions—in 1737 and 1750—he remained in his diocese until 1752, dutifully fulfilling his ecclesiastical functions. Whereas he was an absentee Dean of Derry, he was very much a full-time Bishop of Cloyne. Indeed his commitment to the well-being of those in his diocese—Catholic as well as Protestant—was exceptional for the time.

Berkeley's writings from 1735 to the last, in 1752, reflect his practical philanthropic concerns. Thus, in the year he published the *Defence of Free-Thinking in Mathematics* (1735), he also published the first part of the *Querist*, and in the following two years two further parts were published. The *Querist* is composed—apart from the short Advertisement in later editions—entirely of questions, numbering nearly 600 in the last authorized edition of 1752. It expounds Berkeley's views on economic and social issues, especially those relating to Ireland.[1] Although it has little direct bearing on his philosophy or theology, the *Querist* has interesting links with *Alciphron*, the *Analyst*, and *Defence*. Berkeley had started using the query form in *Alciphron* vii. 7, which he then continued, more formally, in the *Analyst* and *Defence*. Of even greater interest is the connection between Berkeley's emotive account of religious mysteries in *Alciphron* vii and his account of money in the *Querist*.

Queries 21–35, 469–84, and 566–72, especially, suggest that Berkeley looked on money as a system of operative signs; and this hypothesis is supported by the fact that in *Alciphron* vii. 5 he speaks of counters as signs, and in the *Querist* he identifies counters with money (see nos. 23, 25, 40, 47, 308, 310). A piece of physical money, for example, a tenpence, and a particular audible word, like 'hello', are artificial signs which, because of their agreed meaning or credit, can do useful things—like buying a stamp or greeting a friend. Once money is considered as a sign, it will follow that those monetary signs are to be preferred which are most manageable, and most appropriate to the corresponding economic operations. This is so, because such signs will facilitate those operations, for example, purchasing, or, in economic terms, the signs will promote circulation and industry (see nos. 425, 445, 460). As paper money is more manageable than hard money, Berkeley preferred it (nos. 440 and 445); for the same reason, it would seem, he preferred a decimal currency—as early as 1749.[2] Both cases represent an improvement in monetary symbolism or notation.

In Berkeley's Ireland some of the coins, or monetary signs, were scandalously inappropriate to the operations which they were presumably intended to facilitate. The country had a superabundance of gold coins, while there was a serious lack of small denomination

---

[1] For a helpful collection of essays on Berkeley's economic views and their Irish context, see Clark, Garland, ii; also see P. Kelly, 'Ireland and the Critique of Mercantilism in Berkeley's *Querist*', in *Hermathena* 139 (1985), 101–16.

[2] *Life*, 213, and *Querist*, no. 572.

coins, pennies and sixpences, to assist in the common minor transactions, such as buying bread or lending a shilling (see nos. 231, 482, 485). Berkeley was keenly aware of this problem. In numbers 469 to 487, in particular, he stresses the need for a greater number of small coins, because they are 'fitter for common use' than those large monetary signs, such as gold coins (nos. 475–6). His long-term solution to such currency problems was a national bank, which, somewhat like rational theology in his theological system (see above, Ch. 6), was to 'fortify', 'promote', and regulate appropriate (economic) practice (see nos. 314, 425, 588).

That Berkeley viewed money as a system of operative signs also, I suggest, assisted him in freeing himself from the then dominant Mercantilist theory of money. According to this theory— to which Locke subscribed—a piece of money possessed value because it contained, or had an inseparable connection with, precious metals. Now, just as Berkeley rejected Locke's theory of meaning, so he denied that there was a necessary connection between the value of money and precious metal (nos. 26, 35, 251, 426–7, 445). An artificial system of monetary signs—such as paper money issued by an accredited national bank—could facilitate the desired economic operations, thereby giving that money its value (nos. 226, 440, 450). Berkeley's linguistic model directed his attention towards the essentially operative character of monetary signs and away from the less essential issue of the composition of these signs (nos. 37, 460, 472–4, 567). As words could have meaning without ideas, so money could have value without gold. Thus the emotive theory unravelled not merely religious and metaphysical mysteries (as we saw in the previous chapter) but economic ones as well.

Berkeley's general approach to economics may be usefully compared to his general approach to philosophy, as expressed in the Introduction to the *Principles*. Why, he asks, are we unable to understand the world adequately? Now, according to some philosophers, the cause of this is 'the obscurity of things' and/or the 'imperfection of our understanding': our finite faculties are not 'designed by nature to penetrate into the . . . constitution of things', and particularly not infinite things (sect. 2). Berkeley rejects this view, however, and for a theological reason: God would not have implanted in people a 'strong desire for know-ledge, which he had placed quite out of their reach' (sect. 3). (Berkeley uses the same premise, indeed almost the same words, in one of his arguments for immortality, which I examined in Chapter 3 § IV.) But then why *have* we failed to understand what is? Berkeley's answer in the Introduction is that we have been hindered by a faulty notion and use of language—for example, that all words stand for ideas, that general words stand for general ideas.

Berkeley pursues the same line of enquiry in the *Querist*. Why have people, particularly the Irish, failed to achieve material pros-perity? His answer is: because they have, as we have seen above, misunderstood and misused the language of money or monetary signs. But after this point, the comparison becomes more compli-cated. For, unlike most people, the Irish do not seem to have 'a strong desire' for material prosperity. The native, Catholic Irish are 'indolent and supine' (*Querist*, no 357), content with 'dirt and beggary' (no. 19); and the Anglo-Irish are wedded to foreign and artificial luxury (nos. 102–4, 140–1, 150–1, 524). The natural appetites of both native Irish and Anglo-Irish have been corrupted by 'fashion' and 'custom', the two forces which exert a powerful influence on appetite (nos. 9–10, 17). So in this case, not only must the monetary language be rectified, but so, too, must fashion and (ultimately) appetite. Once this is done, prosperity should follow, since the natural resources in Ireland are present in abundance (nos. 123–4, 133–4, 138).

A year after he issued the final part of the *Querist*, Berkeley published his *Discourse Addressed to the Magistrates . . . occasioned by the enormous Licence, and Irreligion of the Times* (Dublin, 1738). It concludes his campaign against the free-thinkers. Its specific cause, according to Stock, was

. . . an impious society called Blasters, which this pamphlet put a stop to. [Berkeley] expressed his sentiments on the same occasion in the

[Irish] house of lords [in 1737], the only time he ever spoke there. The speech was received with much applause.[3]

The *Discourse* was Berkeley's last published work before *Siris* (1744), which it resembles in its extensive use of authority—something altogether lacking in his early works of 1709–13, although present to some extent in *Alciphron*. In the *Discourse* Berkeley writes:

> Religion is the centre which unites, and the cement which connects the several parts or members of the political body. Such it hath been held by all wise men from the remotest times ... (*Works*, vi. 210)

He then goes on to quote such 'wise men' as Aristotle, Zaleucis, Machiavelli, Philip of Comines, Harrington, but above all Plato (pp. 213–15), the philosopher who plays a central role in *Siris*. The proposition that religion is necessary for social order, that 'Obedience to all civil powers is rooted in the religous fear of God...' (p. 208), is one that Berkeley had consistently held in some form since *Passive Obedience*; but there, as he tells us in section 2, his argument is based on reason rather than on authority.

II

The fallow period between the *Discourse* and *Siris*, 1738–44, is noteworthy but not unprecedented in Berkeley's authorial career. There was a similar although not quite so fallow period after the *Three Dialogues* (1713), from which finally issued his utopian *Proposal* (1724) for St Paul's College, Bermuda. In each case Berkeley thought long and hard before going to press with his bold proposals for Bermuda in 1724 and for tar-water in 1744; and there was a similarly long period of reflection and preparation, earlier on, before he published his daring philosophy in 1709/1710. I suggest that there is also a deep connection between these three remarkable projects, a connection which has not been hitherto

---

[3] See *The Works of George Berkeley* (1784), i, p. xx. For a recent note relating to the *Discourse* and Blasters, see W. H. McGowan, 'Did Berkeley write *The Irish Blasters?*', *Berkeley Newsletter* (1982/3), 1–4.

noticed by Berkeley's biographers, but which we can see with the help of the fountain symbolism which I described in Chapter 5 § II. Berkeley's most elaborate preoccupation with this symbolism was in his American venture. However, he also uses a fountain image at the end of the *Three Dialogues* to sum up the movement of thought from scepticism to the common sense of immaterialism. Appropriately, it is Philonous who speaks the piece:

You see, Hylas, the water of yonder fountain, how it is forced upwards, in a round column, to a certain height; at which it breaks and falls back into the basin from whence it rose: its ascent as well as descent, proceeding from the same uniform law or principle of *gravitation*. Just so, the same principles which at first view lead to *scepticism*, pursued to a certain point, bring men back to common sense.[4]

This persistent use of the same water imagery is striking, and it will appear even more so, I think, when we consider Berkeley's third and final crusade: the medical idealism of tar-water. For (apart from the obvious water connection) here too we find the symbolism, this time in the title of his book. Its full title (first edition) reads: *Siris: A Chain of Philosophical Inquires Concerning the Virtues of Tar-water and Divers Subjects Connected Together and Arising One from Another*. The key passage, where Berkeley glosses the title, is in his *Second Letter to Thomas Prior on the Virtues of Tar-water* (Dublin, 1746), sect. 15:

The virtue of tar-water, flowing like the Nile* from a secret and occult source, brancheth into innumerable channels, conveying health and relief, wherever it is applied; nor is it more easy and various in its use than copious in quality.

*The Nile was by the Ancient Egyptians called *Siris*, which word also signifies in Greek, a chain, though not so commonly used as *Sira* [Berkeley's note].[5]

---

[4] *Works*, ii. 262–3. This image of a vertical or (as it is sometimes called) basin fountain is illustrated in a vignette in the first French translation of Berkeley's *Three Dialogues* (Amsterdam, 1750). There is no evidence, however, that Berkeley had a hand in the vignette. It is reproduced in *Images*, 31.

[5] See *Works*, v. 185. On the varying titles of *Siris* in its different editions, see Luce's 'The Original Title and First Edition of *Siris*', *Hermathena* 84 (1954), 45–58, which established that the word 'Siris' was in the first edition.

The similarity between this passage and the one I quoted (in Ch. 5 § II) from the *Proposal* is striking. In each passage, we have water branching into various rivulets or channels, with extensive and beneficial results. Of course, unlike the *Proposal* metaphor, the Nile simile does not employ a fountain or reservoir, from which the running water issues; instead Berkeley speaks (appropriately enough) of a secret source. But a fountain or reservoir and a source are, in this context, clearly similar. That the title of Berkeley's last important book should (at least in his own mind) suggest a streaming water association is of considerable significance, since the title of a book lends itself to symbolical interpretation.

Berkeley's *Siris* is a tangled chain of medicine, chemistry, philosophy of science, mythology, philosophy, and theology; hence it can be difficult in a short space to do justice to its complexity. The opening, medicinal sections, starting with section 1, are the easiest to follow. Here Berkeley gives his recipe for tarwater. A quart of wood tar is to be mixed in a vessel with a gallon of cold water and left standing until the tar sinks to the bottom. The clear infused water can then be decanted and drunk. After this, things become more complicated. Berkeley is supposed to have said that writing *Siris* cost him more time and pains than any of his other works (Stock, p. 34). *Siris* is certainly more allusive, discontinuous and suggestive than any of his earlier writings. Indeed, it is sometimes hard to see what Berkeley is getting at, particularly in the later, speculative sections of *Siris*. Nor is the task made any easier by the reader's not infrequent uncertainty whether Berkeley is asserting his own opinion or that of some ancient philosopher or theologian.

One may, therefore, miss even *Siris*'s most central doctrines. And this has been the case, I think, with one of its leading theses. The thesis, simply and crudely put, is that tarwater is the closest natural thing to drinkable God. Berkeley never states this directly, nor is it easily discernible in the meandering sections of *Siris*. But the thesis is reasonably clear, and it becomes clearer if our reading of *Siris* is guided by the image of the fountain of living waters (see Figures 4–8).

III

Even the most casual reader of *Siris* notices that Berkeley begins with tar-water and ends with God, indeed the God of the Holy Trinity. (This movement from the mundane to the heavenly gave rise to some of the earliest satirical stabs at *Siris*.[6]) Berkeley suggests both by the title of his book, and also in some of its sections, that there is a chain linking the various sorts of being, the high and low, mind and body, God and tar. The point is nowhere so succinctly expressed as in a poem he wrote on the subject, and which he included in some copies of the second Dublin edition of *Siris* (1744):

> Causes connected with effects supply
> A golden chain, whose radiant links on high
> Fix'd to the sovereign throne from thence depend
> And reach e'en down to tar the nether end.[7]

Yet even these lines do not fully reveal the intimate connection between tar-water and God. To appreciate this connection we need to look carefully at some of the links of *Siris*.

(1) Fire, thinks Berkeley, is the natural element closest to God; and this he justifies by citing authorities—mostly ancient—who associate God and fire. Thus the Stoics 'conceived God to be an intellectual and fiery spirit' (sect. 172); the Magi 'worship God as present in fire' (sect. 184); and Berkeley stresses that 'there are many passages in the Holy Scripture that would make one think the Supreme Being was in a peculiar manner present in the element of fire' (sect. 186). Berkeley mentions the burning bush at Mount Sinai, Ezekiel's visions of 'fire and brightness, lamps, burning coals of fire', Daniel's vision of God's throne appearing 'like a fiery flame, and his wheels like burning fire.' (ibid.; also see sect. 187). Berkeley also argues that God operates on the world through the medium of fire; and that this pure fire is to God what the animal spirits are to man (sects. 156 and 163). Thus

---

[6] For example, in the *Gentleman's Magazine* of March 1747, 146, there is a poem entitled 'On the Bishop of Cloyne's *Siris*, which after treating of the virtues of TAR, enters upon the sublime mysteries of the Trinity'.

[7] *Works*, v. 226; these are the last four lines of Berkeley's poem, entitled 'On Tar'.

in section 291 he states: '. . . that a divine Agent doth by His virtue permeate and govern the elementary fire or light . . . which serves as an animal spirit to enliven and actuate the whole mass, and all the members of this visible world'.

(2) Berkeley then argues that tar-water is the substance closest in nature to fire which can be safely consumed by living organisms; for fire need not be manifest as flame (sect. 192), and it 'mixeth with all bodies, even water' (sect. 195). The next crucial links in the argument are to be found (or, one might almost say, they lie hidden) in sections 211 and 212. Berkeley tells us that the

Pythagorean philosophers thought there was a certain pure heat or fire, which had something divine in it, by the participation whereof men became allied to the Gods. And according to the Platonists, heaven is not defined so much by its local situation as by its purity. The purest and most excellent fire, that is heaven, saith Ficinus [1433–99]. And again, the hidden fire that everywhere exerts itself, he calls celestial. (sect. 211)

Here we have one of Berkeley's many identifications of fire and divinity, combined with an identification of heaven and purity; which, given the fountain imagery (described in Ch. 5 § II) was probably a deep motivating force behind the Bermuda project. Of course, I should immediately note that Berkeley does not make these identifications himself; he merely quotes others as making them. Nor does he identify tar-water with fire, either himself or by means of his various authorities.

(3) But what Berkeley does only partially in section 211, he does more fully in the next section. He begins section 212 with a categorical statement: 'This is the general source of life, spirit, and strength, and therefore of health to all animals, who constantly receive its illapses cloathed in air, through the lungs and pores of the body.' Plainly, he has moved here from stating the views of others to a confident assertion of his own views. The abruptness of the movement is highlighted by the opening words. What, the reader might well ask, is the antecedent of 'This . . . general source of life . . .'? Looking back on section 211, he will have to conclude that it is 'the common mass of celestial fire', a notion

that Berkeley had ascribed to Marsilius Ficinus, but which he is now adopting as his own. Section 212 then continues:

The same [fiery] spirit, imprisoned in food and medicines, is conveyed into the stomach, the bowels, the lacteals, circulated and secreted by the several ducts, and distributed throughout the system . . . Plato, in his *Timaeus*, enumerating the ignited juices, names wine in the first place, and tar in the second. But wine is pressed from the grape, and fermented by human industry. Therefore of all ignited juices purely natural, tar or resin must in his account be esteemed the first.

Tar, then, has of all natural substances the closest affinity to celestial fire, which fire is the source of life and is most closely identified with God, heaven, and purity. Of course, with the first link of this crucial chain we are back to authority in the person of Plato. It is Plato who thinks that tar is the natural fluid closest to the life-giving fire. But in *Siris* Plato is Berkeley's hero; thus there is every reason to think that Berkeley does believe that tar-water is liquid, drinkable fire (sects. 216–18). The importance of sections 211 and 212 is not so much that they convey novel information, but that they provide the contiguous links of the chain in Berkeley's curious argument, an argument that leads to the conclusion that tar-water is, in effect, drinkable God. Thus tar-water is a panacea or catholicon simply because, as Berkeley elsewhere states, its 'virtues are *divine*'.[8] Section 212 also introduces a distinction between good natural fire, i.e. tar-water, and bad unnatural fire (wine), which echoes, I believe, the earlier comparison between the fountain of living water and the broken cisterns.[9]

---

[8] This phrase is taken from 'On Tar' (*Works*, v. 225), my emphasis. Of course, 'divine' could be read as a metaphor for, say, marvellous; but in the light of the sections of *Siris* I have quoted above, I should press for a more literal interpretation.

[9] See above, Ch. 5. The antithesis of tar-water and fermented and distilled liquors is to be found in nearly all of Berkeley's tar-water writings, but most importantly in *Siris*, sects. 66, 103–7, and (especially) 217. Thus tar-water is said to produce 'a calm and steady joy like the effect of good news, without that sinking of spirits which is a subsequent effect of all fermented cordials'. It is 'permanent', 'benign', 'consistent'; whereas distilled spirits are 'sporadic', 'pernicious', 'fitful'. And of course, anticipating William Cowper on tea, tar-water is said 'to warm without heating, cheer but not inebriate' (sect. 217); cf. Cowper's *The Task* (1789), iv. 38–40.

Once one realizes the significance of the fountain of living waters, it is difficult to overlook its connection with tar-water. St Paul's College, Bermuda, which was to be a 'fountain or reservoir of learning and religion', God's vehicle for purifying America, had been defeated. But from its ashes issued tar-water, the universal purifier of mankind. Whether consciously or unconsciously, Berkeley must surely have regarded tar-water as the fulfilment or redemption of the Bermuda project. His firm belief in providence and in the providential nature of his projected college must have disposed him to expect some important outcome from the failure of his project. Thus in a letter of 29 March 1730, when the future of his college was beginning to appear gloomy, Berkeley wrote: 'God governs the world and knows his own times and seasons: it is our duty to endeavour not to be unserviceable in this our day and patiently leave the event to Providence' (*Works*, viii. 207). And in a letter written one year later, when the impending failure of the project had become all to clear to him, he wrote: 'This disappointment which long lay heavy on my spirits I endeavour to make myself easy under, by considering that we even know not would be good or bad . . .' (*Works*, viii. 212). Tar-water also had a clear connection with the project: for it was either in or from America that he heard of its use as a medicine.[10] To be sure, twelve eventful years intervened between his return from America and the publication of *Siris*, and these years are punctuated by some of his liveliest writings. But that should not deflect us from seeing the continuing potency of the Bermuda project and the profound underlying relationship between it and the tar-water episode.

One final, poetic, piece of evidence supporting my interpretation should also be mentioned. I have quoted from two of Berkeley's poems—on the Bermuda project (in Ch. 5) and on tar-water (above)—and have suggested that (not unnaturally) he allowed his mind freer rein in his verse. Hence it is of interest to observe that the idea of a 'golden age' in the Bermuda poem of 1726 seems to reappear more concretely as a 'golden chain' in the tar-

---

[10] See my 'Mrs Berkeley's Annotations', 22–3, 27, and Ian Tipton, 'Two Questions on Bishop Berkeley's Panacea', *Journal of the History of Ideas* 30 (1969), 204–7.

water poem of 1744. As the 'virtues of tar-water flowing like the Nile . . .' replaced the 'fountain or reservoir of learning and religion . . .', so the 'golden age' was superseded by the 'golden chain'. And as the fountain of St Paul's College was to stream 'through all parts of America . . . purging away ill manners and irreligion . . .', so *Siris*'s tar-water is said to branch 'into innu- merable channels conveying health and relief'. The source and origin in each case is the same—the Deity—and the general hoped-for effect of both can, I have suggested, be summed up in the word 'purity'.

Seeing tar-water as a sort of phoenix or metamorphosis of St Paul's College helps to explain how one of the most rational of men could seriously think that he had found a panacea. An adequate explanation is not, I think, to be found in either the gullibility of the age or the state of medical science in Berkeley's time. Yet this seems to be the opinion of a number of distinguished Berkeley scholars: T. E. Jessop, the most recent editor of *Siris*, and also A. D. Richie and Ian Tipton. According to Jessop: 'In claiming that it [tar-water] was probably a panacea . . . he belonged to his age: in his time even physicians of standing had their 'catholicons', and there was very little science against them, and the old alchemistic faith behind them.'[11] Yet this judgement seems belied by Berkeley's own words in the *First Letter to Thomas Prior on Tar-water* (Dublin, 1744). Thus in section 11 he states candidly:

The great objection I find made to this medicine [tar-water] is that it promises too much. What, say the objectors, do you pretend to a *panacea*, a thing strange, chimerical and contrary to the opinion and experience of all mankind?

To which Berkeley answers: 'I freely own that I suspect tar-water is a panacea.' Yet in section 22 his uneasiness about proposing tar- water as a panacea reasserts itself: 'After all that can be said, it is most certain that a panacea sounds odd, and conveys somewhat

---

[11] *Works*, v, pp. vi–vii; A. D. Richie, 'George Berkeley's *Siris*', *Proceedings of the British Academy* (1954), 44; and Tipton, 'Two Questions', 219–23.

shocking to the ear and sense of most men, who are wont to rank the universal medicine with the philosopher's stone and the squaring of the circle . . . '. This does not suggest that either Berkeley or his age were in any way disposed in favour of panaceas.

No doubt, Berkeley's successful experimentation with tar-water (which he details in *Siris*) led him to the plausible conclusion that he had found a useful medicine; and his hope that it would prove a healthy substitute for intoxicating drinks was another good reason for endorsing it.[12] It should also be noted, in fairness to Berkeley, that by a panacea he did not mean 'a medicine which cures all individuals', since that—as he himself points out—is not consistent with mortality. What he does mean is a 'medicine that cures or relieves all different species of distempers' (*Works*, v. 175). Yet, in the final analysis, none of these mitigating factors satisfactorily explains how Berkeley was led, in the first instance, to entertain the ' shocking' notion, 'contrary to the opinion and experience of all mankind', that he had stumbled upon a uni-versal medicine. Seeing tar-water as the fulfilment or redemption of St Paul's College does, I believe, go some way towards explaining this.

IV

Siris was probably Berkeley's most popular book in his own lifetime.[13] Of all his works, it made the greatest immediate impact. However, as Ian Tipton has observed, this was not caused by the

[12] This practical aim has not, I think, been recognized by Berkeley scholars; yet it is developed throughout Berkeley's writings on tar-water, particularly in *Siris*, sects. 66, 103–8, 212, 216–17. The theme then reappears in the *First Letter to Prior*, sect. 25, and in the *Second Letter*, sects. 8–10; there are also passing references to it in various private letters and in the 1752 'Farther Thoughts' (*Works*, v. 215–17); see also above, n. 4. Berkeley's wish that tar-water would become an alternative to distilled drinks was endorsed by *The Dublin Journal* (see 14 May 1751) and by the scientist Stephen Hales, who says in *An Account . . . of Tar-water* (2nd edn., 1747) that tar-water 'was never more wanted than in the present Age, to counter-act that great Bane of Mankind' (pp. 25–6). Eventually beer and tea filled the need for a cheap alternative to the 'great Bane' of gin and whiskey.

[13] For a lively account of *Siris* and its printing history, see Keynes, *Bibliography*, 116–30.

more speculative parts of *Siris* (roughly the last third).[14] It was Berkeley's practical recommendations of tar-water in the early sections of *Siris*—precisely the sections that are now no longer taken seriously—that excited interest in the contemporary literature.

Yet there is one notable exception—in the Irish reception of *Siris*. Here the important figure is Robert Clayton, Berkeley's one-time lieutenant in the Bermuda project, who effectively abandoned the project on becoming Bishop of Killala in 1730.[15] Although Berkeley was probably disappointed by Clayton, the two men seem to have been on reasonably friendly terms at least in 1737, since in that year Clayton (now Bishop of Cork and Ross) introduced Berkeley in the Irish House of Lords. After noting that Berkeley and Clayton were bishops of adjoining dioceses between 1735 and 1745, Luce writes:

Clayton in later life came under suspicion of unorthodoxy, and whether the friendship was clouded thereby we do not know; but if the much-discussed *Essay on Spirit* (1750) is by Clayton, it points to a breach; for its opening comments on Berkeley's philosophy are neither friendly nor true.   (*Life*, 84)

In the light of new evidence that Clayton was indeed the author of the *Essay* and that Berkeley expressed his approval of it a breach does seem likely.[16]

Clayton's *Essay* (which went through five editions in two years) contains references to a number of ancient and a few 'modern' writers. Berkeley, however, is the only writer mentioned who was alive when the *Essay* was published. He is considered twice: once by name, in section 1, and again as the author of *Siris*, in section 9 of the *Essay*. The first mention links Berkeley with Malebranche

[14]   See 'Two Questions', 218.
[15]   In a letter from Rhode Island, 20 July 1730, Berkeley writes with characteristic generosity: 'I have not heard from Dr. Clayton since he was made Bishop. I take him to be a man of worthy views and heartily wish success to his endeavours of being useful in that station since we are not likely to see him in this part of the world' (*Works*, viii. 210).
[16]   See my 'Berkeley, Clayton and *An Essay on Spirit*', *Journal of the History of Ideas* 32 (1971), 369–70.

and Spinoza, and probably encouraged the monistic interpretation (or misinterpretation) of Berkeley's philosophy. Section 1 reads:

The Opinion of *Spinosa* was, that there is no other *Substance* in Nature but God: That Modes cannot subsist, or be conceived, without a Substance: That there is nothing in Nature but Modes and Substances: and that therefore every Thing must be conceived as subsisting in God. Which Opinion, with some few Alterations, hath been embraced and cultivated by *P. Malebranche* and Bishop *Berkeley*.

Clayton does not elucidate this judgement; nor does he cite any of Berkeley's works in support of it. Yet it is likely (as we shall see) that he had *Siris* in mind. However, virtually the same charge was made and defended at some length by Chevalier Andrew Ramsay in his posthumously published *Philosophical Principles of Natural and Revealed Religion* (Glasgow, 1748). According to Ramsay, Berkeley is 'the most refined Spinosist that ever was'.[17]

Whether Clayton's interpretation of Berkeley was influenced by Ramsay, I do not know. But in the light of Clayton's own curious theory of spirits, which he develops in the *Essay*, it is not difficult to see why he should want to discredit Berkeley and Malebranche by allying their views with 'the Spinosian impiety', as Ramsay puts it (p. 247). Since Clayton's theory has some bearing on his remarks on Berkeley's philosophy, and also probably on Berkeley's opinion of the *Essay*, a few words about the theory should be useful.

Clayton accepts the independence of mind and body: 'It is beyond the reach of human abilities to explain, how these two different kinds of existence, the active and the inactive, can have an influence, or can possibly affect each other' (sect. 8). But this is not to say, as some followers of Descartes did say, that God is the one true cause of the latter or the co-ordinator of both: '[because] *Nothing can act where it is not*, that Power whereby any

---

[17] Ramsay argues that both the 'enthusiastic notion of Malebranche' and the 'Berkelean scheme' favour Spinosism (p. 248). For denying that bodies are real agents 'tends necessarily to prove, that God is the only agent in nature; and this opinion leads naturally to Spinosism, because it induces us to believe that God is also the only substance in nature . . .' (p. 243).

body continues in [or resists] Motion, is . . . the effect of some concomitant Spirit' (sect. 8). Therefore, Clayton believes, every piece of matter has—united to it—an individual spirit, which governs and effects its movements. His theory might be described as a pluralistic version of occasionalism.

The degree of intelligence and power of a spirit depends, it would seem, on the kind of material system to which it is united. It is even possible, Clayton thinks, that all the innumerable created spirits are 'equally perfect'; the difference in their actual degree of intellect and power may only be the result of the particular 'formation of their bodily organs' (sects. 25–6). In any case, he argues, the real spirit, in man at least, is greatly superior to its human embodiment. The first step of his argument is interesting. Perhaps following Malebranche, Clayton states that the 'Power, which is constantly working within us, to form and preserve the regular Disposition of our bodily Organs, and to change the Food which we eat, into Blood, into flesh and into bones . . . is manifestly above our comprehension' (sect. 22). He then goes one step further, applying this analysis to voluntary human action as well: '. . . when we have a Mind to move a Finger, or a Leg, that Part of the human Understanding, which is under our Direction, is capable of doing no more than the Power of willing it; but how to perform this Action, it is as ignorant as the Beast in the Field' (sect. 23). For convenience, I shall call this the occasionalist problem.[18] It might be restated this way: men have neither the intelligence to understand nor the power to affect the involuntary or voluntary motions of their bodies. How then do these motions come about?

It is not, I think, in the statement of the problem that philos-ophers such as Clayton, Malebranche, and Hume differ, but in their solution to it. As Hume nicely expressed it in his *Treatise of Human Nature* (1739):

The small success, which has been met with in all attempts to fix this power, has at last oblig'd philosophers to conclude, that the ultimate

---

[18] I do not mean that it was a problem for the Occasionalists. They knew, or thought they knew, the answer. It was, so to speak, a rhetorical problem.

force and efficacy of nature is perfectly unknown to us, and that 'tis in vain we search for it in all the known qualities of matter. In this opinion they are almost unanimous; and 'tis only in the inference they draw from it, that they discover any difference in their sentiments. (Bk. I, pt. 3, sect. xiv)

Clayton's own inference from, or solution of, the occasionalist problem would be rejected by Malebranche and Hume. His argument proceeds as follows. Because 'nothing can act where it is not', and since 'God may communicate to the Works of his Hands, such Portions of His own Attributes, as are greatly beyond the comprehension of Mankind to conceive . . .' (sect. 29), Clayton infers that fingers and hearts are moved by superhuman concomitant spirits, which possess the power to affect such complicated motions. For Clayton, therefore, this plurality of spirits solves the occasionalist problem. Occasionalism's *deus ex machina*, as it were, is transformed by Clayton into *dei ex machina*, a vast hierarchy of spiritual beings embodied in varying degrees of intellect and power.

Malebranche, however, would argue that the physical world, at least, is under the immediate direction of the Deity alone; and, with one exception, so would Berkeley. If the monism, in this sense, of Malebranche and Berkeley is right, then clearly Clayton's pluralism is wrong. And I should note that at least one philosopher in Ireland held that Berkeley was right. For this 'monistic' aspect of Berkeley's thought was endorsed in an article in the Dublin *Literary Journal* of 1745. And it is particularly noteworthy that the writer does so by quoting from *Siris*, sect. 237, that all the properties of bodies 'are Effects only of the "immediate Action of an incorporeal Agent, who consults, moves, and disposes all Things according to such Rules, and for such Purposes, as seem good to him"'.[19] Clayton rejects this; for him it is not one 'incorporeal Agent' but many agents that activate the physical world. Hence it seems likely that by invidiously associating Berkeley's

---

[19] *A Literary Journal*, ed. J. P. Droz (5 vols.; Dublin, 1743–8), ii. 2, 23–4. The article is by D. G. S., who might be Berkeley's friend and correspondent Dean GervaiS.

philosophy with the extreme and notorious monism of Spinoza, Clayton was indirectly arguing in the *Essay*'s first section for his own pluralistic philosophy.

Malebranche's solution to the occasionalist problem is monistic. The divine causation alone solves the problem. Now Berkeley accepts, with qualification, both the problem and Malebranche's solution. His qualified statement of the occasionalist problem in *Siris*—which should be compared with the first part of Clayton's— is as follows:

> It must be owned, we are not conscious of the systole and diostole of the heart, or the motion of the diaphragm. It may not nevertheless be thence inferred, that unknowing nature can act regularly, as well as ourselves. The true inference is, that the self-thinking individual, or human person, is not the real author of those natural motions. And, in fact, no man blames himself if they are wrong, or values himself if they are right. The same may be said of the fingers of a musician . . . (sect. 257)

We can see from this that it is only involuntary bodily motions that Berkeley takes to be problematic. Here is the rest of the quotation from *Siris*, sect. 257 and then 258, in which Berkeley sets forth his guarded occasionalist solution:

> . . . it being evident that what is done by rule must proceed from something that understands the rule; therefore, if not from the musician himself, from some other active intelligence, the same perhaps which governs bees and spiders, and moves the limbs of those who walk in their sleep.
>
> Instruments, occasions, and signs . . . occur in, or rather make up, the whole visible Course of Nature. These, being no agents themselves, are under the direction of one Agent concerting all for one end, the supreme good. All those motions, whether in animal bodies or in other parts of the system of nature, *which are not effects of particular wills*, seem to spring from the same general cause with the vegetation of plants—an aetherial spirit actuated by a Mind.

I have drawn attention by italics to Berkeley's qualification of the Malebranchian solution to the occasionalist problem. Although 'the whole visible course of nature' is 'under the direction of one agent', namely God, Berkeley is careful here to except 'those motions' which are 'effects of particular wills', namely finite minds or persons. This was also, as we have seen in Chapter 2, Berkeley's view in the *Principles* and in entry 548 of the *Commentaries*, where he clearly distinguishes his position from the more monistic occasionalism of Malebranche: 'We move our Legs our selves. 'Tis we that will their movement. Herein I differ from Malbranch.'

If Hume thought that Berkeley was one of those philosophers who 'conclude, that the ultimate force and efficacy of nature is perfectly unknown to us', he was mistaken. Berkeley holds that we do know something of this force. As he says in *Siris*, sect. 291: 'We are conscious that a spirit can begin, alter, or determine motion.' Similarly, Clayton's interpretation of Berkeley as a pantheist or monist was mistaken. Yet, as we have also seen in Chapters 2 and 3, it is not so easy to see how Berkeley could justify his theory of spirits, particularly against criticisms from a Humean point of view.

In section 9 of the *Essay*, Clayton contends 'that Resistance is something more than bare Inability, or a Want of Power, or a Negation of Spirit, as the Author of (7) *Siris* asserts it only to be'. (In his note '(7)' he refers to '*Siris*, Sect. 290'.) Clayton seems to have held the theory, which was elaborated in detail by Andrew Baxter, that bodies could no more resist motion than cause it; because, to use Baxter's quaint phrase, they are composed of 'poor sluggish matter'.[20] Here again Clayton seems to be defending his own theory by attacking Berkeley: for if resistance were a 'Negation of Spirit', then Clayton's spirits would become, in that context (see *Essay*, sect. 8), superfluous.

Although this is the only explicit reference to *Siris* in the *Essay*, there is reason to believe that *Siris* is more generally in the background of the *Essay*. I suspect that Clayton appropriated some of the content of *Siris*. One example is the opening of section 11 of the *Essay*, which reads: 'All nature, therefore, seems to be animated, or alive.' In section 291 of *Siris* Berkeley writes: 'We see all nature alive or in motion.' Both writers are led from this observation to

---

[20]   Baxter, *Enquiry into the Nature of the Human Soul* (London, 1745), i. 88.

a consideration of spirits. And, it will be remembered, that Clayton had only two sections previously—in sect. 9—criticized section 290 of *Siris*. This is unlikely to be a coincidence.

There is another reason for thinking that *Siris* is in the back-ground of the *Essay*. In a pamphlet published in 1754 Clayton openly admits that Berkeley influenced some of the *Essay*'s subject-matter:

As to the doctrine of the Platonick or Pythagorean Trinity etc. the author of the *Essay on Spirit* would never have troubled his head with such a rhapsody of nonsense, if some great names, such as Cudworth and Berkeley, had not first produced them in confirmation of the Athanasian doctrine of the Trinity.[21]

Clayton could only be alluding here to *Siris*, sects. 252 and 360–5; for nowhere else does Berkeley try to show that (as he puts it in sect. 361) 'the notion of a Trinity is to be found in the writings of many old heathen philosophers'. The use which Clayton made of *Siris*, and his explicit reference to it, also confirm that *Siris* was probably the main source for his monistic inter-pretation of Berkeley's philosophy.

Until recently scholars were unaware of Berkeley's opinion of the *Essay*, or that he had been drawn into the heated controversy that followed the *Essay*'s publication. One of Clayton's antagonists was Dr Thomas McDonnell, a clergyman in his own diocese of Clogher, who had replied to Clayton in *An Essay towards an Answer to the Essay on Spirit* (Dublin, 1753) in which he makes some complimentary references to Berkeley.[22] Clayton rejoined with *Some Remarks on Dr McDonnell's Essay* (1754) in which he states that 'those [Irish] bishops, who have hitherto shewed them-selves most virulent against the *Essay* . . . are the least knowing

[21] *Some Remarks on Dr McDonnell's Essay towards an Answer . . . to the Essay on Spirit* (Dublin, 1754), 34.

[22] See his pp. 9, 11, 235–6. About Clayton's assertion in the *Essay*, sect. 1, McDonnell says: 'Whether he [Spinoza] lives in the writings of P. *Malebranche* or Bishop Berkley [*sic*], it is not my present purpose to enquire. But if they have adopted any thing valuable in him, (and what is there so depraved, that hath not in it some-thing worthy of preservation?) he, of those two learned men, who is amongst us, will doubtless be able to maintain and defend it.' (p. 2).

of the whole Bench . . .' (p. 34). McDonnell replied in a *Short Vindication* (Dublin, 1754), where he prints a letter he received from Berkeley on the *Essay*, which he introduces as follows:

> If a strong contempt and an avowed diapprobation of the *Essay* . . . be what its author means by *virulence*, I know of none of the bishops, who then adorned the Bench, that expressed himself so strongly against it, as that confessedly learned and ingenious prelate, the late bishop of Cloyne: one whom even this gentleman allows to be a great name.

McDonnell then prints the letter, apparently the last extant one we have by Berkeley, written on 7 May 1752, three months before he left Cloyne for Oxford. In it, Berkeley says:

> The Weakness and Presumption of the Book stiled an *Essay on Spirit*, render it undeserving any serious Answer. I find there are some anony⁄mous persons who have treated it in a ludicrous Manner.[23] But if you are minded to confute it seriously, I make no Doubt of your being singly an Over⁄match for such a Adversary.[24]

There is another surprising link between Berkeley's *Siris* and Clayton's *Essay*. In the first chapter of his notorious novel *Chrysal: or, the Adventures of a Guinea* (London, 1762) the Irish writer Charles Johnston quotes and uses theories both in *Siris* and the *Essay* as scaffolding. In short, there is a spirit, called Chrysal, which was assigned to a bit of gold 'upon first feeling the influ⁄ence of the [quoting *Siris*] "etherial fire of the sun, the general minister of the divine commands"'. The piece of gold is then mined, becomes a guinea, is passed from person to person, and narrates his (often shocking) experiences.

Of all Berkeley's writings, *Siris* has probably had the most associations with literature, attracting a great number of distin⁄guished literary figures, including Henry Fielding, Thomas De Quincey, S. T. Coleridge, Charles Dickens, and, in our own century, W. B. Yeats. William Blake, as is generally known,

---

[23] Berkeley may be alluding to, among other pamphlets, *A Modern Preface* [to the *Essay*] *put into Plain English by Way of Abstract, for the Use of the Poor* . . . (Dublin, 1752).

[24] See McDonnell, *A Short Vindication*, 21; McDonnell notes that Berkeley's letter 'lies in the bookseller's hands for the satisfaction of those who desire to see it'.

annotated a copy of *Siris*; although his marginalia are less appre-
ciative than one might and some have thought.[25] *Siris* also inspired
at its publication more poems than any of Berkeley's other
writings, although most of these were mere doggerel, poking fun at
a bishop meddling out of his profession—to use Berkeley's own
phrase—and into medicine.[26] This is the theme of the shortest
poem, called 'Tit for Tat, or Divinity and Physick at War':

> The bishop's book annoys the learned tribe,
> They threaten hard; we'll preach, if you prescribe.[27]

But in the war of verse about tar-water there was a ready reply
from one of Berkeley's supporters:

> . . . if he is a soul's director,
> Be of the body no protector?

as well as a more sustained one, in a larger compass:

> Is B—rkl—y's reas'ning, sense and diction
> To pass for nought but cant and fiction,
> And 'cause thou can'st not understand him,
> Do'st thou with incoherence brand him?[28]

V

Siris has also had admirers in more recent times. Thus it has been
hailed by Fraser and John Wild as the 'consummation' of, or
new departure in, Berkeley's thought; and George Sampson describes it as 'certainly the most amazing work in the literature of
British philosophy'.[29] And yet it is hard to see a coherent picture

[25] See e.g. Katherine Raine, 'Berkeley, Blake and the New Age', in *Thought* 51 (1976), 356–76.

[26] See the Advertisement to the 1750 edition of the *Querist*, in *Works*, vi. 103.

[27] Printed in the *London Magazine* (1744), 614.

[28] The preceding six lines are from a poem in the *London Magazine* (1744), 406. For other poems about tar-water, see *Gentleman's Magazine* (1745), 160, (1747), 146, (1752), 578; *Newcastle Courant* (1744), nos. 2646 and 2648; and *Universal Magazine* (1748), 223.

[29] See Wild, *George Berkeley* (Cambridge, Mass., 1936), ch. 16—one of the more ambitious discussions of *Siris*; Berkeley, *Complete Works*, ed. A. C. Fraser (Oxford, 1901), iii. 117–18; *The Works of George Berkeley*, ed. G. Sampson (London, 1989), iii. 198. For a recent scholarly study of the philosophy of science in *Siris*, see G. Moked, *Particles and Ideas: Bishop Berkeley's Corpuscularian Philosophy* (Oxford, 1988).

in *Siris*'s multiplicity of hints, reflections, and glosses on (as its subtitle expresses it) 'diverse subjects connected together and arising one from another'. However, this is not to say that Berkeley had adopted this unsystematic style of writing for no purpose. In his 'Primary Visitation Charge' at Cloyne, about 1736, he recom﹣ mends something similar to his clergy as a helpful technique for bringing Roman Catholics over to Anglicanism: 'Occasional discourse, I say, that imperceptibly glides from one subject to another, may be so conducted by a prudent person to those topics he hath a mind to treat of, as if they naturally arose from what went before . . .' (*Works*, vii. 164). Berkeley then goes on to make what seems to be his last pronouncement on persuasive strategy:

. . . a subject, [he tells his clergy] which if proposed at once might shock, being introduced by degrees might take: . . . what comes as it were from chance is often admitted, while that which looks like design is guarded against: and he who will not seek instruction may nonetheless receive it. (ibid.)

Berkeley seems to have been employing something like this strategy in *Siris*; thus in section 350 he says:

The displeasure of some readers may perhaps be incurred by surprising them into certain reflections and inquiries for which they have no curios﹣ ity. But perhaps some others may be pleased to find a dry subject varied by digressions, traced through remote inferences, and carried into ancient times, whose hoary maxims . . . scattered in this essay, are not proposed as principles, but barely as hints to awaken and exercise the inquisitive reader . . .

Berkeley's message in the later philosophical and theological part of *Siris* may lie more in its apparently random hints, therefore, than in any coherent position or system. In section 296 he seems to say that he is unable to express directly what he knows:

There is, it must be owned, a mixture of obscurity and prejudice in human speech and reasoning. This is unavoidable, since the veils of prejudice and error are slowly and singly taken off one by one.

This may be an allusion to his strategy of gradual revelation (com﹣ pare, e.g. *TVV*, sect. 35). The metaphor of undressing error is also not new; it is to be found as early as entry 737 in his philosophical notebooks: 'To view the deformity of Error we need only undress it.' What does seem new is that Berkeley longer regards himself as entirely in control: 'It may, therefore, be par/doned if this rude essay doth, by insensible transitions, draw the reader into remote inquiries and speculations, that *were not, perhaps, thought of* either by him *or by the author at first setting out*' (sect. 297, my italics). Perhaps the main difference between the early Berkeley and the author of *Siris* is that the former thought he could express the naked truth in a coherent form, if he wished, whereas the latter was no longer so confident.

Berkeley's uncertainty comes out fairly clearly at the end of *Siris*: '. . . imprisoned like oysters . . . in this mortal state we must be satisfied to make the best of those glimpses within our reach' (sect. 367). His diffidence is expressed most eloquently in the next and final section:

368 The eye by long use comes to see even in the darkest cavern: and there is no subject so obscure but we may discern some glimpse of truth by long poring on it. Truth is the cry of all, but the game of few. Certainly, where it is the chief passion, it doth not give way to vulgar cares and views; nor is it contented with a little ardour in the early time of life, active perhaps to pursue, but not so fit to weigh and revise. He that would make real progress in knowledge must dedicate his old age as well as youth, the later growth as well as first fruits, at the altar of Truth.

Cujusvis est errare, nullius nisi insipientis in errore perseverare. Cicero[30]

Is Berkeley alluding to himself here? Is he suggesting that in *Siris* he has now seen 'fit to weigh and revise' his youthful 'first fruits', his early philosophy? This has been the opinion of some com/mentators, most notably John Wild; but it has been forcefully opposed by A. A. Luce. The subject is a wide and complex one, as it involves Berkeley's views on matter, perception, causality, abstraction—on all of which, Luce maintained, there was no retraction. There is one topic in this debate, however, on which I should like very briefly to comment, since it could be seen to

[30] That is: 'Any one may err, but no man unless he be a fool should continue in error'; the quotation is from Cicero's *Philippics* 12. 2.

bear on my account (in Ch. 6) of his theology. This is Berkeley's commitment to rational theology. According to Wild, Berkeley's theological thought was originally deistic but it became increasingly more fideistic and sceptical. Wild's argument for this dubious thesis is thin on evidence but strong on speculation, often more obscure than *Siris* itself.[31]

One clear reason Wild had for his interpretation, however, was the evidence of Berkeley's manuscript sermons, particularly that on 1 John 2, which Wild was the first to print. In his introductory note Wild observes:

The new anti-Deistic movement in Berkeley's thought is made manifest. His constant omission of the Deistic phrases 'natural light' and 'natural religion' is particularly significant. (op. cit. 521)

The systematic deletion of these phrases in the manuscript is indeed remarkable as is the note affixed to Berkeley's 1751 sermon on the will of God: 'Mem. Leave out all those Passages wch relate to the Light of Reason.' But the hand that did the deleting and wrote this note was not, as Luce was able to show, Berkeley's. The person who did the revising (or inspired it) was almost certainly John Ellis, who was (ironically) a Dublin follower of Berkeley's old theological opponents, Browne and King. For just above the note or memorandum is Ellis's (just legible) signature and the comment: 'Vide Ellis's Knowledge of Divine Things from Revelation [London, 1743]'.[32]

VI

Between *Siris* and his last published essay, 'Farther Thoughts on Tar-water'—included in his *Miscellany* (London, 1752)—Berkeley was chiefly concerned with promoting tar-water. Within a month of publication, *Siris* and tar-water had become the rage. As Luce notes:

The work passed through at least six editions in the first year . . . it was translated, in whole or part, into French, Dutch, Portuguese, and

---

[31] *George Berkeley*, esp. 466–73.
[32] See my 'Culmination and Causation', 264 n. 11.

Spanish . . . Tar-water leaped into fame on both sides of the Channel . . . Do you sell tar-water? a man asked an apothecary; tar-water, was the reply, why, I sell nothing else. (*Life*, 200–1)

Berkeley's involvement with tar-water is shown in the letters and poems he published on the subject. Much of his time after 1744 was also taken up with patients in Cloyne and elsewhere. Writing to his friend Samuel Johnson, he remarks: 'My correspondence with patients who drink tar-water obliges me to be less punctual in corresponding with my friends'(*Works*, viii. 302).

Berkeley did have other interests, however, and he did publish other works in this period. These were short works on social issues, relating particularly to his Roman Catholic countrymen. The most important of these is *A Word to the Wise, or an Exhortation to the Roman Catholic Clergy of Ireland* (Dublin, 1749), which may be read as a sequel to the *Querist* (to which it was appended in the 1750 edition.) It begins disarmingly:

Be not startled, Reverend Sirs, to find yourselves addressed to by one of a different communion. We are indeed (to our shame be it spoken) more inclined to hate for those articles wherein we differ, than to love one another for those wherein we agree. (*Works*, vi. 235)

Berkeley had stated his views on Roman Catholicism in a private letter of 1741 to Sir John James, who had accompanied him to America and was now proposing to become a Roman Catholic.[33] Berkeley's critique of Catholicism is along fairly conventional Protestant lines. It is in his attitude to his Catholic countrymen, however, that he is generally thought to be unusually liberal and in advance of his times. One reason for this opinion is the appre-ciative reply of the Roman Catholic clergy of Dublin to his *Word to the Wise*. First printed in the *Dublin Journal* in November 1749 and reprinted in later editions of the *Word to the Wise*, the Catholic clergy here returned 'their sincere and hearty thanks to the worthy [author]; assuring him, that they are determined to comply with every particular recommended in his address . . .' (*Works*, vi. 248).

[33] For Berkeley's letter, see *Works*, vii, 143–55. In the Bermuda Group (see Fig. 7) James is standing next to Berkeley.

Yet there were some who had serious doubts about the *Word to the Wise*; and at least one clergyman found it difficult to publicize these doubts, as the following extract of a letter shows. The letter, dated 24 March 1749, was written to the antiquarian, Charles O'Conor of Balangare (1710–91), most of whose writings were aimed at improving the legal and economic conditions of his fellow Irish Catholics.

I saw lately a Manuscript, intitled, An Answer to the Bishop of Cloyne's [*Word to the Wise, or an*] Exhortation . . . it is written by a Clergyman, who . . . [has] detailed the obstructions which the Bishop's Scheme must meet with, while the Laws which have been enacted against us continue in Force: He has incontestably showed that Sloth and Idleness are no more peculiar to our Countrymen, than they are to any other People on Earth, and that those who are now remarkable, e.g., the Dutch, French, &c, for their industry and economy, wou'd in our Circumstances be whatever we are. He will indeed, if he appears in Print, rescue us in the Judgmt of the Candid from the Obloquy and Scandal thrown upon us by those whom self-interest has biased agt us. . . . This Answer is in a Printer's Hands, who I believe, is too cautious to publish it; He tells me the Author is determined to be at the expense of an Impression and take copies with him to the Country he lives in (the North) rather than it sho'd be totally suppressed.[34]

As there is no record that such an Answer to Berkeley was published, we must assume that it was suppressed. In the *Word to the Wise* Berkeley himself mentions certain 'obstructions' or 'discouragements', as he calls them, which may 'act as a bar against all endeavours for exciting [the Irish Catholics] to a laudable industry'; for example, ineligibility to buy land, exclusion from civil employments, and 'hardness of the landlord' (*Works*, vi. 240–1). But these discouragements should not prevent the humbler Catholics from achieving a modest prosperity; for the real obstacles to prosperity, he holds, are the uncleanliness and laziness of the people: 'our poor Irish are wedded to dirt

---

[34] The letter is in the Royal Irish Academy, Dublin, B. I. 1; for details, see my 'Berkeley and his Catholic Countrymen', *Long Room* 16/17 (1978), 26–8.

upon principle', they are 'distinguished above all others by sloth, dirt and beggary' (ibid. 242). Perhaps Berkeley's concern for purity (as expressed in the fountain imagery) helps to explain his aversion to dirt.

However, he is even more severe on the sloth of his countrymen, with regard to which the 'Dutch, English, French, or Flemish cannot match them'. This unpleasant message is repeated—one might say rubbed in—throughout the *Word to the Wise*. On nearly every page sloth is castigated in some new form: Berkeley speaks of 'innate hereditary sloth', 'sin and folly of sloth', 'gentle spirit of sloth', 'matchless sloth bred in every bone', 'beloved sloth', 'shackles of sloth', 'odious sloth', and 'sweet dream of sloth'. It is hardly surprising that some found this unacceptable, and that the Northern clergyman (mentioned in the letter to O'Conor) wished to rescue his countrymen from such obloquy. For if in Berkeley's view 'material well-being requires moral grit'—to quote Jessop's vigorous formula (*Works*, vi. 233)—it is also worth insisting that moral grit may be difficult without a just social order—something that was absent in Berkeley's Ireland.

Berkeley was not concerned to point out the legal and economic injustices suffered by the Catholics (and, to a lesser extent, the Presbyterians). His liberal statements are based on considerations of expedience rather than morality. His pragmatic liberalism comes out in the *Querist*, which contains his first published views on the Irish Catholic question. His opinion in query 191 on allowing Catholics to attend Trinity College is fairly typical:

Whether, in imitation of the Jesuits at Paris, who admit Protestants to study in their colleges, it may not be right for us also to admit Roman Catholics into our college, without obliging them to attend chapel duties, or catechisms, or divinity lectures? And whether this might not keep money in the kingdom, and prevent the prejudices of a foreign education?

The *Querist* was sympathetically received by Irish Catholics, such as O'Conor, who exploited it in their campaign to weaken the oppressive Penal Laws. In pamphlets published between 1751 and 1771 O'Conor gratefully acknowledged Berkeley's liberal sentiments, often referring to and quoting from the *Querist*. In the first of these pamphlets, *Seasonable Thoughts relating to our Civil and Ecclesiastical Constitution* (Dublin, 1751), he writes: 'A few Berkleys, in every Communion, would restore us to that spirit . . . of true Christianity, which one hath labored, so apostolically to revive' (p. 8). In 1756, O'Conor pays a similar tribute to Berkeley, which links Berkeley with Clayton. Reflecting on how the evils of religious conflict in Ireland might be cured, O'Conor says that it must 'be the work of long time; and . . . proceed partic-ularly from the virtue and superior talents of . . . some rare spirits, who, like a BERKELEY, or a CLAYTON, take the lead in human knowledge . . .'.[35] And in *The Touchstone of Patriotism, in a Series of Interesting Queries to the Publick* (Dublin, 1756), a work clearly modelled on Berkeley's *Querist*, O'Conor asks 'Whether Bishop Berkeley's hints in respect of our College have been sufficiently attended to, and whether he may not be supposed to have been a competent judge in such matters?' (no. 24; see also nos. 35–65). Catholic writers certainly wished to find principles of toleration and reconciliation in Berkeley's writings. An amusingly misguided example of this can be seen in Arthur O'Leary's 'Essay on Toleration'. Here O'Leary (1729–1802)—who was personally acquainted with Berkeley's brother, Robert (1698–1787)—asserts that 'the immortal Berkeley, bishop of Cloyne, has proved by arguments hitherto unanswerable, that there is no demonstration for the existence of one single body in nature. He has reconciled the Catholic and Protestant philosophers and divines, about the real presence, by cutting off, at one blow, both body and place.'[36]

In 1750 Berkeley issued his shortest work. Its original title page reads: 'Maxims Concerning Patriotism. By a Lady'. We know that Berkeley was the author, because he included the *Maxims* in his *Miscellany, containing several Tracts . . .* (1752), 'by the Bishop of Cloyne'. Berkeley's editors, Fraser and Luce, have

---

[35] See *The Principles of the Roman Catholics* (Dublin, 1756), 8. Clayton was cam-paigning in the 1750s not only to make the Thirty-Nine Articles less restrictive for Irish Anglicans, but also to soften the penal laws against Roman Catholics.

[36] *Miscellaneous Tracts* (London, 1791), 383.

suggested that the original ascription to 'a lady' may mean that the Bishop's wife, Anne, contributed some of the maxims, or helped to collect them. Although these suggestions are plausible, they have become less compelling since the recent discovery, mentioned in Chapter 4, that Berkeley was responsible for the *Ladies Library* (1714), since it also is described as 'written by a Lady'.

Little seems to be known about the *Maxims*. Their publication was probably prompted by the battle of books which raged in Ireland in 1749, for and against Charles Lucas (1713–71), the 'Wilkes of Ireland'. Lucas was in the line of the so-called 'patriots'—earlier figures were Molyneux and Swift—who urged the rights of Ireland against the British ministry or court party. Berkeley seems to have been unusual in siding with neither party in the *Maxims* and in the *Querist*. 'Patriot' was then, as it is now, a controversial and emotive term. In the *Maxims* Berkeley is trying to provide ways to identify 'true' patriots. There are 42 maxims in the last (1752) edition; here are two samples:

15. To be a real patriot, a man must consider his countrymen as God's creatures, and himself as accountable for his acting towards them.
22. Ibycus is a carking, griping, closefisted fellow. It is odds that Ibycus is not a patriot.

No. 22 recalls *Alciphron* vii. 30, where Berkeley speaks of 'that meagre minute philosopher Ibycus' and his 'carking and cheating'—a correspondence which would alone have suggested Berkeley's authorship of the *Maxims*.

VII

Apart from performing his normal episcopal duties, Berkeley devoted considerable attention to improving the material and economic conditions at Cloyne, where he set up a spinning school and tried to establish the manufacture of linen. According to his wife, he was also unusually active at home, especially in raising their children: 'He made home pleasant by a variety of employ-ments, conversation and company; his instructive conversation was delicate, and when he spoke directly of religion (which was seldom) he did it in so masterly a manner, that it made a lasting impression.'[37]

Berkeley's life in Cloyne was largely uneventful, although it was disrupted in 1745 by the second Jacobite uprising, which prompted him to raise a troop of horse and write two public letters—one to his own clergy, the other to the Catholics of his diocese—urging them not to support the Jacobite cause. In the same year he was offered the wealthy Bishopric of Clogher by Lord Chesterfield (1694–1773), who was then Lord Lieutenant of Ireland. That Berkeley refused the offer has been long known; but the letter of 25 June 1745 in which he did so has only recently come to light: 'Quiet and content', he writes, 'have nailed me down to this corner, to which I am also riveted by an indisposition that ill consists with moving from place to place . . . This hath kept me these eight years past from seeing Dublin . . .'.[38]

Apart from that visit to Dublin (in 1737), to take his seat in the Irish House of Lords and to speak against the Blasters, Berkeley had not been away from his diocese since becoming bishop in 1734. In the summer of 1750 he made one other brief excursion, this time to Killarney for a holiday with his family and friends. Upon his return, he is reported to have told a friend 'to whom he was describing its beauties that the utmost exertion of all the powers of art might repair a ruined Versailles, but that God alone could make a Killarney'.[39]

By this time, however, Berkeley's health was failing badly; and it must have received a severe blow in March 1751 with the death of his favourite son, William, then fourteen, whose loss 'was thought to have struck too close to his father's heart'.[40] These words of Stock are confirmed by Berkeley's letter to Bishop Benson (1689–1752), written shortly after the event. The letter, probably his most poignant and deeply touching, deserves, to be quoted here:

---

[37] Letter by Mrs Berkeley to her son, George, c.1760; in *Life*, 181. For a detailed account of the Cloyne period, see *Life*, chs. xi–xiv.

[38] The letter is printed in my 'Mrs Berkeley's Annotations', 24.

[39] J. Prior, *Life of Edmund Malone* (London, 1860), 15; the anecdote is contained in a letter of 1765.

[40] See *Works of Berkeley* (1784), i, p. lxxxv n.

I was a man retired from the amusement of politics, visits, and what the world calls pleasure. I had a little friend, educated always under mine own eye, whose painting delighted me, whose music ravished me, and whose lively, gay spirit was a continual feast. It has pleased God to take him hence. God, I say, in mercy hath deprived me of this pretty, gay plaything. His parts and person, his innocence and piety, his particularly uncommon affection for me, had gained too much upon me. Not content to be fond of him, I was vain of him. I had set my heart too much upon him—more perhaps than I ought to have done upon anything in this world. (*Works*, viii. 304)

In August 1752 Berkeley and his family left Cloyne for Oxford, where he was to spend his last months. His primary aim seems to have been to supervise the education of his son George, but he also apparently took the opportunity to publish (or republish) in London two books: a new and revised edition of *Alciphron* (1752) and his *Miscellany* (1752). The *Miscellany* contains only one new work by him: 'Farther Thoughts on Tar-Water'. Berkeley's last moments, as recorded in the *London Evening-Post*, were not unfitting:

We hear from Oxford, that the following remarkable circumstances attended the death of the good Bishop Berkeley. His Lady was reading a Sermon to him on Sunday evening [14 January 1753], & before it was finished, she looked up & saw him dead in his chair: he was perfectly well when the Sermon begun, & had made many observations upon it in the course of the reading.[41]

---

[41] *The London Evening-Post*, 23–25 January 1753. While Stock says (p. 38) that it was a sermon by Dr Sherlock, Mrs Berkeley states that she was reading 1 Cor. 15; see *Biographia Britannica* (2nd edn., London 1784), iii, Addenda and Corrigenda.

8

Epilogue: *Ecce Homo*

I

'When the multitude heard, they were astonished at his doctrine'; or so runs the inscription commemorating Berkeley in the Trinity College Chapel, an inscription which might be reformulated 'When the biographers heard, they were fascinated by his life'; for George Berkeley, the man, has attracted many biographers. These include at least one major poet, a British Prime Minister, a psychoanalyst, and a famous novelist. And yet, amidst the diversity, the work of three biographers—Stock, Fraser, and Luce—stands out.

Stock was the pioneer; his *Account of the Life of . . . Berkeley* was first published in 1776 and reissued three times within the next eight years.[1] As Stock was Berkeley's foremost biographer in the eighteenth century, so Fraser established himself as the leading Berkeley scholar of the nineteenth century by his massive 1871 *Life and Letters of Berkeley*. Fraser set a precedent not only for high scholarship but also for longevity; and in both he was followed by his great successor, Luce, who, like Fraser, lived into his nineties.

Luce's biographical preeminence rests firmly on the *Life of Berkeley*, universally accepted as authoritative since its appearance in 1949. Drawing skilfully on the primary evidence—much of which he himself brought to light—Luce there reveals Berkeley as a man of strong sense, 'sane, shrewd, efficient' (p. 1), a picture

---

[1] After a second edition in 1777, a new edition—called *Memoirs of . . . Berkeley*—was published in 1784 and also prefixed to Berkeley's *Works* (1784). The *Works* were then reprinted in 1820, 1837, and 1843.

that complements his common-sense reading of Berkeley's philosophy. Among the factors that helped the biography to achieve its
magisterial position—a position never attained by the philosophical
reading—was Luce's deep appreciation of his predecessors. On
Stock and Fraser he comments:

> Stock had access to family information, and he laid the foundations
> upon which later biographers have built, but his [*Account*] was too
> slender and brief. Fraser had more success. His *Life and Letters* is a
> mine for biographers . . . but [its] portrait of Berkeley lacks depth and
> tone, and in some features is untrue. (*Life*, p. v)

Even more untrue, according to Luce, was the first biographical
essay on Berkeley, printed in the *British Plutarch* in 1762. Luce
scathingly describes it as a 'pretentious, and irresponsible account
. . . the source of the general misconception of the man, the *fons
et origo mali*':

> The Memoir contains at least three definite errors in fact which can be
> easily refuted. . . . Its picture of Berkeley in his student days is absurd;
> he is a recluse and the butt of the college, and is by some regarded as
> 'the greatest dunce in the whole university'; here we have the well-
> known, but baseless, tale, told with gusto, of him and his [student]
> chum, Contarini [*sic*], agreeing to hang one another for a while in turn
> that they might experience the sensations of . . . dying. . . . The Memoir
> contains a few interesting and possibly true statements which are not
> found elsewhere; but . . . it looks like a piece of ignorant hack-work
> without a vestige of authority. . . . That a bantering record of this great
> man . . . should have been the first to appear and should have set the
> tone for later studies is a matter for keen regret. (*Life*, pp. 2–3)

Luce's own portrait of Berkeley as 'the man of affairs, sane,
shrewd, efficient' is in clear opposition to this early Memoir. But
Luce was also reacting to another, more recent misrepresentation,
as he saw it, namely, to the picture of Berkeley which emerges in
the work of W. B. Yeats, particularly in the poet's *Diary* of 1930
and in his fifteen-page introduction to Hone and Rossi's *Bishop
Berkeley*, published in the following year. For Yeats the real
Berkeley was 'that fierce young man', a visionary and radical

who 'proved all things a dream'.[2] Indeed, according to Yeats, there were two Berkeleys. Berkeley was 'idealist and realist alike'. He 'wore an alien mask'. Only in his student notebooks, the *Philosophical Commentaries*, 'is Berkeley sincere . . . the bishop was a humbug'.[3] Luce's comment, in a word, is 'nonsense': Yeats's assertions, he says, are 'charming, inconsequent nonsense, sparkles of poetic fancy without any foundation in fact. There was only one George Berkeley in actual life; he never wore a mask, and he was transparently honest and single-minded.'[4] Luce told me that he sent Yeats a detailed critique, to which the poet did not, however, reply.

II

Curiously, Yeats and Luce each focused his biographical animus on one or the other of two Berkeley portraits hanging in Trinity College. Thus Yeats exclaimed: 'I hate what I remember of his portrait [Figure 11] in the Fellows Room [now the Senior Common Room] at Trinity College; it wears a mask kept by . . . painters . . . of the eighteenth century for certain admired men.'[5] 'That philanthropic serene Bishop, that pasteboard man never wrote the [*Philosophical Commentaries*].'[6] (One wonders what Yeats would have said had he learned that this hated portrait, by James Latham, appeared in 1985 on an Irish postage stamp commemorating the philosopher.) The portrait Luce disliked he explicitly associated with Yeats. 'The false Berkeley Yeats knew is the Berkeley of legend . . . it is the long-haired, languishing visionary depicted in that mural decoration [Figure 12] which does duty as

---

[2] J. M. Hone and M. M. Rossi, *Bishop Berkeley: his Life, Writings and Philosophy*, with an Introduction by W. B. Yeats (London, 1931); see Introduction, p. xv; also see *Variorum Edition of the Poems of Yeats* (London, 1957), 'Blood and the Moon', p. 481.

[3] W. B. Yeats, *Pages from a Diary written in Nineteen Hundred and Thirty* (Dublin, 1944), 38–41; Introduction, pp. xxiii, xxvi.

[4] *Berkeley's Immaterialism*, p. viii.

[5] Introduction, p. xvi, and *Images*, 89.

[6] *Pages from a Diary*, 38. For a helpful account of Yeats's connection with Berkeley, see D. T. Torchiana, *W. B. Yeats and Georgian Ireland* (Evanston, Ill., 1966), 222–65.

Fig. 11. Portrait of Bishop Berkeley by James Latham, *c*.1738. Oil on canvas in an oval, 73.5 × 61 cm.

portrait of Berkeley in the Examination Hall of his College . . .'[7] It is 'the stage philosopher peering into infinity' (*Life*, 248).

Of course, Luce's own biographical portrait of Berkeley was formed by many forces, positive as well as negative. Among the positive ones are the statements of Berkeley's wife and daughter-in-law, the researches of Benjamin Rand; more negatively, the work of Hone and Rossi and also John Wild. But the main negative influence was what we may call the Goldsmith/Yeats

---

[7] *Berkeley's Immaterialism*, pp. viii–ix, and *Images*, 96.

Fig. 12. Portrait of George Berkeley by Robert Home, c.1783. Oil on canvas, 277 × 175 cm.

picture of Berkeley. I call it that, because we now know that Oliver Goldsmith (1730–74) wrote that first notorious Memoir, 'the *fons et origo mali*'.[8] This discovery of Goldsmith's authorship by his editor, Arthur Friedman, has a direct bearing on the credibility of

---

[8] Goldsmith, *Collected Works*, ed. Arthur Friedman (Oxford, 1966), iii. 35.

that earliest Memoir and, of course, on our understanding of Berkeley. Luce did not know that Goldsmith was the author of the first Memoir. Nor should anyone, I imagine, if an apparently unique copy of the first printing had not been noticed by Friedman in the Huntington Library at San Marino, California. For the 1762 Memoir, as we now know, was originally printed in 1759/60 in the *Weekly Magazine: or, Gentleman and Lady's Polite Companion* (London), a short-lived periodical in which Goldsmith published some of his earliest verse.

More decisive still, there is a crucial phrase in the first printing of the Memoir that was omitted from the later reprints known to Luce, Yeats, and others. It occurs in the long, circumstantial hanging episode. Here we learn that, having witnessed a public execution, Berkeley became curious to know 'what were the pains and symptoms' the hanged man experienced on such an occasion. He therefore arranged with a student friend that they should assist each other in the experiment, and that 'at a signal agreed upon' the assistant would take his friend down. So Berkeley, who was to go first, was 'tied up to the ceiling, and the chair taken from under his feet, but soon losing the use of his senses, his companion', Contarine, waited so long to assist Berkeley that

as soon as he was taken down he fell senseless and motionless upon the floor. After some trouble however he was brought to himself; and observing his band [exclaimed] bless my heart, Contarine, you have quite rumpled my band.[9]

Now in the *Weekly Magazine* the writer not only names Berkeley's companion, but says that it was Contarine 'from whom I had the story'. Who, then, was this Contarine? There has been only one Contarine at Trinity College and that was the Reverend Thomas

---

[9] 'Some Original Memoirs of the late famous Bishop of Cloyne', repr. in Goldsmith, *Collected Works*, iii. 35, and Garland, vol. 1. I, 172. One would like to know more of the hanging episode, but Goldsmith provides the only account or direct reference to it. There is, however, an enigmatic entry in Berkeley's notebooks which may advert to the incident. The incomplete entry, which has puzzled all Berkeley scholars, is on folio 95 and reads: 'August 28th 1708 [wit *crossed out*] the Adventure of the Shirt . . .'. Now as 'band' in eighteenth-century usage was an alternative for shirt, Berkeley may have been adverting here to the hanging incident.

Contarine (b. 1683) who entered College in 1701—a year after Berkeley—and graduated in 1706. Equally important, this Thomas Contarine was the uncle and patron of Goldsmith; indeed, he helped to pay Oliver's expenses at Trinity. Goldsmith refers to his uncle in the *Deserted Village* (1770) in the line: 'More skilled to raise the wretched than to rise'[10]—in which he may be alluding not only to his uncle's generosity but also to his skill in hanging poor Berkeley up to the ceiling, but evading the proposal (as the Memoir puts it) when it was his 'turn to go up'.

On the Memoir's authorship, Friedman notes: 'Of the small number of men who would be employed in writing for the *Weekly Magazine*, it is highly improbable that anyone except Goldsmith himself would have known his uncle, who spent his [entire] life in Ireland.'[11] But why, one might ask, was the crucial phrase 'from whom I had the story' omitted from the *British Plutarch* reprint? The answer, I believe, is that because its biographies were presented in the first person plural it would have been absurd for the *British Plutarch*'s piratical editors to have written 'and from whom we had the story'.

Once we allow—as I think we must—Goldsmith's authorship of the Memoir, we can no longer regard it as, to quote Luce's judgement, 'a piece of ignorant hack-work without a vestige of authority'.[12] For not only could Goldsmith have drawn on his generous uncle Contarine—at whose house he often stayed after leaving College—but he could also have gleaned biographical information from another well-placed relative, the Reverend Isaac Goldsmith, who was Dean of Cloyne from 1736 to 1769—in other words, during fifteen years which Berkeley was Bishop. The Memoir's credibility has also been bolstered recently from another source. One of its (apparently) dubious statements has been corroborated, I think, by the independent testimony of Berkeley's

---

[10] The identification was first made in Charles O'Conor's *Memoirs of the Life ... of the late Charles O'Conor of Balangare* (Dublin, c.1796), 186.

[11] *Collected Works*, iii. 37.

[12] It is worth noting that although Luce dismissed the Memoir's hanging story as a 'baseless tale' and 'silly' (*Life*, 3, 34), in his earlier *Berkeley and Malebranche* (1934), 7, he seems to accept the story.

wife. In the Memoir, Goldsmith had asserted that 'Dr Pepusch, an excellent Musician [was] engaged in [Berkeley's] design to establish a College in Bermuda, and actually embarked in order to put it into execution, but the ship being cast away the design unhappily was discontinued'.[13] Because the final part of this statement was known to be untrue, the initial part has also been rejected. Yet in her annotated copy of Stock's *Account of Berkeley*, Mrs Berkeley notes that 'one of the first composers and performers in Music of that time had engaged to come' to Bermuda—a ref- erence, I take it, to John Christopher Pepusch (1667–1752), who arranged the music for Gay's *The Beggar's Opera*.[14]

My conclusion is that Goldsmith's picture of Berkeley cannot now be confidently dismissed. Moreover, his picture of Berkeley fits, in some measure, with that of Yeats; for the youthful visionary, who proved all things a dream, might indeed appear absurd and comical to his fellow students. He might well seem, as Goldsmith put it, 'the greatest genius or the greatest dunce in the whole univer- sity . . .', a fool to those 'slightly acquainted with him', a 'prodigy of learning and good nature to those who shared his intimate friendship'. And while we may not have the two Berkeleys, as claimed by Yeats, we at least have two very different views of him. The Goldsmith and Yeats accounts cohere, too, in another inter- esting respect. It is the young, Trinity-College Berkeley whom Goldsmith and Yeats both see as solitary and especially childlike. The later Berkeley becomes in Goldsmith's Memoir more sober;

---

[13] See Garland, vol. 1. I, 174. All further quotations from Goldsmith's Memoir will be from this volume.

[14] See my 'Mrs Berkeley's Annotations', 20, 27. Another piece of new evidence which seems to support the Memoir is to be found in an unnoticed 'Last Will' of Berkeley's daughter-in-law, now in the Trinity College Library, MS 3530; here Eliza speaks of 'the poor insane Son and Daughter of Bishop Berkeley' (fo. 20), who are elsewhere identified as 'Henry Berkeley Esq, eldest son of Bp Berkeley and his sister Mrs Julia Berkeley . . .' (fo. 8). Berkeley was survived by three children: Henry, Julia, and George (the husband of Eliza). Little or nothing has come down to us of Henry and Julia— certainly nothing of their insanity. Yet there may well be a hint of it in the Memoir, where Goldsmith mentions that Berkeley drank tar-water 'in abundance himself, and attempted to mend the constitution of his children by the same regimen: this, however, he could never effect, and *perhaps his desire of improving their health and their understanding, at which he laboured most assiduously, might have impaired both*' (Garland, vol. 1. I, p. 179, my italics).

whereas for Yeats, he becomes more circumspect about revealing his true self. In later years, Yeats claimed, Berkeley's deeper, more anarchic self appears 'but in glimpses or as something divined or inferred'.[15] Perhaps the agreement and coherence of Goldsmith's and Yeats's pictures come out most clearly when they are juxta- posed to Luce's portrait of the straightforward Berkeley, 'sane, efficient, shrewd', the man with vision but in no sense a visionary.

III

Who, then, saw the real Berkeley? Here I should note that our knowledge of Berkeley is probably very limited. Like other promi- nent eighteenth-century figures, he seems to have kept himself to himself. Certainly, he was not given to self-revelation, particularly about his early life. Thus virtually the only personal details we learn of his childhood are from his two (private) notebook entries: that he was 'distrustful at 8 years' old and that he had an 'unac- countable turn' in harmonizing with the opinions of others.[16] Nor have we many more details of his student life, for our main source for that period is Goldsmith's Memoir, such as it is. Berkeley wrote no account of his life; and very few letters, comparatively speaking, have come down to us. Thus we do not have even one letter or note between Berkeley and any member of his family. Luce published two hundred and seventy letters in 1956; since then about twenty new letters have been discovered. But compare that to the published correspondence of Berkeley's two colleagues in the triumvirate of British Empiricism—about fifteen hundred letters for Locke, six hundred letters for Hume— and one sees how small the extant Berkeley correspondence is. Yet it is from this source that Luce's portrait is mainly drawn.

For Yeats, on the other hand, the real Berkeley, the angry young rebel behind an 'alien mask', is to be seen in Berkeley's student notebooks. Only once, Yeats wrote, was Berkeley 'free, when, still an undergraduate [and young Fellow] he filled . . . [his

---

[15] *Pages from a Diary*, 41.
[16] See above, Ch. 1 § I, and Ch. 2 § I.

notebooks] . . . with snorts of defiance' (*Diary*, 41). Yeats delighted particularly in those four snorts in which Berkeley wrote 'We Irishmen', for 'That', Yeats declared, 'was the birth of the [Irish] national intellect; and it aroused the defeat in Berkeley's philo﹣ sophical secret society of English materialism, the Irish Salamis' (ibid. 51). Luce, however, disputed this, arguing that when Berkeley wrote 'We Irishmen', he simply meant 'we ordinary folk, shrewd judges of fact and commonsense'.[17] Luce also argued against Yeats's other fond belief that Berkeley belonged to a secret society devoted to immaterialism. Both issues are a little complicated, but I think it is likely that Luce was right: Yeats was carried away by wishful thinking.

Plainly, a follower of Yeats will not find it easy—even given the new Goldsmith identification—to dislodge Luce's sturdy por﹣ trait. For not only is it drawn skilfully from the available primary evidence, but it is broadly supported by earlier biographers, notably by Stock and (with qualification) Fraser, and, more recently, by Lord Balfour—in his introduction to Berkeley's *Works* (1898)— and Benjamin Rand. Neither Goldsmith nor Yeats could lay claim to their wide acquaintance with Berkeley's life and writings. Luce's picture of the straightforward, sane Berkeley has been confirmed also in a detailed book by Ben﹣Ami Scharfsten on the psychology of philosophers. There Berkeley appears as one of the most normal philosophers of the past three hundred years.[18] And yet, probably the poets did see something that the scholars missed.

The question is complicated. For one thing, some of Goldsmith's statements tend to support Luce's disagreement with Fraser on the Cloyne period. For whereas Fraser portrayed Berkeley as the 'recluse of Cloyne'—'a caricature', according to Luce's *Life* (p. 186)—Goldsmith paints a picture more gregarious and more in line with that of Luce. 'The gentlemen of the neighbourhood and he [writes Goldsmith] preserved the closest intimacy; and

---

[17] See *Philosophical Commentaries*, 226, and Torchiana, *W. B. Yeats*, 237–8.

[18] Ben﹣Ami Scharfstein, *The Philosophers: Their Lives and the Nature of their Thought* (Oxford, 1980), 182; for a not dissimilar judgement, see J. O. Wisdom, *The Unconscious Origin of Berkeley's Philosophy* (London, 1953), 227.

while [the Bishop] cultivated the duties of his station, he was not unmindful of the innocent amusements of life: music he was particularly fond of, and always kept one or two exquisite performers to amuse his hours of leisure.' (Memoir, 179). About one such performer, the Italian musician Pasquilino, we have a story from Berkeley's daughterinlaw which adds colour to Goldsmith's picture and weight to Luce's case against Fraser. One day at dinner, we are told, the Bishop mentioned that he had disposed of a great many concert tickets for Pasquilino among his neighbours, to which the Italian replied with a bow: 'May God *pickle* your Lordship.' After the laughter of the company subsided, the poor Italian said, 'Vell, in de grammar dat my Lord gave me... it is printed, *pickle*, to keep from decay.'[19]

My serious point in all this is to emphasize that we are not being asked to choose between two clearcut, rival pictures of Berkeley. It is not as though Luce, Fraser, and Stock saw one Berkeley, whereas Yeats and Goldsmith saw another. A further difficulty is that given Yeats's impressionistic sketch—in some ways almost a prose poem—it is not altogether clear how completely it differs from that of Luce. I take it, however, that the hanging episode, recorded by Goldsmith, agrees with Yeats's picture.[20] And so, too, does the young Berkeley's description of himself in his notebooks, no. 465, as 'young', 'vain', and 'an upstart'.

The image this 'snort of defiance'—to use Yeats's phrase—conjures up is of a rebellious young man, and it is supported by Archbishop King's testimony, which I quoted in Chapter 1, about Berkeley's irregular ordination; from which it seems that King—who, it is generally agreed, was a shrewd judge of character—saw the young Junior Fellow as vain and rebellious. But this is still a long way from the subterranean Berkeley, whom Yeats describes as 'solitary, talkative, ecstatic, destructive'.[21]

[19] *Poems by... GeorgeMonck Berkeley* (1797), p. ccccxii.
[20] Berkeley's hanging experiment may be one of the earliest premeditated investigations into what are now called N.D.E.s, or Near Death Experiences. His experiment may also be connected with his views on time and death; see above, Ch. 3 § V.
[21] Introduction, p. xvi.

However, consider the following dictum of Berkeley recorded by his wife Anne. The Bishop's 'maxim', she says, 'was that nothing very good or very bad could be done until a man entirely got the better of fear of *que dira-ton*—but when a man has over-come himself he overcomes the world and then is fitted for his Master's use—.'[22] I find this maxim revealing, particularly when taken with another, this time recorded by Percival: '"I know not what it is to fear," said Mr Berkeley, "but I have a delicate sense of danger".'[23] Both dicta seem to reveal a duality. In the first, there is what people say, public opinion, the world or the worldly; this one must cease to fear if one is to do something either very good or very bad. The other suggests that Berkeley had a natural lack of fear—but of what? I am tempted to combine the two and say that he was naturally fearless of *que dira-ton*, of what the world says, and that this helps to explain those three bold crusades which largely constitute his life and career: his attempt to reform philosophy in early life by proving the non-existence of matter; his scheme in middle age to establish a missionary college, to ameliorate British society in the New World; and, finally, his advocacy of tar-water as a universal medicine.

Any of these three projects might have marked its originator as a Don Quixote. Yet that caricature simply does not fit Berkeley. For in each of his three idealistic projects we clearly see the prac-tical man and cautious reasoner, the man with his feet set firmly on the ground, who anticipates and answers our best objections. Berkeley was no romantic like his immaterialist follower Shelley, carried away by a noble idea in the blaze of its inception. Each of his three projects he publicized only after he had privately deliberated for at least two years. So, while Berkeley may naturally have lacked fear of public opinion, he knew what was needed to persuade others, to alter public opinion. As he tells us, he had 'from childhood an unaccountable turn' that helped him 'to win another over to his opinion' by seeming 'to harmonize with him

---

[22] 'Mrs Berkeley's Annotations', 22.
[23] First published by Luce in 'More Unpublished Berkeley Letters and New Berkeleiana', *Hermathena* 23 (1933), 28.

at first in his own way of talking'. We have seen this strategy in operation (in Chs. 2 and 3) particularly in his early philosophical works; and from his wife's statements and those in his 'Primary Visitation', he seems to have still had the 'turn' in middle age. Naturally unworldly, perhaps, Berkeley none the less had a delicate sense of what was required if the world was to be changed. In the non-philosophical sense, at least, he was both an idealist and a realist.

There is nothing languid, dreaming, or visionary in the way that he campaigns for his immaterialism, his Bermuda college, or his universal medicine. And yet, the goals were extraordinary and astonishing—as Berkeley himself recognized. That he should seriously entertain and publicly defend them—this strikes me as visionary and child-like. Yet once we encounter him actually defending them—in his *Principles*, *Proposal*, and *Siris*—then we feel that he is the very paradigm of reason. Hume seems to have felt something of this when he said of Berkeley's philosophical arguments: *'they admit of no answer and* [yet] *produce no conviction.'*[24] One does have the impression, as Yeats suggests, that Berkeley lived in two worlds. We feel at one moment that his ideas are out of this world, yet at another moment we cannot see what in the world is wrong with them.

Berkeley's friends, too, seem to have perceived and been struck by the way he combined innocence and experience, shrewdness and selflessness. Thus in 1713 Richard Steele wrote to him: 'Till I knew you, I thought it the privilege of angels only to be very knowing and very innocent'—a tribute supported by Bishop Atterbury, who said of Berkeley: 'So much understanding, so much knowledge, so much innocence, and such humility, I did not think had been the portion of any but angels till I saw this gentleman.'[25] Pope's better-known line—'To Berkley, ev'ry Virtue under Heav'n'—dulls rather than sharpens what I take to be the crucial insight: that Berkeley united the (seemingly) incompatible

---

[24] See above, Ch. 2 § II.
[25] *Works*, vii. 176–7, and *Letters by Several Eminent Persons deceased including John Hughs* (London, 1772), ii. 2.

virtues of worldly wisdom and childlike innocence. Certainly Swift saw Berkeley's innocent and unworldly side when in 1724 he described him as 'an absolute philosopher with regard to money, titles, and power'.[26] Yet Thomas Blackwell, Berkeley's Scottish friend, was plainly impressed by his other side when he wrote:

I scarce remember to have conversed with [Mr Berkeley] on [any] art, liberal or mechanic, of which he knew not more than the ordinary practitioners . . . With the widest views, he descended into . . . minute detail . . . I have known him to sit for hours in forgeries and founderies to inspect their successive operations.[27]

Perhaps Berkeley's capacity to unite other-worldly idealism with this worldly practicality helps to explain the extraordinary impression he made on the London wits. Thus, there is the story told by Pope's friend, Lord Bathurst, about a meeting of the Scriblerus Club at his house, where all the members rallied Berkeley on his Bermuda scheme:

Having listened to all the lively things they had to say, [Berkeley] begged to be heard in his turn; and displayed his plan with such an astonishing and animating force of eloquence and enthusiasm, that they were struck dumb, and, after some pause, rose up all together with earnestness, exclaiming—'Let us all set out with him immediately [for Bermuda]'.[28]

I am inclined, then, to agree with Yeats that there was a deep, unworldly, childlike side to Berkeley. But Yeats was wrong to suppose that Berkeley the Bishop was a humbug. For the deep Berkeley was inextricably bound with the religious man, the Christian, whose aim, as Mrs Berkeley says, was to be 'fitted for his Master's use'. That comes out clearly in his powerful defences of Christianity against its most formidable critics, and in his three bold crusades, all of which are deeply motivated or guided by his religion. Indeed, it is in his fearless commitment to Christianity

---

[26] Swift, letter of 3 Sept. 1724 to Lord Carteret. In a letter to the Earl of Oxford, 14 Aug. 1725, Swift describes Berkeley as 'a true philosopher . . . but of a very visionary virtue'; *Correspondence of Swift*, ed. F. E. Ball (London, 1910–14), iii. 212–13, 262.

[27] *Memoirs of the Court of Augustus* (Edinburgh, 1755), ii. 277–8.

[28] See Joseph Warton, *Essay on . . . Pope* (London, 1782), ii. 240 n.

that we see him at his best and (it must also be said) at his worst: in his biblical endorsement of slavery; his approval of kidnapping for the sake of converting the American Indians; in his theological rejection of all rebellion, no matter how tyrannical the ruler; in his intolerant attitude to free-thinkers. And yet these defects or shades (to paraphrase his words in *Principles*, sect. 152) serve to set off the brighter parts of his religious character, as well as adding conviction to it.

IV

Where can the real Berkeley be found? One answer is to go first to the Latham portrait (which Yeats disliked) and then to the painting by Home (which Luce disliked). Yet that would be facile. The Home painting (Figure 12) is an imaginative recreation, with no real authority; whereas there is every reason to believe that Bishop Berkeley did sit for the Latham portrait (Figure 11). Similarly, there can be little doubt that Berkeley sat for Luce's biographical portrait, given its judicious use of his correspondence and other hard evidence. Neither Goldsmith nor Yeats inspires such confidence. Goldsmith was well known for mixing truth and fantasy. Similarly, Yeats's judgements are often based on intuition, as when he asserts that with Berkeley 'we feel perhaps for the first time that eternity is always at our heels or hidden from our eyes by the thickness of a door'[29]—an assertion which must prompt the question: Is this biography or poetry? And yet for all that, more than a suspicion remains, as I have tried to show, that there was a deeper Berkeley which neither Latham nor Luce has captured, but of whom Goldsmith and Yeats have caught a glimpse.

[29]   Introduction, pp. xxi-xxii.

Bibliography

Manuscript material (not mentioned in *Life* or *Works* of Berkeley)

Berkeley, Anne, Annotations in J. Stock, *An Account of the Life of Berkeley* (1776); Trinity College, Dublin, Library, MS 5936.

Berkeley, George, Letter of 5 September 1728, possibly to Bishop Gibson; auctioned by Swann Galleries, New York, 10 May 1979.

—— Summary of Metaphysics, *c*.1729; Johnson Collection, Columbia University Library.

—— Letter to Bishop Gibson, 15 March 1730/1; Lambeth Palace Library, Fulham Papers, vol. xvii.

—— Letter to Robert Wilmot, 25 June 1745; Yale University, Osborn Collection.

—— Sermon on the Will of God, 1751, with annotations by J. Ellis; British Library, Add. MS 39306.

Berkeley, Eliza, Last Will, 1793–1800; Trinity College, Dublin, Library, MS 3530.

King, William, Letter to Bishop Ashe, 27 March 1710; Trinity College, Dublin, Library, MS 750/11.

Reilly, Michael, Letter to Charles O'Conor, 24 March 1749; Royal Irish Academy Library, O'Conor Papers, B. I. 1.

Steele, Richard, Papers on the *Guardian*; British Library Add. MS 61688.

—— Contract with Jacob Tonson for *Ladies Library*, 15 October 1713; Yale University, Osborn Collection.

Tyrrell, Duke, Letter to Robert Molesworth, 14 May 1716; Public Records Office, London, State Papers Ireland 64/374.

Printed Material

Analecta Hibernica (Dublin, 1931).

BIBLIOGRAPHY

ARMSTRONG, D. M., *Berkeley's Theory of Vision* (Melbourne, 1960).
—— and MARTIN, C. B. (eds.), *Locke and Berkeley* (New York, 1968; Garland, xiv). [Cited as Armstrong]
AYER, A. J., Language, *Truth and Logic* (London, 1936).
BAILEY, N., *An Universal English Dictionary* (10th edn., London, 1742).
BARKER, N., 'Typography and the Meaning of Words: the Revolution in Layout of Books in the Eighteenth Century', in G. Barker and F. Bernhard (eds.), *Buch und Buchhandel in Europa im 18. Jahrhundert* (Hamburg, 1981), 127–65.
BAXTER, A., *An Enquiry into the Nature of the Human Soul* (2 vols.; 3rd edn., London, 1745).
BAYLE, P., *The Dictionary, Historical and Critical*, ed. and trans. P. Demaizeaux (5 vols.; 2nd edn., London, 1734–8.
BEATTIE, J., *Essay on the Nature... of Truth* (3rd edn., Dublin, 1773).
BELFRAGE, B., 'A summary of Berkeley's Metaphysics in a Hitherto Unpublished Berkeleian Manuscript', *Berkeley Newsletter* 3 (1979), 1–4.
—— 'A New Approach to Berkeley's Philosophical Notebooks', in E. Sosa (ed.), *Essays on the Philosophy of George Berkeley* (Dordrecht, 1987).
BENNETT, J., 'Berkeley and God', *Philosophy* 40 (1965), 207–21.
BERKELEY, G., *The Works of George Berkeley*, ed. with a *Life* by J. Stock (2 vols.; Dublin, 1784).
—— *The Works of George Berkeley*, ed. G. Sampson (3 vols.; London, 1898).
—— *Berkeley's Complete Works*, ed. A. C. Fraser (4 vols.; Oxford, 1901).
—— *Berkeley's Philosophical Commentaries generally called the Commonplace Book, An Editio Diplomatica*, ed. A. A. Luce (London, 1944).
—— *The Works of George Berkeley*, ed. A. A. Luce and T. E. Jessop (9 vols.; Edinburgh, 1948–57).
—— *The Philosophical Commentaries*, ed. G. Thomas, with notes by A. A. Luce (Ohio, 1976).
—— *George Berkeley's Manuscript Introduction*, ed. B. Belfrage (Oxford, 1987).
—— *Berkeley: Philosophical Works*, ed. M. R. Ayers (1975; new edn., London, 1989).
BERKELEY, G. M., *Poems by the Late George-Monck Berkeley*, ed. with a preface by E. Berkeley (London, 1797).
BERMAN, D., 'An Early Essay concerning Berkeley's Immaterialism', *Hermathena* 109 (1969), 37–43.

—— 'Some New Bermuda Berkeleiana', *Hermathena* 110 (1970), 24–31.

—— 'Berkeley, Clayton and *An Essay on Spirit*', *Journal of the History of Ideas* 32 (1971), 367–78.

—— 'On Missing the Wrong Target', *Hermathena* 113 (1972), 54–67.

—— 'Mrs Berkeley's Annotations in her Interleaved Copy of *An Account of the Life of Berkeley* (1776)', *Hermathena* 122 (1977), 15–28.

—— 'Berkeley and his Catholic Countrymen', *Long Room* 16/17 (1978), 26–8.

—— 'Berkeley's Philosophical Reception after America', *Archiv für Geschichte der Philosophie* 62 (1980), 311–20.

—— 'Bishop Berkeley and the Fountains of Living Waters', *Hermathena* 128 (1980), 21–31.

—— 'Berkeley's Prophecy', *The Scriblerian* 13 (1980), 38–9.

—— 'Cognitive Theology and Emotive Mysteries in Berkeley's *Alciphron*', *Proceedings of the Royal Irish Academy* 81 (1981), 219–29.

—— 'Enlightenment and Counter-Enlightenment in Irish Philosophy', *Archiv für Geschichte der Philosophie* 64 (1982), 148–65.

—— 'The Culmination and Causation of Irish Philosophy', *Archiv für Geschichte der Philosophie* 64 (1982) 257–79.

—— 'Berkeley and King', *Notes and Queries* NS 29 (1982), 528–30.

—— 'Berkeley and the Moon Illusions', *Revue Internationale de Philosophie* 154 (1985), 215–22.

—— 'George Berkeley: Pictures by Goldsmith, Yeats and Luce', *Hermathena* (1985), 9–23.

—— 'The Jacobitism of Berkeley's *Passive Obedience*', *Journal of the History of Ideas* 47 (1986), 309–19.

—— 'Berkeley's Semantic Revolution', *History of European Ideas* 7 (1986), 603–7.

—— 'Die Debatte über die Seele', in J. P. Schobinger (ed.), *Grundriss der Geschichte der Philosophie: Die Philosophie des 17. Jahrhunderts* (3 vols.; Basle, 1988), iii. *England*.

—— *A History of Atheism in Britain: from Hobbes to Russell* (1988; London, 1990).

—— (ed.), *George Berkeley: Eighteenth-Century Responses* (New York: Garland, i. 1–2, 1989).

BERMAN, D., and CARPENTER, A., 'Eighteenth-Century Irish Philosophy', in S. Deane (gen. ed.), *The Field Day Anthology of Irish Writing* (3 vols.; Derry, 1991).

Biographia Britannica, A. Kippis (ed.) (5 vols.; 2nd edn., London 1778–93).

BLACKWELL, T., *Memoirs of the Court of Augustus* (2 vols.; Edinburgh, 1755).

BOSWELL, J., *The Life of Samuel Johnson* (3 vols.; Dublin, 1792).

BRACKEN, H. M., 'Berkeley on the Immortality of the Soul', *The Modern Schoolman* 37 (1960), 77–94, 197–212.

—— *The Early Reception of Berkeley's Immaterialism, 1710–1733* (1959; rev. edn., The Hague, 1965).

—— 'Bishop Berkeley's Messianism', in R. H. Popkin (ed.), *Millenarianism and Messianism* (Leiden, 1988.)

BROOK, R. J., *Berkeley's Philosophy of Science* (The Hague, 1973).

[BROWNE, P.], *A Letter in Answer to ... Christianity not Mysterious* (3rd edn., London, 1703).

—— *Procedure, Extent and Limits of the Human Understanding* (London, 1728).

—— *Things Divine and Supernatural Conceived by Analogy with Things Natural and Human* (London, 1733).

CAJORI, F., *History of the Conception of Limits and Fluxions in Britain* (Chicago, 1919).

CALHOUN, W., *Richard Steele, M. P.* (Baltimore, 1970).

CHAMBERS, E., *Cyclopaedia, or a Universal Dictionary of the Arts and Sciences* (2 vols.; London, 1728).

CHANEY, E., 'George Berkeley in the Veneto', *Bolletino de CIRVI* I. ii (1980), 82–8.

—— 'Architectural Taste and the Grand Tour: George Berkeley's Evolving Canon', *Journal of Anglo-Italian Studies* 1 (1991), 74–91.

CLARK, S. R. L. (ed.), *Money, Obedience, and Affection: Essays on Berkeley's Moral and Political Thought* (Garland, ii; New York, 1989).

[CLAYTON, R.], *An Essay on Spirit* (Dublin, 1750).

—— *Some Remarks on Dr McDonnell's Essay towards an Answer ... to the Essay on Spirit* (Dublin, 1754).

COLLIER, A., *Clavis Universalis* (1713), ed. E. Bowman (Chicago, 1909).

[COLLINS, A.], *An Essay Concerning the Use of Reason in Propositions, the Evidence whereof depends on Human Testimony* (London, 1707).

—— *An Answer to Mr Clark's Third Defence of his Letter to Mr Dodwell* (1708; London, 1709).

—— *A Discourse of Free-Thinking, Occasion'd by the Rise and Growth of a Sect call'd Free-Thinkers* (London, 1713).

COUPLAND, R., *The British Anti-Slavery Movement* (London, 1964).

[COWARD, W.], *Farther Thoughts concerning Human Soul* (London, 1703).

CREERY, W. (ed.), *George Berkeley: Critical Assessments* (3 vols.; London, 1991).

A Defence of Natural and Revealed Religion: being...Lectures founded by Boyle... (3 vols.; London, 1739).

DODDRIDGE, P., *Course of Lectures...*, ed. S. Clark (London, 1763).

DOWNEY, J., *The Eighteenth-Century Pulpit* (Oxford, 1969).

DROZ, J. P. (ed.), *A Literary Journal* (5 vols.; Dublin, 1744–8).

DUDGEON, W., *Several Letters to...Jackson from William Dudgeon* (London, 1737).

ENGLE, G. W. and TAYLOR, G. (eds.), *Berkeley's Principles of Human Knowledge: Critical Studies* (Belmont, Calif., 1968). [Cited as Engle]

Essay, see under Locke, J.

An Essay on the Existence of Matter (London, 1751).

FLEW, A., *The Logic of Mortality* (Oxford, 1987).

——'Was Berkeley a Precursor of Wittgenstein?', in W. B. Todd (ed.), *Hume and the Enlightenment: Essays Presented to Ernest Campbell Mossner* (Edinburgh, 1974).

FOOTE, H. W., *John Smibert, Painter* (Cambridge, Mass., 1950).

FRASER, A. C., *Life and Letters of George Berkeley* (Oxford, 1871; Garland, x).

FURLONG, E. J., 'How much of Steele's *Guardian* 39 did Berkeley write?', *Hermathena* 89 (1957), 76–88.

——'An Ambiguity in Berkeley's *Principles*', *Philosophical Quarterly* 14 (1964), 334–44.

——'Berkeley and the Tree in the Quad', *Philosophy* 41 (1969), 169–73.

——'Some Puzzles in Berkeley's Writings', *Hermathena* 120 (1976), 68–71.

——and BERMAN, D., 'George Berkeley and the *Ladies Library*', *Berkeley Newsletter* 4 (1980), 4–13.

Guardian, see under Stephens, J. C.

Garland = G. Pitcher (gen. ed.) *The Philosophy of George Berkeley* (15 vols.; New York: Garland Publishing, 1988–9).

GAUSTAD, E., *George Berkeley in America* (New Haven, Conn., 1979).

GOLDSMITH, O., *Collected Works of Oliver Goldsmith*, ed. A. Friedman (5 vols.; Oxford, 1966).

GRANT, R., and TRACY, D., *A Short History of the Interpretation of the Bible* (2nd edn., London, 1984).

GREENE, D., 'More on Berkeley's Prophecy', *The Scriblerian* 14 (1981), 58.

GREY, D., 'Berkeley on Other Selves: A Study in Fugue', *Philosophical Quarterly* 4 (1954), 28–44.

HALES, S., *An Account . . . of Tar-Water* (2nd edn., London, 1747).

HAMILTON, W., *The Dangers of Popery and Blessings Arising from the Late Revolution* (Dublin, 1723).

HERBERT, G., *The Temple: Sacred Poems* (London, 1674).

[HERVEY, Lord], *Some Remarks on the Minute-Philosopher* (London, 1732).

[HOADLEY, B.], 'A Vindication of Lord Shaftesbury's Writings . . . against the Author of . . . Alciphron', *London Journal* (10 and 17 June, 1732).

HONE, J. M. and ROSSI, M. M., *Bishop Berkeley: his Life, Writings and Philosophy*, with an introduction by W. B. Yeats (London, 1931).

HOPPEN, T., *The Common Scientist in the Seventeenth Century: A Study of the Dublin Philosophical Society 1683–1708* (London, 1970).

HOUGHTON, R., BERMAN, D., and LAPAN, M., *Images of Berkeley* (Dublin, 1986).

HUME, D., *A Treatise of Human Nature* (1739), ed. L. A. Selby-Bigge (Oxford, 1967).

——— *A letter from a Gentleman to his Friend in Edinburgh* (1745), ed. E. C. Mossner and J. V. Price (Edinburgh, 1967).

——— *An Inquiry concerning Human Understanding* (1777), ed. C. W. Hendel (Indianapolis, 1955).

HUTCHESON, F., *Inquiry into the Original of our Ideas of Beauty and Virtue* (1725; 3rd edn., London, 1729).

Images, see under Houghton, R., *et al.*

JESSOP, T. E., 'Berkeley and Contemporary Physics', *Revue Internationale de Philosophie* 7 (1953), 101–33.

——— *Bibliography of George Berkeley* (2nd edn., The Hague, 1973).

JOHNSON, S., *Samuel Johnson: His Career and Writings*, ed. H. and C. Schneider (4 vols.; New York, 1929).

[JOHNSTON, C.] *Chrysal: or, the Adventures of a Guinea* (4 vols.; London, 1762).

KANT, I., *Critique of Pure Reason*, trans. N. K. Smith (London, 1968).

KELLY, P. H., 'Ireland and the Critique of Mercantilism in Berkeley's *Querist*', *Hermathena* 139 (1985), 101–16.

KEYNES, G., *A Bibliography of George Berkeley . . . His Work and Critics in the Eighteenth Century* (Oxford, 1976).

KING, W., *Europe's Deliverance: A Sermon* (Dublin, 1691).

—— *Origin of Evil*, trans. and ed. E. Law (3rd edn., Cambridge, 1739).

—— *A Great Archbishop of Dublin, William King 1650–1729 . . . His Autobiography. . .*, ed. C. S. King (London, 1906).

—— *King's Sermon on Predestination*, ed. A. Carpenter, with an introduction by D. Berman (Dublin, 1976).

KLINGBERG, F., *The Anti-Slavery Movement in England* (New Haven, Conn., 1926).

KUPFER, J., 'Universalization in Berkeley's Rule Utilitarianism', *Revue Internationale de Philosophie* 28 (1974), 511–31.

LECKY, W. E. H., *History of England in the Eighteenth Century* (5 vols.; (London, 1892).

Letters of Several Eminent Persons deceased including John Hughes (London, 1772).

Life, see under Luce, A. A.

LOCKE, J., *An Essay Concerning Human Understanding* (1690), ed. P. Nidditch (Oxford, 1975).

—— *The Correspondence of John Locke*, ed. by E. S. De Beer (8 vols.; Oxford, 1976–89).

LUCE, A. A., 'More Unpublished Berkeley Letters and New Berkeleiana', *Hermathena* 23 (1933), 25–53.

—— 'Is there a Berkeleian Philosophy?', *Hermathena* 25 (1936), 184–210.

—— 'The Philosophical Correspondence between Berkeley and Johnson', *Hermathena* 56 (1940), 93–112.

—— 'Berkeley's Essays in the *Guardian*', *Mind* 52 (1943), 247–63.

—— *Berkeley and Malebranche: A Study in the Origins of Berkeley's Thought* (1934; new edn., Oxford, 1967).

—— *The Dialectic of Immaterialism: An Account of the Making of the Principles* (London, 1963).

—— *Berkeley's Immaterialism: A Commentary on the Principles* (1945; New York, 1968).

—— *The Life of George Berkeley* (1949; repr. with a new introduction by D. Berman, London, 1992).

—— 'The Original Title and First Edition of *Siris*', *Hermathena* 84 (1954), 45–58.

—— 'Another Look at Berkeley's Notebooks', *Hermathena* 110 (1970), 5–23.

MABBOTT, J. D., 'The Place of God in Berkeley's Philosophy', *Journal of Philosophical Studies* 6 (1931), 18–29.

MCCABE, J., *A Rationalist Encyclopedia* (London, 1948).

MCDONNELL, T., *An Essay towards an Answer to the Essay on Spirit* (Dublin, 1753).

—— *A Short Vindication of ... the Essay towards ...* (Dublin, 1754).

MCGOWAN, W., 'Did Berkeley Write *The Irish Blasters?*', *Berkeley Newsletter* 6 (1982/3), 1–4.

MALEBRANCHE, N., *Treatise Concerning the Search After Truth*, trans. T. Taylor (London, 1694).

MEDE, J., *His Works, Corrected and Enlarged* (London, 1664).

MILL, J. S., 'Berkeley's Life and Writings', in Mill, *Collected Works*, vii, ed. J. M. Robson (Toronto, 1978).

MOKED, G., *Particles and Ideas: Bishop Berkeley's Corpuscularian Philosophy* (Oxford, 1988).

MOLESWORTH, R., *An Account of Denmark as it was in the Year 1692* (1694; Glasgow, 1745).

MOLYNEUX, W., *Dioptrica Nova* (London, 1692).

MORGAN, M., *Molyneux's Question* (Cambridge, 1977).

[O'CONOR, C.], *Seasonable Thought relating to our Civil and Ecclesiastical Constitution* (Dublin, 1751).

—— *The Principles of the Roman Catholics* (Dublin, 1756).

—— *The Touchstone of Patriotism, in a Series of Interesting Queries to the Publick* (Dublin, 1756).

O'CONOR, C., *Memoirs of the Life ... of the late Charles O'Conor of Balangare* (Dublin, c.1796).

O'LEARY, A., *Miscellaneous Tracts* (London, 1791).

OLSCAMP, P. J., *The Moral Philosophy of George Berkeley* (The Hague, 1970).

OSWALD, J., *Appeal to Common Sense* (Edinburgh, 1766).

PAPPAS, G., 'Abstract Ideas and the *Esse* is *Percipi* thesis', *Hermathena* 139 (1985), 47–62.

PARKS, S., 'George Berkeley, Sir Richard Steele and the *Ladies Library*', *The Scriblerian* 12 (1980), 1–2.

PEARCE, Z., *Sermon Preached before the Society for the Propagation of the Gospel in Foreign Parts ... on 20th of February 1729* (London, 1730).

PITCHER, G., *Berkeley* ('Arguments of the Philosophers'; London, 1977).

PITTION, J. P., BERMAN, D., and LUCE, A. A., 'A New Letter by Berkeley to Browne on Divine Analogy', *Mind* 78 (1969), 375–92.

PLATO, *The Republic*, trans. Paul Shorey (2 vols.; Cambridge, Mass., 1969).

POPE, A., *The Works of Alexander Pope*, ed. W. Warburton (9 vols.; London, 1757).

——*Pope: Poetical Works*, ed. H. Davis (London, 1966).

POPKIN, R. H., 'Berkeley and Pyrrhonism', *Review of Metaphysics* 5 (1951), 223–46.

POPPER, K., 'A Note on Berkeley as Precursor of Mach and Einstein', *British Journal for the Philosophy of Science* 4 (1953), 37–45.

PRIOR, J., *Life of Edmund Malone* (London, 1860).

RAINE, K., 'Berkeley, Blake and the New Age', *Thought* 51 (1976), 356–76.

RAMSAY, A., *Philosophical Principles of Natural and Revealed Religion* (Glasgow, 1748).

RAND, B., *Berkeley and Percival* (Cambridge, 1914).

——*Berkeley's American Sojourn* (Cambridge, Mass., 1932).

REID, T., *Enquiry into the Human Mind* (Edinburgh, 1764).

RITCHIE, A. D., 'George Berkeley's *Siris*: The Philosophy of the Great Chain of Being and the Alchemical Theory', *Proceedings of the British Academy* 40 (1954), 41–55.

RUSSELL, B., *History of Western Philosophy* (New York, 1964).

RYLE, G., *The Concept of Mind* (1949; London, 1966).

SCHARFSTEIN, B./A, *The Philosophers: Their Lives and the Nature of their Thought* (Oxford, 1980).

SCOTT, W. R., *Francis Hutcheson: His Life, Teaching and Position in the History of Philosophy* (Cambridge, 1900).

SMITH, A., *Essays on Philosophical Subjects* (Dublin, 1795).

STEELE, R., *Apology for Himself* (London, 1714).

STEPHEN, L., *History of English Thought in the Eighteenth Century* (2 vols.; London, 1876).

STEPHENS, J. C. (ed.), *The Guardian* (Lexington, Ky., 1982).

[STOCK J.], *An Account of the Life of George Berkeley... With Notes, Containing Strictures upon his Works* (London, 1776; Garland, i. 1).

SWIFT, J., *The Works of Jonathan Swift*, ed. W. Scott (19 vols.; London, 1883).

—— *Correspondence of Jonathan Swift*, ed. F. E. Ball (6 vols.; London, 1910–14).

—— *The Poems of Jonathan Swift*, ed. H. Williams (3 vols.; Oxford, 1958).

TEMPLE, W., *Miscellanea, the Second Part* (5th edn., London, 1705).

TIPTON, I., 'Two Questions on Berkeley's Panacea', *Journal of the History of Ideas* 30 (1969), 203–24.

—— *Berkeley: The Philosophy of Immaterialism* (London, 1974).

TOLAND, J., *Christianity not Mysterious* (London, 1696).

TORCHIANA, D. T., W. B. *Yeats and Georgian Ireland* (Evanston, Ill., 1966).

Touchstone; or paradoxes brought to the Test (London, 1732).

[TRENCHARD, J. and Gordon, T.], *Cato's Letters* (4 vols.; 5th edn., London, 1748).

TURBAYNE, C. M., *The Myth of Metaphor* (New Haven. Conn., 1962).

—— 'Berkeley's Two Concepts of Mind', *Philosophy and Phenomeno-logical Research* 20 (1959), 85–92; 22 (1962), 577–80.

—— (ed.), *Berkeley: Principles, Text and Critical Essays* (Indianapolis, 1970). [Cited as Turbayne]

TYRELL, D., *The Established Church Vindicated* (Dublin, 1716).

URMSON, J. O., *Berkeley* (Oxford, 1982).

VESEY, G., *Berkeley* (Open University text; Milton Keynes, 1982).

WARNOCK, G., *Berkeley* (1953; London, 1969).

WARTON, J., *Essay on the Genius and Writings of Alexander Pope* (2 vols.; London, 1782).

WILD, J., *George Berkeley* (Cambridge, Mass., 1936).

WINKLER, K., *Berkeley: An Interpretation* (Oxford, 1989).

WINTON, C., *Richard Steele, M.P.* (Baltimore, 1970).

WISDOM, J. O., *The Unconscious Origin of Berkeley's Philosophy* (London, 1953).

WITTGENSTEIN, L., *Tractatus Logico-Philosophicus*, trans. D. F. Pears and B. F. McGuinness (London, 1969).

YEATS, W. B., Introduction to J. M. Hone and M. M. Rossi, *Bishop Berkeley* (London, 1931).

—— *Pages from a Diary written in Nineteen Hundred and Thirty* (Dublin, 1944).

—— *The Variorum Edition of the Poems*, ed. P. Allt and R. K. Alspach (London, 1957).

Index